AT HOME IN
DOGWOOD MUDHOLE

———

VOLUME ONE:

NOTHING THAT EATS

PRAISE FOR AT HOME IN DOGWOOD MUDHOLE

Faith, family, farming, hard money, and Southern history. Those are the core themes that coalesce into Franklin Sanders' newest book, an autobiographical collection of essays titled *At Home in Dogwood Mudhole*. As back-to-the-land books go, this one is unique. Over the course of generations (going back some 200 years) commercial-industrialism has almost completely destroyed the agrarian traditions that once epitomized not only the South, but all of America. But there is good news as a growing remnant of concerned people are returning to the land, establishing small farms and homesteads, and rediscovering the manifold virtues of agrarian-based life. The Sanders family is among them. — HERRICK KIMBALL

At Home in Dogwood Mudhole is an agrarian epic—no, *the* agrarian epic—a tale of the odyssey of Franklin Sanders and his family making their way toward home—that is, back to the land and the farming life of their forebears in Middle Tennessee. The tale is told with vivid and unflagging immediacy, courage, wisdom, Christian faith, and good humor. Franklin Sanders is a gifted writer and original thinker who avoids two of the most common American faults: spiritless practicality and easy sentimentality. The land teaches us, writes Sanders, that "life is not science, it is mystery." This is the kind of writing that the late Southern philosopher M.E. Bradford called "hard pastoral," neither preachy nor sentimental about the demanding life on the land but aware of its deeper rewards. The "hard pastoral," Bradford further avowed, is one of the hallmarks of great Southern literature. Add to this that Volume 1 is what they call these days a "page-turner," difficult to put down, and in *At Home in Dogwood Mudhole* we have a lasting achievement with many lessons for us all. — CLYDE WILSON

I once asked Franklin during *The Solari Report* how he and Susan learned how to farm. His honest reply was: "We killed a lot of animals." I could feel our urban subscribers sit back in their chairs! One of my favorite essayists once referred to the power of never giving up in a difficult, imperfect world: "What we all need is the courage to proceed in the face of our own nauseousness." It is essential not to give up or start drinking when your truck rolls over your favorite dog. — CATHERINE AUSTIN FITTS

AT HOME IN
DOGWOOD MUDHOLE

———

VOLUME ONE:

NOTHING THAT EATS

FRANKLIN SANDERS

FOUR RIVERS, INC.

Reno, Nevada

At Home in Dogwood Mudhole
Volume One: Nothing That Eats

Published by Four Rivers, Inc.
          9120 Double Diamond Parkway, Suite 4549
          Reno, Nevada 89521 USA

Edited by Fiona McNeill
Book design and author photograph by Collin Houseal

First printing, 2012
Printed in the United States of America

ISBN Trade Paperback: 978-1-938817-06-9
ISBN PDF: 978-1-938817-07-6
ISBN Mobipocket: 978-1-938817-08-3
ISBN ePub: 978-1-938817-09-0

Library of Congress Cataloging-in-Publication Data

Sanders, Franklin (1947-)
At Home in Dogwood Mudhole. Volume One. Nothing That Eats.
1. Memoir—Farming. 2. Self-reliant living. 3. Southern States—History.
4. Agrarianism. 5. Tennessee—History. 6. Homesteading. I. Title.

FOR SUSAN,
MY BELOVED HEROINE

ALSO BY FRANKLIN SANDERS

Heiland

Paul Schneider: The Witness of Buchenwald
translated from Rudolf Wentorf's German original

The Next Great Depression Survival Manual

FORTHCOMING TITLES

Volume Two: Best Thing We Ever Did

Volume Three: The Sage of Dogwood Mudhole

CONTENTS

SECTION ONE

LEAVING MEMPHIS FIVE MILES AT A TIME

SECTION TWO
LIVING IN THE COUNTRY CHANGES YOU

SECTION THREE

LEARNING CURVE

SECTION FOUR

A REAL FARM

LIST OF PLATES

All photographs by friends and members of the Sanders family.
Maps hand-drawn by Franklin Sanders.

ACKNOWLEDGEMENTS

People fudge a lot when they say "this book wouldn't have been possible except for the help of" and then list everybody they know from the president to the second assistant tire checker. You can, however, believe me and take it to the bank when I tell you that this book would never have seen the light of day unless my friend Nick Bull had spent much of his summer gathering the files. Unaided by my guide, encourager, and book developer Fiona McNeill, the book would still be moldering old newsletters and electrons whizzing around in computers. She understands elegant simplicity, and allowed me to reach for it. If I failed, it wasn't her fault. My friend Collin Houseal is, I suspect, not only a supremely talented graphic artist but also a clairvoyant who reads my mind at will. Dear Sara Hill spent long hours proof-reading, missed ne'er an error and bettered much. I thank my children Liberty, Justin, Wright, Christian, Mercy, and Zachariah for occasionally chipping in where my memory was missing, and my wife Susan who put up with my late nights and other bothers. And I am grateful for all the denizens of Dogwood Mudhole, fowl, beasts, children, in-laws, and grandchildren, who have taught me everything I know worth knowing.

SOUTH

MEMPHIS

MAGIC ROAD
HWY 64
X Previtt's
X Crossroads

SHILOH
SAVANNAH

MURFREESBORO

FT. Donelson
FT Donelson
MIDDLE TENNESSEE
NASHVILLE

NATCHEZ
TRACE
Doomhole
Windmill
LAWRENCEBURG
V CROSSROADS
OF DIXIE

TENNESSEE RIVER

Chattanooga

— TENNESSEE —

viii

PREFACE

When I tell people that I live at Dogwood Mudhole, Tennessee, they look askance and smirk. They believe I am pulling their leg, but I'm not. In the *Tennessee Atlas and Gazetteer* you will find Dogwood Mudhole just east of the Natchez Trace Parkway.

How could any place deserve such an astounding name? Dogwood Mudhole is not a town, not a village, not even a store, just a crossroad now where Suck Stem Branch Road tees into Little Fish Trap Road, which is the original Natchez Trace. When the federal government built the Natchez Trace Parkway in the 1930s, they altered the route of Natchez Trace, moving it a half mile to the west.

The Trace was the first post and military road built in the old Southwest frontier, running from the Cumberland River at Nashville to the Mississippi at Natchez along a trail long used by game and Indians. Before steamboats took over, farmers from the Ohio River Valley would ferry goods down the Mississippi in flatboats, sell the goods at Natchez or New Orleans along with the boats, then take the Trace north to their homes. Passing through wild Chickasaw and Choctaw country, the Trace was a hive of bandits lying in wait for the pilgrims returning from Natchez with bulging wallets. One of the worst haunts stretched through impenetrable scrub oak thickets north of the Tennessee River crossing at Colbert Ferry, Alabama. A few miles' travel north takes you into Wayne County, Tennessee.

Dogwood Mudhole lies on the original Natchez Trace, a low spot on top of a ridge surrounded by dogwood trees. When it rained, the road became a mudhole, but one suspects that, given the area's reputation, the resident bandits gratuitously watered the road to bog down wagons and travelers, thus easing the hard work of waylaying them.

Still, I love the name, because it serves as a metaphor and reminder of our condition, the world lost but heaven promised. In the depths of mud, there is grace. Out of grace—grows a garden.

This world was originally ordained to be a garden, but Adam turned it into a mudhole. He overthrew grace and peace and contented steward-ship for self-rule and rebellion. Spreading out from the Garden, sin has worked its miracle, transforming the whole world into a mudhole. *Oh*, it may be a mudhole hidden by gardenias, but behind the blooms it remains a mudhole. Mankind turned a garden into a mudhole, and some of us are doing that still.

The legend of the dogwood teaches that it was once a great, tall tree, so broad and strong that wood from its trunk was used to make the cross. Humiliated and crushed by grief and shame, the dogwood pleaded with God never again to let it grow large enough to make a cross. God granted the dogwood's wish, and marked her flowers forever, a white cross with hands, feet, and heart tinged red with Christ's wounds.

So here we are, all of us—you, too—at home in Dogwood Mudhole, sunk in the mire of the world but surrounded always by the promise of resurrection, the assurance of grace, and the hope of glory. That hope transforms the mudhole back into a garden.

No, I am not ashamed to confess I live in Dogwood Mudhole.

A DECADE OF FARMING

I did not write this book as a memoir looking back on events and imposing some kind of meaning after the fact. Rather, I wrote these let-ters once a month for sixteen years, recounting our family news for the "Dear Readers" of *The Moneychanger*, my monthly newsletter. Together

these monthly letters paint a picture, but only as life does, adding experience, wisdom, and faith along the way. Life happens; later you figure out what it means.

Life before Dogwood Mudhole was hard. Renting house after house big enough for seven kids and my untamable gardening ambitions, fighting the government over whether or not gold and silver sales were taxable, and facing Y2K's potential dissolution of the financial and monetary systems. The end of the world as we knew it was constantly approaching. We were in a hurry to get to our own land and start learning to farm before we ended up with nowhere to live, no business, no means of income, and many mouths to feed. But we weren't pushed. We went because we *wanted* to go.

Like most folk from Tennessee, my wife and I are only two generations removed from farming. Rank amateurs, we had to relearn all that forgotten lore to reclaim a way of life—and a lot else besides. When we bought our land here, what we thought would happen didn't, and what did happen we didn't expect. We weren't just about to survive Y2K or another Great Depression. We were about to find that our children would move back to the land with us, learn to farm, build their homes on our land, that we would teach our grandchildren to milk cows, and somewhere down that road lose forever the nuclear-family suburban model and re-root our family in Tennessee, deep in the same soil that we worked so hard to rebuild from the very first year.

We have now lived, three generations all piled up on each other, over a decade at Dogwood Mudhole, and at last we have a place of our own on the face of the earth. Do we own it, or does it own us? I'm content either way. Tennessee is where I am from and it is where I stay, until they plant me, too, in this ground. Living in a rented house in the city and living on your own land that teems with life that you nurture—it's the difference between Tennessee and the moon. Life here on the farm is unpredictable, hard in so many unsuspected ways, but never as hard as it used to be.

THE HUNDRED YEAR HORIZON

Everything we do here at Dogwood Mudhole looks at a one hundred year horizon. When we left the city, my family and I, we planned to build and live here for more than a hundred years, a life outside the modernist world. I don't mean something Luddite by any means. We have computers and satellite dishes. What I mean is a community with farms that will last more than a hundred years. I tell them this at least once a week—that we must take everything that we do with *The Moneychanger* and put it into the farm. *The Moneychanger* will end. That is only natural. I am the only one who can write it, and it will end. But the farm—and my grandchildren—will still be here. We moved around a lot before we came here, but to our children and their children and their children's children, we leave something else: a place all their own in the world, a place unlike any other. A place they belong.

Franklin Sanders
Dogwood Mudhole, 2012

LEAVING MEMPHIS FIVE MILES AT A TIME

A THIRTY DOLLAR DOG

"*G*et *a border collie*," I prodded, hinting at the same birthday present I had been unsuccessfully promoting for three years.

More than money, more than fame, more than a big car, I wanted a border collie. A few years ago I saw sheep dog trials for the first time. One short session left me a hopeless border collie addict. When you've seen man and animal work with one mind and heart, you've discovered something new in the world, something boundlessly worthy. I had to have that.

Without ever fully confessing my passion, long before every gift-giving occasion I take up the border collie lament.

My family just won't get the message. I still get ties with hand-painted views of Port-au-Prince and battery-powered devices that chew the sweater-boogers off your cardigans. I saw my opportunity.

Our dog Scruffy had died, and this was my moment. We had never been adopted by a dog before, but Scruffy paid us that honor. He appeared out of nowhere, and he and Zachariah, my eight-year-old, became instant friends. Scruffy was part beagle, part rabbit, and the most loving dog I have ever known. When I stepped out the door for a walk in the morning, you'd have thought I was a pork roast the way he trembled and quivered. When I worked in the garden, he'd loaf in the tall grass, or lie on his back in the cool, freshly turned dirt, patiently watching and waiting for me to finish so we could get on to something more worthwhile. Scruffy wasn't here long, but we were glad to have him.

You'd have thought that living on a rented five-acre lot here outside Memphis surrounded by similar lots, there wouldn't be much traffic, and there wasn't, but I just couldn't break him of chasing cars. He'd see one coming and crouch down in the ditch, then spring out as the car roared by. He didn't know that sometimes cars pull trailers. Ignorance kills.

Our three youngest, Zachariah (8), Mercy (10), and Christian (12), were away at camp. My wife Susan and I just didn't know how to tell them—especially Zachariah—about Scruffy. We have another dog, Sparky the Labrador. He's been around ten years. He's a fixture. His muzzle and paws are gray now, he lost one eye to a snake several years ago, and his arthritis slows him down. He used to stay up all night, barking at cornered possums. The possums would play dead in the garbage bin. They were too stupid to get up and run, and Sparky was too stubborn to stop barking. Now he just lies around most of the time, scratching all night under the window next to our bed and indulging all the other bad habits (better left unmentioned) he is too old to break. Sometimes I think he's smarter than I am.

We just had to get another dog before the children came back. Susan, along with three of our eldest, Justin (18), Worth (16), and Wright (14), got out the want-ads and began to search.

I quickly fell behind. Susan ruled out a border collie as soon as she saw what they cost. She landed instead on an ad for some mixed Labrador/Dalmatian pups. "What a mess," I argued. "A Labrador likes water, and a Dalmatian chases fire trucks. All that dog'll be good for is to chase wet fire engines."

"What about a Bengal tiger?" I added hopefully. "We could keep him in the front yard, and that way we'd all get some exercise sprinting from the front door to the car."

Blast it, there is *no* eight week old dog on earth that isn't cute, not even those awful, wrinkled Chinese things that come with enough skin for two dogs. We drove up to the man's house, and we must have had a sign on our car door that said "Suckers Drive This" because he was waiting for us and opened the gate. Out bounced this black puppy with a black-spotted white mask, spotted belly, white paws, and a white–tipped tail. Right then and there before my thunderstruck eyes my own wife, the woman who hands me a quarter when I tell her I need some money for gas, the same woman who raises silk worms in her purse because they need a quiet, dark place where nobody ever disturbs them, before I could even say "that dog wouldn't make a decent set of earmuffs," that woman whips out *two tens and two fives* and puts them in that man's hand without so much as a shriek of pain or a single word about the county poor farm!

I know when I'm licked. I retreated to my second line of defense: naming the dog. "How about Eugene?" I said.

"Nope," she answered, "that dog looks like a *Jack*." And you know, since I've been watching him a while, he does look like a Jack.

Now how did she know that?

JULY 1995

Jack is either a Dalmador or a Labramatian. And yes, Zachariah was greatly surprised when he arrived home from camp to find a new puppy. Our one-eyed Labrador, Sparky, is tickled to have him around jumping all over him and gnawing his legs and ears. Sparky bears it all genially, glad of the attention.

I thought Jack was smart until last Sunday. I was lying on the deck reading when Jack mistook me for Sparky and sank his needle-fangs into my earlobe. Much to my credit, Jack is still alive today.

AUGUST 1995

Sparky is laboring manfully to teach Jack good manners, but Jack is just as oblivious to Sparky's instructions as he is to everybody else's.

Sparky has some bad habits of his own, which Jack is picking up nicely. Sparky likes to push open the front door with his nose, and head through the house for the back door. The first kid who spots him cries, "Dog in the house!" and this sets off a Keystone Cops chase as Sparky tears through the house with kids streaming after him.

How do I know Sparky knows what he's doing? If no child raises the hue and cry, Sparky merely saunters through the house, and sits down before the back door, waiting for you to let him out. With diabolical cunning, Sparky has instructed Jack in this same intrigue.

We have been moving east a few miles at a time for the last decade. Started out in mid-town Memphis on a 90' x 180' lot in a 1904 house. Gardened in flower beds, and wowed passers-by with our beautiful border plant. Car pulls up to the curb, rolls down window: "What is that exotic ground cover?"

"Sweet potatoes," I reply with smug innocence.

By now we are outside the city limits, on five wooded acres with a half-acre garden. In a couple of centuries we'll be at the Atlantic.

TWO-CAR FAMILY

W hy do I do it to myself?
In a feat of piloting worthy of Mark Twain, I stopped at a country store to ask directions. Seven thirsty kids piled out of two cars, mimicking Ma and Pa Kettle's westward progression during the Depression. I bought a map in Waynesboro to make sure Meridian didn't ensnare us again as it had on our way south through Tennessee to Alabama. But by 10 p.m. we found ourselves lost near the Alabama frontier looking for Lauderdale.

For vacation last year we rented a van and in ten days logged 2,500 miles traveling with seven children from Memphis to the North Carolina Outer Banks, down to Wilmington, and back. This year we logged about the same number of miles.

We just did it in five days instead of ten.

We set out on a Friday 245 miles to Waynesboro, Mississippi, which is not on the Gulf, but you can throw a rock at it from there and hear a splash. We stayed overnight for a friend's wedding, then left Saturday evening about 8:00 p.m. and headed north to Lake Barkley State Park in Kentucky. We left *in a caravan*, I might add, because we have too many grown children to fit into one car, now that two of my five sons are six foot two and more.

In the dark I found the Toomsuba-Lauderdale Road, took the correct *unmarked* left turn at the critical moment, and emerged from the inky black night into the welcoming glare of the largest gas station I've ever seen, *smack* on Highway 45. One hundred and ninety miles later we pulled into a motel at Corinth, almost on the Tennessee line. It was 1:00 a.m. Sunday morning. Car Number Two was still following.

After a brief sleep, we passed through my father's ancestral home in McNairy County, Tennessee. Seven Sanders brothers moved there in the 1820s from east Tennessee. Unbeknownst to them, they would find themselves split between North and South in the middle of a battleground.

We kept on driving, following General Nathan Bedford Forrest's favorite invasion routes into west Tennessee and Kentucky, where he armed and outfitted his troops at Yankee expense. Since the Southern government had so few weapons and supplies, he just invaded and supplied his army from his enemy's stores. Born in middle Tennessee, raised in Tippah County, Mississippi, and untrained in warfare, General Forrest became, in the opinion of William T. Sherman and Robert E. Lee, the greatest general of the war, a hero bearing in himself all the best and worst traits of his people. We drove through Parker's Crossroads, where Forrest had nearly beaten one Yankee army when another one unexpectedly caught him in the rear. Unruffled, he ordered his men to "Charge both ways!" and escaped. Forrest summed up his formula success thus: "Get there first with the most men." Once you read your first paragraph about him, you're hooked. Driving through Tennessee, history calls from every corner.

From Parker's Crossroads, we pushed on to Paris, Tennessee (don't think France!), about a hundred miles as the crow flies, but we aren't crows and didn't by any means fly. Sometime before the end of the day we made it to beautiful Lake Barkley Lodge for a reunion with Susan's five brothers and sisters and their families. We had logged about three hundred miles in twenty hours, counting the ten hours we merely wasted sleeping and eating in Corinth. Forrest would have been proud. We didn't get there first, but we certainly had the most—most miles, most hours in the car, most children.

Lodging next to a lake with seven kids for three days is no vacation, I'll promise. If you want rest, this is like somebody giving you a cookie

7

when you're hungry. It doesn't satisfy your hunger; it infuriates it. My children brought in-line skates. The hotel is two levels of rooms opening onto long, smooth sidewalks. Are you putting this together? Since it is a state-run lodge, all fun is strictly forbidden, skating included. It was a sidewalk, perfectly smooth, long, shaded, begging for skaters. My kids don't understand the state, and wouldn't care if they did. I don't understand the state and wouldn't care much, either.

We visited Fort Donelson National Battlefield and the noble Confederate monument there, which reads: "Somewhere here our unknown dead lie unburied, with arms unstacked forever, with colors that cannot be furled." I read these words and turned away from a burden too heavy to bear.

The Confederacy's woes began at Fort Donelson in February 1862, when two squabbling generals buffaloed themselves into surrendering 13,000 men needlessly and laid bare Tennessee's breast to Yankee General Ulysses S. Grant, paving the road to the Battle of Shiloh and defeat in the approaching April. Then fell Memphis to a Union river fleet in June. For the rest of the war, except for Forrest's raids, most of west Tennessee and much of middle and east Tennessee remained in Yankee hands. In middle and east Tennessee, bitter and savage partisan fighting took place, worse than in any other place except Missouri.

In west Tennessee, things were not much better. At Purdy, in McNairy County, the home to my father's people, lived the Union partisan Fielding Hurst, who committed atrocities against his own neighbors that don't bear retelling. I have a personal stake in visiting these battlefields. Of the seven brothers in my grandfather's grandfather's generation who settled there in the 1830s, one sided with the Union. Right as the war ended, within days of Lee's surrender, Union partisans shot another of my great-great grandfather's brothers, old and grey-bearded as he was, because he sneered at them and their horses, alluding no doubt to their horse-stealing ways. Somebody bushwhacked the Unionist brother that same day, probably in revenge. My grandfather's father, Rook Sanders, took the hint and decided it was time to move to the county's southernmost extremity, as near as he could get to Mississippi without crossing the line out of Tennessee. That's where my father grew up.

Next, with all my children not yet arrested by park rangers, we loaded back into the cars and headed home for Memphis. Saturday we turned around and drove three and a half hours to Heber Springs, Arkansas, this time for my mother's family reunion. I take my children to these reunions not merely because I want to torture myself driving and burning up tires and gasoline, but for a better reason. To my shame, as a young man I stupidly skipped them all, despised them, and cut myself off from my own people and place. Some of those folks have died, and only they knew the dead I never got to meet. Dead and living, I threw away my chance to know them, and to know that part of who I am. I don't want my children to follow my error. Most of all, I want them to know their people and place. I want them to know who they are.

By the time we got home Sunday afternoon, I was begging to go back to work. My fun bank was plumb full.

FIVE BOYS AT WORK

When your children reach sixteen and the feed bills jump, you may begin wondering what they are good for. Here's one example. These are our five boys (out of seven children) along with a friend, equipped for work. Our two wood-burning stoves eat three cords of wood every winter. Justin (19, kneeling) and Worth (17, right rear) can split red oak *far more efficiently* than I can. We're breaking in Wright (15, middle rear), and even Christian (almost 13, with cap) and Zachariah (almost 9, with chainsaw) pitch in loading and unloading. Zachariah wanted to wield an ax, so I bought him a little hatchet to split kindling.

ARE YOU TOO BUSY?

A friend called to apologize for not finishing something he had long promised. "I should have gotten it done, but I've been *so busy,*" he explained.

I'm sure he was, but then, who isn't busy? Who doesn't have more than he can do? With a twinge of guilt, I realized "busy" is usually a smokescreen for my own procrastination, or my real priorities, usually misplaced.

Susan reminds me often that every day God gives us time enough to finish the work he has appointed for us. God gives us peace. We work; then we rest. We don't have to work seven days a week; we work six, but he pays us for seven. Our success does not depend on our efforts, but on Christ in whom we rest.

If you hear me say, "I'm too busy," hang up or hit me in the head with a hammer. I have just as much to do as God knows I need. I will delight in my work all day, then delight in the rest that God gives me. Whatever remains, I'll get to it tomorrow. Work makes up only *part* of our lives.

Another acquaintance forcefully reminded me of Man's Greatest Excuse for not spending time with his family. "But I don't have time to spend with my family! Don't I work hard to provide for them?" Thus we men wrap ourselves with the invincible mantle of self-righteousness to defend ourselves from every failure to spend time cherishing our wives and bringing up our children. We want to work at everything but love. It won't wash, because we all know we *like* working, and we're just camouflaging our self-indulgence as devotion to duty. I can never forget a sign that used to hang on a building on Central Avenue in Memphis: "No other success can compensate for failure in the home."

Time robs us too quickly of those tender years when wife and children need our presence and love. Yes, I know it's not tender when you've been broiling in a car for three hours and the fighting kicks up in the back seat, or when you leave one behind at a gas station. But underneath plays a hope that they will remember all this and delight.

A FOUR HUNDRED DOLLAR DOG

It happened Wednesday night. Jack was hit by a car!

No sooner had I shut my eyes than Zachariah came running in, crying and yelling that Jack had been hit by a car. I was exhausted. I had to speak twice that week at the Great Revival in the Southern Armies Conference, barely had time to put together a speech, give it, and dodge the bricks from my listeners before I had to leave immediately on Thursday to speak in Wichita. On top of that I was finishing a newsletter all week. I was burning the candle at both ends and in the middle with a blow torch.

Wednesday evening after supper I lay down on the couch to grab a couple minutes' sleep and prepare myself for staying up most of the night to finish my next speech. We live on a country road with very little traffic, so the children often play there. Jack was with them after supper, and a passing car had hit him.

I ran down to the road to find Jack bloodied and knocked out, his leg obviously broken and who knew what else. We slipped some towels under him and lifted him gently onto a piece of plywood, then loaded him into the station wagon. I did my best to keep working regardless, knowing that Justin (19) and Worth (17) were taking Jack to the vet.

When the vet finally called, the news wasn't good. It cost nearly two hundred bucks just to get him x-rayed, and then all we knew was that he had a broken leg. The x-ray didn't tell us anything about ruptured spleen, ruptured bladders, or other internal injuries. Surgery to repair the break would cost somewhere between five hundred and eight hundred dollars.

What could I do? This thirty dollar dog was fast becoming a thousand dollar dog, and I have seven kids and a wife to feed. There's a limit, and it looked like Jack had reached his. It would cost fifty dollars to "put him down," said the vet. Susan, our resident penny-pincher and -stretcher, didn't need to say anything to me. I understood the choices all too well. But when she ventured a word on economics, I made everything worse by losing my temper.

I finally got to bed at 3:00 a.m., my work finished, but still agonizing about that dog. By the time I woke up, a possibility had hatched in my head. Susan had to leave at 6:30 a.m. to take the newsletter to the printer, and I had to speak at 9:00 a.m. If Jack was still alive, I would get Justin to pick him up and take him to our regular vet in Collierville.

I made the arrangements and called the vet. She was quite understanding when I explained that I just couldn't spend an exorbitant sum on Jack. When I returned from my speech, with the clock now ticking for me to get to the airport, I called her again.

The only thing wrong, she said, was his leg. Both the tibia and fibula were fractured. She could operate and install a plate for $350, or tape it into a wire splint for $175. He would recover completely, so there was no need to put him down.

Poor Jack was taped up into a splint and arrived safe at home after I'd already arrived in Wichita. Now that I had time to think, I began to ask myself why an otherwise sane person would willingly spend almost 400 bucks saving a thirty dollar dog.

OCTOBER 1995

JACK'S BACK

After the car hit and nearly killed him, Jack is back and in fine fettle. We had to keep his leg splinted for six weeks, then keep him quiet for one

week more. Jack was a puppy when he was hit, but just about doubled his size while he was penned up. He's so happy to be free he spends most of his time running, and can jump five feet high from a flat-footed start.

UNCONDITIONAL LOVE

A few days ago our old one-eyed Labrador, Sparky, stopped eating and just laid around in the sun in the front yard. After a couple of days he moved down to the lake bank across the road, and that was the last I saw him alive. The children found him in the bushes. He had passed peacefully away. We buried him next to the lake where he loved to swim and chase ducks.

When I was growing up, I never had a dog all my own. Until Scruffy came to live with us last spring, I had never known dogs, or at least never paid them any mind. Before we lost him to a speeding car, Scruffy's faithful and unconditional love had astonished—almost unnerved—me. I did nothing to deserve it (I wasn't even the designated dog-feeder), but he lavished affection on me just the same. When I worked in the garden, he would lie in the grass for hours, content just to be near me and await my will.

Unmerited, faithful, unconditional love: that's what Jack, Scruffy, and Sparky have shown me. God revealed himself in these three dogs. These lowly creatures—*dogs*—had shamed and surprised me with a devotion so pure, so intense, so unchanging, and so self-forgetful that I had no choice but to love them back. I loved them because they first loved me.

Was I foolish to spend so much money to save a thirty dollar dog?

I reckon it depends on the dog.

SHOOTOUT AT ELMWOOD

The Walk through Elmwood Cemetery kept us running, and almost (literally) killed Zachariah and me. More of that below.

For over 150 years Memphis has buried its dead in Elmwood Cemetery. In its eighty acres, over 70,000 Memphians are laid to rest. Elmwood joined the Robert E. Lee Sons of Confederate Veterans Camp of Memphis to sponsor a walking tour of the Cemetery. Elmwood was founded in 1852, just nine years before the War began. Let's get that name straight. Some call it the Civil War, but not here in the South. Some in the South call it the War Between the States, to make the point that every state was sovereign. I call it the War for Southern Independence, because the men who fought this War looked back to their grandfathers in the American Revolution by calling it their "Second War for Independence." From Memphis to Mobile, from Charleston to Shreveport, Northern armies carried on a war of annihilation against Southern civilians, demolishing in four years the rules of warfare that Christian civilization had thus far spent eighteen centuries observing. Don't expect me to call the war Civil because there wasn't anything "civil" about it.

The Walk recreated the lives of ten people buried in Elmwood who were active in that War for Southern Independence. Volunteer actors in authentic dress portrayed Memphians buried there. On a circuit of a quarter-mile, the actors presented five-minute monologues that brought to life the War as it played out in our home city of Memphis. Yes, I did have a part. I played Joseph Shepherd, a Memphis merchant who died in prison here after the Yankees accused him of trading with the Confederacy. Susan was a guide.

I wasn't too sure about this project until I read the scripts. The heroic lives of these uncommon men and women will move you to tears. They did me.

Joseph Shepherd originally opposed the War. General William T. Sherman's persecution of civilians under the Yankee occupation of Memphis—arbitrary searches and arrests, harsh martial law, and cruel imprisonment in filthy, death-dealing conditions—changed his mind. Shepherd was finally arrested for surreptitiously trading with the Confederacy, his

property was seized, and he was thrown into the Irving Block Prison where malnutrition, cold, and disease killed him. He is buried at Elmwood.

Susan made everything we wore except Justin's hat, shirt, and vest, and my hat, shirt, and frock coat. (Okay, she didn't make Justin's boots, but she did make her own hat and Mercy's). Susan made my period trousers and shawl collar vest, and I bought the frock coat (an exact replica) at Jarnigan's in Corinth. Frock coats have no exterior pockets, but they do have two pockets in the tails, handy if you are a contortionist. Susan made her own dress out of green brocade. Old Hot Needle Hattie, as her daddy used to call her, was still sewing the night before the Walk.

We set out to create a historical reenactment, but the actors were so carried away by their parts that we ended up creating a work of art. Something changed. When we played our parts, we were no longer acting, we were carried away. We became those people, alive again and face to face with our hearers. Spectators were moved to tears. It was a hard sell, but I persuaded Justin to play an unknown Confederate soldier in the Walk through Elmwood. He was a little damp to light, but once he caught fire he did a great job, and has become an enthusiastic reenactor. He's from Tennessee. I wouldn't expect anything else. Blood tells.

You enter Elmwood Cemetery over a humpbacked, single lane bridge with high walled sides. As you come off the bridge, a wide paved area a hundred yards long and fifty yards wide stretches out where all the cemetery roads converge. On the big day the actors showed up at 5:30 a.m. for a local morning TV show. I took eight-year-old Zachariah with me. By 7:00 a.m. we had finished with the first TV show and were waiting for the next station's camera crew to set up.

Fifteen of us, including women in hoop skirts, were standing about a hundred yards from the bridge. I realized Zachariah had disappeared, and turned to look for him.

About that time I heard what was either gunshots or a car backfiring. I looked to the bridge. A black Camaro came racing toward me at sixty miles an hour, full bore, backfiring and dragging its muffler. It was headed straight for the crowd of actors. Everyone stiffened with shock. At the last second the driver veered off and disappeared down one of the cemetery roads.

I looked back at the bridge just in time to see Zachariah ambling over it toward me. "Where have you been?" I shouted. "Come here, quick!"

Zachie ran over the bridge, and had no more than stepped off when another car zoomed over. This one slowed down long enough for the two riders to ask where the Camaro had gone, because he had side-swiped their car. Somebody pointed down that lane, and the second car took off after the Camaro.

We hustled Zach and the women into the cemetery office building. Seven minutes later the black Camaro appeared again, having circled through the cemetery and found no way out.

Gary Hood, the Walk organizer is also a Sheriff's deputy. He also happens to be descended from General John Bell Hood, of the Confederate States Army. *Robert E. Lee's* General Hood, a brave, aggressive, reckless general who lost the use of his arm at Gettysburg and lost a leg at Chickamauga. Gary Hood stepped in front of the speeding Camaro and raised his hand to stop, but the driver just gunned it.

Gary jumped aside, pointed his .45, and shot out the front tire and then put a bullet through the engine block.

The Camaro squealed around the corner on a flat tire and front hub, then vanished back into the cemetery, smoking all the way.

Police cars began to pour over Elmwood bridge. I counted nine in a row, then a pause, then three more, pause, another three. Fifteen cars in all. You'd have thought the cemetery had been baited with donuts. They got their man. They also got the two poor fellows whom he had side-swiped, arresting them and locking them in squad cars too. Them they eventually let go. I confess: I don't always understand the logic of law enforcement.

SOUTHERN HERITAGE DAYS

This beautiful lady is my wife Susan, photographed last Memorial Day at the Confederate Ball. Memorial Day, you may or may not know, was begun by Southern ladies when they began decorating the graves of Confederate and Union soldiers in Meridian, Mississippi, in springtime. The practice quickly spread to other Southern states. Thus, around this time every year the *Southern Heritage Society* hosts Southern Heritage Days, ending with the magnificent Confederate Ball. This year the Ball was hosted by the Great Moments of the Great Battles of the Civil War Reenactment. I'm wearing the uniform of my reenactment group, the First Tennessee Light Artillery. I must confess that I have no generational connection to that unit, but a practical one, i.e. I know the man who bought the cannon for the unit and he drafted me. The uniform is wool, slightly thicker than your electric blanket and overcoat combined, but amazingly cool even in the sun. Once you sweat clean through it, it's cool as a wet blanket.

Don't get riled or get your Yankee dander up. If any War Between the States reenactments are staged near you this year, grab your kids and *go.* A unique way to teach your children history, reenactments give you an eyewitness's understanding. You experience the very sights and smells and sounds of the war. And if you ever get a chance to attend a Confederate Ball, *don't miss it.* I dance almost as well as I pilot space capsules, but there's always a dance master—or mistress—to make it easy. You *will* have a *ball.*

Every summer Lloyd Sprinkle, a Baptist pastor from Virginia who reprints classic Southern books, sponsors a conference, "The Great Revival in the Southern Armies." This year "How the South Became the Bible Belt" takes place in Memphis in August. Fifteen great speakers, historians amateur and professional, and no admission.

Some people don't understand why I make the effort to attend these conferences and reenactments. Mississippi writer William Faulkner summed up the Southern perspective when he wrote, "The past is never dead. It's not even past." If you read Andrew Nelson Lytle's *A Wake for the*

Living, you understand that if you take pains to know and love them, the dead aren't dead. Lytle was born and grew up in middle Tennessee and north Alabama, descended from the first settlers, and he knew most of them in person. When he was past ninety, he wrote *A Wake for the Living* retelling all the memories and stories about his folks. I love these people not because they were good and true and noble. A lot of them weren't. I love them because they are mine, as nature obliges every man to love his own flesh. Like it or not, they made me, and they live on in me. Can I know myself if I don't know them?

In the 1930s, along with eleven other Southerners, including Robert Penn Warren and John Crowe Ransom, Lytle published a book called *I'll Take My Stand*, warning the South that she ought to carefully ponder the bargain she was about to make in giving up her own agrarian culture for the homogenized industrial one proffered by the North.

I thought I knew a lot about Southern culture and history when I started down this road. I had a college education and several years of graduate work. In fact, I didn't know anything much worth knowing, and have to throttle back my anger over what I never was taught, the history and wisdom of statesmen and of keen students of human nature and valuers of love and family and eternal things and of the painful, prickly truth at all costs. The value of tasting life and loving, instead of gobbling your way through.

CHRISTMAS TRADITIONS
OLD AND NEW

JANUARY 1996

Christmastime shredded my schedule. Can you imagine how a knot in a shoelace feels when you pull it through the eyelet? That's how I felt over Christmas, but I survived, and even remembered once again to buy my wife a present. (I have never *in fact* forgotten, although I have once or twice brushed perilously close.) Almost forgetting is one of our Christmas traditions. Now a tradition is not a rut. A rut is doing the same things year after year because you don't have enough imagination to do anything new. A tradition is something you do once and discover a joy so deep that you do it again, Christmas after Christmas, to keep on savoring it and make it last.

We always cut a cedar tree in the woods. Last year, Susan nearly killed me for cutting one fourteen feet tall. It took her a day to decorate, and a day to put it all away. However, I did remember to buy my wife an anniversary present—16 December 1967—*and* a Christmas present.

This year we had a fourteen-*and-a-half*-foot Christmas tree. If that sounds like excess, it probably is, but it's a real heart-stopper when first you lay eyes on it. Besides, after twenty-eight years, we have so many ornaments it takes a tree that big to display them all. She won't admit it, but I think Susan secretly enjoys unpacking those ornaments, because every one carries a storied memory.

I always cut my own Christmas tree, and thanks to a kind friend, this year's was the best ever. But it's hard to find a well-shaped cedar tree that size. Cedars usually grow in thickets, so it's hard to find one evenly shaped. So you might find one twenty feet tall that's so ugly you wouldn't use it in a coal chute. Usually they're bald or flat on one side, which means you stand with a mouthful of cedar needles for half an hour, twisting and turning the tree while your wife decides which side looks best. You have to find a tree right in the middle of a field by itself, or cut the top out of one forty feet tall.

Me, I don't care anything about Christmas trees. I just do it for the children. (*Right.*)

Susan continued a tradition of sentimentalism when she gave me my own car window squeegee with a built in scrub pad. In the handle there's a neat well for liquid window cleaner. My, I was thrilled to unwrap *that*. I will admit that it was better than a case of motor oil, but I would have preferred industrial strength, antifungal foot powder. *Okay, okay*, I did get a few other nice things.

Justin (19) thought he'd do the family a favor this year, so he got us another puppy. Having enjoyed a full-blooded Labrador for nearly ten years, we are now on a *half*-Labrador streak. Jack the *Dalmador* is half Lab, half Dalmatian. Now we have an *Ozzidor*: half Lab, half Australian shepherd. They named him Bear. Imagine a furry, fat, black basketball with ears and a tail. Jack came to love Bear, once we convinced him Bear wasn't an hors d'oeuvre.

SMITH FARMS BACON

When my mother and daddy used to live in Albertville, Alabama, on their way to visit us for Christmas in Memphis they always stopped by Holly Pond, near Cullman, to buy bacon, ham, and sausage. It probably reminded my daddy of the home-cured bacon his father made. He kept the taste for home-cured ham without learning the craft. The Smith Farms store looks like just another country fruit stand, but they make the very best breakfast sausage you have ever eaten. It's coarse ground, and hidden in the taste there lurks a mysterious acidulous *tang* that perfectly sets off the flavor. Their bacon is made the old fashioned way, not injected with chemicals. It is firm, not mushy. It still has the rind, so after you've eaten the bacon you have something left to chew on. They mail everywhere. **Smith Farms**, 1825 Fourth St. SW, Cullman, AL 35055; (205) 737-0505. Wherever they earn it, I shall enthusiastically give you my endorsements, right down to the names, addresses, and telephone numbers of the roadside joints, mom-and-pop-, family-, and real-people-run businesses that I patronize. Otherwise, God forbid, what alternatives will you have to Walmart, Pottery Barn, and Burger King.

For reasons unclear to me, a lot of people think Southern country food is boring food. It's not, and I don't say that just because I grew up eating it. You eat it and tell me. My grandmother started cooking when she was five, standing on a stool to reach the stove. She made fried pies— her own inimitable pastry stuffed only with her own home-dried, *never canned*, tangy fruit, then fried to brown perfection on a hot dry skillet. Not boring, any more than the holy grail of smoked meats, bacon—or the apotheosis of pork, country ham—is boring. No, this is high art, as high as the culinary art can reach, and worth cherishing.

When I was a little boy my father's grandfather had a smokehouse, a dark place of mystery, pregnant with the smell of wood smoke, meat hung high above, and the secrets of the craft. He knew how to cure hams and bacon, but to my sorrow, that was yet another skill my school education left out.

A TIME TO PLAN

Though I'm not a farmer, I like to think like one. Winter, I hope, has now done its worst. Time to pull out the seed catalogs and plan a garden. We have another tradition. After Christmas passes, I list everything in the seed catalog I want to buy. Susan then takes the list and edits it down, throwing out the Peruvian purple potatoes, spaghetti squash, and forty-eight varieties of cayenne. Just once I'm going to catch that order before she mails it. I've got to see purple potatoes growing before I die. Besides, you can never have too much garden. My children think you can, but my ambition knows no bounds.

FEBRUARY 1996

A SONG OF JOY

Mercy is eleven years old, and she is what you might call a "loud" child. When she's busy working in her room or playing outside, she unconsciously starts singing, and the volume keeps twisting higher and higher. The way Susan explains it, her little heart just overflows and it has to come out somewhere, so she sings.

The Psalms tell us that when God approaches his creation, the trees dance for joy, and the hills skip like little lambs. How could it be otherwise? Their Master approaches, and the whole creation trembles and shivers, not from fear, but from joy over what and who he is.

Ever notice a dog when his master comes home? That dog is so happy he trembles and shivers all over. He jumps and dances for joy. He just can't help himself.

In our wretched fallen world sin and death mar everything. How easy it is to be cast down, focusing on the sorrow! But the *leitmotif*, the recurring, all-covering theme of the universe is not defeat, but *victory*. Not sorrow, but *joy*. That joy stirs even unsinning angels to sing unbrokenly one mighty hymn of joy in their Creator. If even the brute, unwitting creation shivers with the same joy, uncontrollably dancing—then what joy are we capable of, we who are created in his image?

"O, sing unto the Lord a new song!" exclaim Psalms 96 and 98 (Authorized Version). May we all be blessed enough to have our hearts overflow into song.

WHEN THE SANDERS
LEFT FARMING

MARCH 1996

I can't seem to stay out of Georgia this year. I will speak for Alexander Stephens Day in Crawfordville, Georgia, hundreds of miles from here. "Little Alec," as he was called, was the dyspeptic vice president of the Confederacy. I'll be the one with a goatee, gray planter's hat, and black frockcoat. If you don't know who Alexander Stephens was, you might not enjoy it. If you do know of "Little Alec," you'll be interested to hear what I have to say about "Why the South is under Attack." The attack on the South has nothing to do with racism. It has everything to do with social change by intimidation, destroying Southern culture by perverting symbols like the flag most associated with the South, filling them with alien meaning. The flag actually incorporates the Saint Andrew's Cross, a reminder of the South's Christianity, but also of her Scottish and Scotch-Irish heritage. B.Y.O. Flag.

Back in Memphis, we'll be staging another Walk through Elmwood Cemetery. This year's Walk will feature General Nathan Bedford Forrest and his family and friends. Forrest, his wife, and family were originally buried there. In 1904 he and his wife were re-interred in the base of his statue in Forrest Park, a few miles away. What fascinates me most about Forrest is that he effortlessly leapt from common life—successful, but

27

common—into greatness. Forrest has captured my interest and won't turn it loose. The more I learn about him, the more I want to learn.

Shiloh Battlefield and McNairy County lie between where we live outside Memphis and Huntsville, so we stopped at Selmer, the McNairy county seat, for forty-five minutes' worth of quick genealogy on my father's family, who settled there in the 1820s. My father's parents are buried in the graveyard at Shiloh Church, with his father's mother. The church was built on that site long before the 1862 Battle of Shiloh took place. When we parked to visit the graves, I noticed a historical marker I had never seen before. The 11th Louisiana Infantry and Bankhead's Battery, forces of the Confederate States of America, had been positioned there on April 7, 1862. Today there's an artillery reenactment group in Memphis by the same name—Bankhead's Battery—and my son Justin happens to be a member.

My father was born in 1910 in Michie, Tennessee, just seven miles from Shiloh. As a boy he would wander through the woods on Saturdays— barely sixty years after the battle—and return home with pockets stuffed with buttons and Minié balls and bayonets and all sorts of artifacts long since disappeared. His mother's father, Benjamin Franklin Sanders, had a farm there, and was a wheelwright. (My grandmother's father and my grandfather's father were first cousins, so my father's mother and father third cousins, both named Sanders.) Moving from Corinth in the south to Shiloh, the Confederate Army had to march right past his door.

I found a Tennessee record that Benjamin Franklin Sanders had signed up for the Confederate Army in 1862 in Columbia, but I found no other record of his service, and no discharge. In the family there was a story that the Confederate government sent him home because they needed wheelwrights worse than they needed another soldier. Time has hidden the truth. I have a picture of him from 1874, from the waist up—bushy beard, piercing eyes, and that sinewy thickness of body that comes from working hard all your life on a farm. I have a picture of my great-grandmother taken the same day. She has her hands folded on her stomach. She was pregnant with my grandmother.

Far as I know, there aren't any of the Sanders family name left in Mc-Nairy County. The War and its aftermath sent a lot of them west to Texas and Oklahoma, then the next generation, like my father, moved away for the sake of work. My daddy never had a taste for farming. He was the youngest boy of five children, and was always in for a good time, but not so enthusiastic about work. When he was about ten, he was supposed to be picking cotton with his brother and sisters, and thought it would be funny to imitate his uncle, who had lost an arm, so he stuck one arm down in his overalls and was limping along picking cotton with one arm. Unbeknownst to him, my grandfather, whose sense of humor lay dormant for months at a stretch, saw a double crime: not working, plus making fun of a crippled uncle. My daddy never saw him coming till that cotton stalk in my grandfather's hand struck him like lightning.

THE MAGIC ROAD

In twenty-eight years of marriage, we had never before worked up enough courage.

The last four months have been brutal as I wrestle with knots that I just can't untangle. These aren't small knots. So far I am now counting ten years of IRS and state persecution in my life, my business, and my church over an issue that I tried to clear up on day one of starting my gold and silver business. That knot seems always hanging over me. So the day after we put the last newsletter into the mail, we finished up one other project and I cleaned off my desk. About noon I told Susan to pack a bag. She told the children she thought we would be back, but wasn't sure *when*, and we climbed into the car and headed east. I wasn't sure *where* we were going, but we were *going*, that much I knew.

HIGHWAY SIXTY-FOUR

We headed for Highway Sixty-four. Sixty-four runs straight across the bottom of Tennessee, from Memphis in the southwest to Chattanooga in the southeast, roughly following the state line. Nearly two centuries ago it was the old stage road. We currently live in a rented house just east of Memphis, so our quickest way to hook up with 64 was to drive east on Highway 57 all the way to Pickwick Lake at the Tennessee River, till the two roads join.

I call Highway Sixty-four the "Magic Road" because it passes through middle Tennessee, some of the world's most beautiful country. I make that boast advisedly, since I have traveled the US, Europe, New Zealand, Australia, parts of Central America, and Illinois. Middle Tennessee is lush and mysterious, with little hills that look like giant's cauldrons overturned on flat valleys and dark hollows hiding mossy secrets.

THE CROSSROADS OF DIXIE

As beautiful as middle Tennessee is, I wasn't prepared for Wayne County. Had someone known we were coming and passed through with busy broom and dustpan to make sure everything was clean and tidy for us? I wanted to stay, but restlessly wanted to keep driving, too, so we pressed on to Lawrence County, leaving behind Waynesboro, "Home of Mark Collie." (Who was Mark Collie, anyway?)

The county seat of Lawrence County, Lawrenceburg, boasts itself as the home of Fred Thompson. This name I vaguely recognized as belonging to a former presidential hopeful, but I wondered at its brag-worthiness. On the way into Lawrenceburg we passed several restaurants, but every

time I suggested we stop, Susan objected that there weren't enough cars parked around them. When we located a motel, I asked the clerk where we could find a good restaurant. "Your *better* restaurant,' she informed me with great confidentiality, "is the Brass Lantern, just outside town."

It was dark by the time we found it, but Susan was satisfied by a parking lot chock-a-block with cars. "Obviously your *better* restaurant," I observed as we climbed out of the car. Okay, the grub *was* edible, but don't look for it in the Michelin restaurant guide.

Lawrenceburg, Tennessee, is the Crossroads of Dixie? Why? Look at the map! It's right there in the middle.

MAMA J LEAVES US TO MIND THE STORE

We weren't hurrying to meet any schedule the next day, so right after we passed into Giles County we stopped at Mama J's, a log cabin store covered with American flags. Now for Susan the word "vacation" means "shopping." She never met a gift shop she didn't like, and I must admit Mama J's had its charms. In addition to the standard tourist bait, the proprietress, "Mama J," offered clever signs and crafts made locally. I learned she grew up in Stuttgart, Arkansas ("Mosquito and Rice Capital of the World"), where my parents had taught school after World War II. To give you a flavor of the people who live in middle Tennessee, while we were browsing, Mama J remembered something she had left undone at home next door, and left us alone in the shop while she ran her errand. I am proud to report that Susan did not shoplift a single trinket or souvenir.

TRACTOR GRAVEYARD AND FRIED PIE HEAVEN

Down the hill into Giles County we drove, and I began to notice that we were passing through Tractor Graveyard, hulks of rusting machinery on both sides of the road. We spied the Green Valley Store and pulled in. Susan's shopping gland was working overtime, but what interested me most were the *homemade fried pies*.

Now your *better* fried pie does not at all resemble the glop-filled, cardboard–skinned, commercial counterfeit. From my grandmother's kitchen I knew that a genuine fried pie is fried in a dry skillet, is at least as big as your hand, and must be prepared from *dried*, not fresh, fruit. Green Valley may have been Tractor Graveyard, but it was Fried Pie *Heaven*.

GILES COUNTY COURTHOUSE

Thus fortified, we resumed our route to Pulaski. The Giles County courthouse, "Built by the Public, Dedicated to Justice," reigns over the square. Built about 1910, it is magnificent. Before we toured the inside, we visited the monument to Sam Davis, a 20-year-old Confederate scout hanged there as a spy during the War. The courthouse is exquisitely ornate, and the upstairs courtroom one of the most interesting I have ever seen (and I have seen the insides of more courtrooms than I ever wanted to). Filled with oak stained dark by the years, it has a gallery or balcony above, and theater seats below, backlit by windows on three sides. The area behind the bar is surrounded by audience on three sides. A shining brass bar-rail rests on squat little balusters, and the jury is seated *in front of* the bench.

We left the courthouse and drove a couple of blocks to the Episcopal Church of the Messiah, built in 1885. These old Episcopal churches are not numerous in Tennessee, but are exceptional for their simple dignity and reverence. Other than a few Presbyterian churches, there are very few that old. In the 1830s Bishop Otey, the first bishop of Tennessee, came from North Carolina to Nashville, packed up a horse, and set out over west and middle Tennessee, planting churches in the wilderness. He died during the War for Southern Independence, and is buried at crenellated St. John's Church at Mt. Pleasant. We never miss a chance to visit one of these churches, and they often hide wonderful surprises. As you enter the sanctuary of Emmanuel Church in LaGrange, golden letters above the altar warn: "Thou God Seest Me."

Back on the square in Pulaski the friendly lady at the Chamber of Commerce told me where to find the Sam Davis Museum, but said it wasn't open all the time. She graciously called the caretaker so we could meet him there. You'd have thought the only reason anybody had come to work in Pulaski that morning was so that Susan and Franklin would feel welcome.

WE MEET JACK DANIEL

We left Giles County and crossed Lincoln County (named for Revolutionary War general *Benjamin* Lincoln—not the other Lincoln). Outside Fayetteville, Highway 50 took us north to the Jack Daniel's Distillery at Lynchburg. Would you believe that two *million* tourists a year visit Lynchburg, population 315? Whether you like whiskey or not, the distillery is something to see. Anyway, you can't *drink* whiskey there, or even *buy* a drink. Moore County is dry for whiskey and has no taverns. Until the General Assembly passed a special act permitting it, you couldn't even buy a bottle of JD at the distillery.

There are *fifty* warehouses built in the hills and hollows of Lynchburg, each holding a million gallons of sour mash (*not* bourbon) whiskey aging in charred oak barrels. Each warehouse is worth $13.5 *million* in federal excise taxes, and another $4.5 million in state taxes. Inside the warehouses it's freezing cold because the whiskey stores the winter cold and won't freeze. Standing in the warehouse, one of the tourists asked our guide, Sammy, if he hadn't ever wanted a job tasting whiskey.

"Nope," Sammy responded positively. "I hadn't never wanted one of them tastin' jobs. I been lookin' for a *swallerin'* job."

I PLAY STRAIGHT MAN TO A MOTEL CLERK

When we finished our tour it was so late that we drove the fifteen miles to Tullahoma looking for a room. We drove up and down the strip, but found only one motel. I went inside to haggle.

"Have you got a room with a king-sized bed?"

"Yes. You can have a room on this side [*pointing to his right*] for $44 a night, or a room on this side [*pointing to his left*] for $59 a night."

"What's the difference?"

"The rooms over here [*left*] have a Jacuzzi."

Back to the car to consult Susan. She and I agreed we could almost *buy* a Jacuzzi for $15 a night, so we opted to sleep Jacuzzi-less. "Don't forget to ask him about the Triple-A discount," Susan warned me. She likes that discount.

"Do you give a Triple-A discount?"

"Nope. I reckon the management figures what with being the only motel in town, we don't have to do that."

By now I was beginning to feel like the straight man in the Arkansas Traveler routine.

> "Does this road go to Little Rock?"
> *"Naw, it don't go nowhere. It just lays there."*
> "How'd your taters turn out this year?"
> *"Didn't turn out at all, we had to dig them out."*
> "Do you know anything?"
> *"No, but I ain't lost, neither."*

"Do you have a continental breakfast?"

"Well, we *will* have, beginning next Wednesday, but I don't guess you'll be here then. The management has had trouble finding somebody to run the restaurant, but they'll have somebody come next Wednesday."

"Okay, never mind breakfast, can you give me a room away from the road, back toward the back?" The motel sat right on the highway, and we didn't want to hear eighteen-wheelers grinding gears all night.

Yeah, I could [pause—*long* pause], but then you'll be right next to the railroad."

"I see what you mean. Well, just give us a room in the middle."

In the end, it was both quiet and clean.

A TRANSPLANTED DELI

Next day we returned to Lynchburg to tour the town square, a.k.a. shop. This fit Susan's conception of proper tourist behavior. In addition to the standard Southern café (believe me, a memorable gastronomic delight you should never pass up), there was also a deli. We were lured to the deli by the sandwich we saw a lady eating in one of the stores. I recognized from his accent that the counterman did *not* hail from Moore County, so I asked him where he was from.

"New Hampshire."

Be that as it may, he made a killer sandwich.

FALLS MILL

We took the back roads from Lynchburg toward Winchester because we wanted to see **Falls Mill Museum of Power and Industry** (134 Falls Mill Road, Belvidere, TN 37306; (615) 469-7161). Built in 1873 as a textile mill, the owners have restored it as a working water-powered grist mill. It was fascinating, with a thirty-two-foot waterwheel and belts and shafts running through the three-story building. They sell stone-ground flours and some of the best grits I have ever eaten. (Store-bought grits, for the uninitiated, aren't worth throwing away.)

We still had enough daylight to make Winchester and more shopping. I stood on the corner, drinking in the American Fascist-style courthouse built in 1936 at the depth of the New Deal. (You didn't think *I* would say the "*height* of the New Deal," now did you?) The New Deal and its Tennessee Valley Authority set out to capture Tennessee's soul with government money. I think they only half-way won, and then only the ugly half.

THE TENNESSEE VALLEY AUTHORITY

This trip greatly restored both of us. I won't wait twenty-eight years to take another adventure. Still, I couldn't altogether shut down my mind from seeing the world in the light of my current troubles. Some things were too obvious. While generally the countryside was prosperous, too many sadly vacant stores on town squares show how spotty that prosperity is. Many rural areas rely, unfortunately, on government-bought prosperity: community colleges, public works projects, welfare, agricultural subsidies. Since politicians can shut these off at a moment's notice, they bring no *permanent* root of prosperity.

The mention of Tennessee Valley Authority always brings to mind a story told me by a former TVA employee. Seems that TVA was sampling pig dung a few years ago, and some of the samples disappeared. The ensuing full-scale investigation revealed the danger to national security inherent in leaving official pig dung samples lying around unsecured, so TVA rented a bank vault to store the pig dung.

For sixty years rural Tennessee has been the battleground in a war for America's soul. How much government money will you take for your soul? Since the New Deal, federal welfarism has waged war on personal independence. Tennessee Valley Authority's fight against private property distils that warfare. (How come nobody ever mentions that Joe Stalin *shared* Roosevelt's interest in rural electrification and hydroelectric power?)

WILL THE SOUTH SURVIVE?

The Tullahoma local newspaper reported that the town was trying to pass liquor-by-the-drink laws to woo "up-scale" restaurants to locate themselves at the interstate interchanges. Such new South boosterism has made heavy inroads into local culture. New South boosterism began in the nineteenth century with Henry Grady, editor of the *Atlanta Constitution* newspaper. Boosters and their legislation promised that all the South needed was to give up everything that makes us the South and become just like the North, and we would all be happy and wealthy (nobody mentions boring). A Chamber of Commerce might conclude that we need to entice more national chains to establish prosperity, but chains and industry move elsewhere, leaving behind unemployment, a victim mentality, and no lasting prosperity. I call this kind of approach "*homo economicus*" anthropology. It reduces everything—and every man—to a question of money. One hundred and twenty years later, the promises still haven't been fulfilled. I don't know whether to laugh, cry, or puke, but I am pretty sure that passing liquor-by-the-drink laws will not bring economic Nirvana to Tullahoma. When you make a bargain to sell your soul, first make sure that the devil can pay.

Will boosterism finally gobble up the South? On the surface, the homogenization of culture that comes with the local economy relying on big business and chain stores means we are steadily being de-Southernized. The whole effect is to homogenize and standardize the landscape. That seems to be proceeding fast, while the people themselves seem unchanged. What's happening at the roots of Southern culture is anybody's guess. On the outside the country here is peaceful, pleasant, friendly, independent, and helpful, but at the same time there's that welfare mentality, some *very* fat people, and loads of government economic intervention.

The courthouses at the heart of each county tell this story of the South eloquently. Giles County's 1910 courthouse retains the integrity of the South's past. In Lawrenceburg sits a hideous 1960s "Modern" courthouse. In Waynesboro looms a 1970s tenement-style concrete slab. In Winchester squats a blocky 1936 "American fascist" look that would gladden the heart of any fascist or Soviet architect. Gone are the stately courthouses, the statues of soldiers holding muskets and facing north, symbols of the community's continuity and long life, and with them fast disappears our local history. In Lawrenceburg nobody really knows who tore down the old courthouse and left the square naked save for the statue of David Crockett (who started his political career here) and the monument to Mexican War veterans (which probably stands here because so many Tennesseans fought for Texas's independence in the 1835 Texas War of Independence against Mexico and later for the United States in the 1848 Mexican War). Both monuments seem strangely out of place without the courthouse. In Waynesboro things wax comical. The builders had stuck metal letters on stalks into the concrete slab reading "Wayne County Courthouse." Some wag stole the C and R and now it reads, "Wayne County Outhouse."

Nevertheless, many of these counties have attracted back-to-the-land, simple-life people, and their roots are permanent so they will recreate permanent prosperity. The land is rich, the people true, the leadership clueless. I could move elsewhere, but Tennessee is my home. Our family could do a lot worse than finding itself at home out here.

Perhaps the fate of the Magic Road says it all. The state is turning Highway Sixty-four into a four-lane, bypassing exquisite little villages like McBurg and big towns alike. I know it's *faster*, but *God help me*, I do love the old road so much better.

A THOUSAND DOLLAR
DOG WITH SOCKS

APRIL 1996

Jack the Dalmador entered our lives as a thirty dollar puppy. Then a car hit him and broke his leg. After all the gauze settled, he was a four hundred dollar dog.

Now he's returned to his bad habits and won't stay out of the road. A few weeks ago a car hit him, knocked him flying through the air, and threw him into a brush pile. He limped and gimped for a week, but was otherwise unhurt.

Then on Palm Sunday we came home from church to learn that Jack was bleeding from a two-inch gash below his ankle. We've doctored on it for a week, smearing the cut with triple antibiotic ointment, bandaging it, and covering it with a sock. Jack is the only dog in Shelby County wearing Argyles. Yesterday I broke down and sent him to the vet for stitches. Jack is now a $648.92 dog, and won't even get stitched till Friday.

When I got that last bill, I looked at him hard and said, "Jack, I've got a limit, and your medical insurance runs out at $999.99."

He just sat there, looking up at me and thumping the floor with his tail.

I'm not sure, but I think as I turned away, I saw him smiling.

JACK IS MENDING

Nearly everybody who calls wants to know about Jack. His wounded ankle has healed, but we never got him stitched up. The vet said there wasn't any point in it. Chalk up another forty-eight dollar office visit. Jack is now a $696 dog.

I'm not sure I have gotten much dog for my money, either. Jack's no thunder-hound. A few nights ago Susan and I drove home through a vicious spring storm. We beat the storm home, and were sitting in the kitchen with the back door open, enjoying the cool breeze and waiting for the storm to hit.

When it hit, so did Jack—the back screen, that is. There was some of the worst rain, lightning and thunder I've ever seen. Jack wouldn't mind me and go to the dog house. He just stood in the downpour at the back door, stubborn as a wet mule. Then lightning struck in our back yard, cracking like a rifle in your ear. Poor Jack... I thought we were going to have to start beating on his chest to get his heart going again. He looked so scared and pitiful we had to let him in.

I'm fairly sure that Jack was a politician in his last life, or at least a professional fund raiser.

A "WALK" WITH JACK

Strange how some things flourish in some years, and others in others. A few years ago it was Garden (a.k.a. Signature) Spider Year. From spring through fall, a bumper crop of big yellow and black spiders decorated every tree and corner with webs. Then it was Possum Grape Year.

This year it's *leaves*. Fall in west Tennessee usually brings the season when the leaves turn brown and fall off, but this year a lot of rain and cool weather have made the trees extraordinarily colorful. Few maples are native here, so we don't get those flashy green shading into yellow, orange, and red, but the sumac and dogwoods turn red, the oaks every shade of orange and yellow, the sweetgums every shade from yellow to deep purple, and the hickories a magnificent glowing gold.

Last Sunday afternoon I wanted to take a walk. The day had dawned rainy and foggy, then cleared, then clouded up again. It was nearly eighty degrees and intensely muggy. I had the children call the dogs into the house, because I didn't want to have to keep up with them. They race ahead and chase cars and generally make themselves pesky.

Halfway around the lake I was enjoying the spicy smell of damp Tennessee woods when I heard something jingle behind me. It was Jack, tongue flailing the air.

Now you can't take a walk with Jack, because Jack won't walk. He runs, and he bounds. Like a rabbit. Or a kangaroo. Jack thinks the command "Heel" means, "Show me yours." If there's another dog *anywhere*, he'll find him and get in a fight. He'd fight a circle saw—no judgment at all.

I grabbed Jack's collar and walked up to the next road headed for my neighbor's. He has thirty acres, most of it pasture, and I knew I could walk there and Jack could run, bound, circle, sniff, and leave messages for other dogs without being run over.

Even overcast days can be beautiful, especially with everything overgrown and luxurious from the summer—grass, weeds, wildflowers—looking like it's been specially arranged for my admiration. We followed through the back pasture all the way to the creek so Jack could have a wade, and then circled back to my neighbor's house.

When we got up to the house, my neighbor was standing outside with his dog, Homie. Jack believes that Homie was created solely for Jack to fight with. After breaking them up, my neighbor showed me the addition he is building on his house. By the time I got back outside, it was just beginning to rain, and I was a twenty-minute walk from home. But it was so warm and muggy that the rain was, believe it or not, *lukewarm*, and just landed with a pleasant cool *plink!* against my skin. It was just getting good and dark. As I walked home, to the west the top of the treeline was barely backlit through the clouds. Time I got home, I was soaked, and trying to figure out which one of us, Jack or me, had had a better time.

Probably Jack, cause I didn't get in a dog fight.

JACK THE BABY

The windows in our bedroom reach the floor, and just outside is our deck. During one storm (always late at night) Jack discovered he could scratch out the screen and climb through the open window into our bedroom.

We're now going on our fourth screen since Jack's discovery. A few nights ago, just as we went to bed, a magnificent thunderstorm broke out. Nothing bothers phlegmatic Bear, the other dog, but Jack quickly assumed his wonted whining position outside our window. At first he says nothing, then you barely hear the strained whine of desperation. "Jack, go get in your dog house." That only encourages him. Louder whining. Scratch on the screen. "Jack! Stop that!"

He knows (I promise, he knows) just about how long it takes me to fall asleep, and waits that long to begin scratching again. I bark, he runs around to the front door to scratch and whine. Then he sneaks back to the window.

Awakened for the twentieth time, I stormed to the front door and tore it open to whack Jack. He slithered in the door and melted into the carpet. "No, you don't! OUT!" Like a cross between a garter snake and a Dalmador, he slithered into the hall, flattened himself into a perfect imitation of a square yard of carpet. "OUT, Jack!" Two more attempts to convince me he was simply a piece of dog-colored carpet likewise failed.

Jack is nothing if not persistent. Okay, I will admit, he finally won. It was either let him in or stay up all night guarding the screens. But I didn't let him into the house proper. Just into the mudroom.

Jack may have won, but I still have my pride.

A YANKEE GIFT FOR CHRISTMAS

MAY 1996

My sons, Justin (19) and Worth (17), don't usually hang out in grave-yards, but in the last Walk through Elmwood they both played William Montgomery Forrest ("Willie"), son of General Nathan Bedford Forrest. Susan was a tour guide. Yours truly played General Nathan Bedford Forrest himself. I had to do it in civilian clothes because I couldn't afford his uniform.

Justin wore a kepi, the flat-topped hat typical of the War for Southern Independence. There's a story behind Justin's hat that proves kind manners grow North and South.

I wanted to give both boys kepis of their own as Christmas gifts, since they're now both interested in reenacting. Last year Justin borrowed mine. A kepi is a flat-topped, visored cap made popular by the French army in the 1830s and adopted by both sides during the War. I called The Quartermaster Shop in Kimball, Michigan—substantially north of the Mason-Dixon line—where I had bought my own uniform for the First Tennessee Light Artillery. They make authentic reproductions. Little did I realize that my uniform had been made to a *custom* order, not stock, so I just ordered two Confederate regulation artillery kepis.

This was pushing up on Christmas, so I was frantic when I received my confirmation and saw that the *regulation* kepi wasn't gray with a red band, like mine, but red with a dark blue band, I called The Quartermaster

Shop. The lady there was understanding, but in the end it was my mistake. The kepis were custom-made, and I admitted that I would get to eat seventy dollars' worth of kepis. I had ordered "artillery" kepis, and those were red, not gray.

Two or three days before Christmas, my package arrived from The Quartermaster Shop. I opened it glumly, and what should I find to my surprise but gray kepis with red bands! On the invoice the lady had written, "I discussed this with my boss, and we decided we would rather you got what you wanted for Christmas." Their thoughtful kindness was the perfect icing on my Christmas. The kindness was all the sweeter because it came from the wrong side of the Mason-Dixon line.

A CONFEDERATE WEDDING

I was driving along country roads swathed in new greenery, like a cathedral with walls and ceiling of green-stained glass. On the long drive home I turned on National Proletarian Radio.

I do this to annoy myself, and because the other stations are even worse. Besides, sometimes they play something other than Bartok. Sometimes they play Bach. As much as I love music, I have no musical pretensions whatever. I play the banjo, but can't read even one note.

It was my morning. Bach's "Toccata and Fugue in D Minor" came on the radio. It was a perfect spring morning, the kind of day that makes you long to get in the car and drive to the end of the earth—*fast*—when you feel so wild you're not sure you'll ever come down again.

As I listened to Bach's music, tears started into my eyes. What a man, to invent such a thing! How far past searching out are the ways of God who could create such a man, who had in him such music!

JUNE 1996

WILT THOU LOVE HER, COMFORT HER, HONOUR AND KEEP HER

In May reenactor friends of ours married, and wanted a period wedding. Some reenactors are *really* serious about reenacting. Bride and groom were dressed in the styles of the period, and many of the guests were too. The bride and groom were married beneath a double stairway in a house built—I am not joking—as a replica of Arlington, Robert E. Lee's home. At the last minute I was dragooned into the choir. Evidently nobody had ever heard me sing. Part of the choir was on the stairs on one side, the rest on the other. This gave me bird's eye view, and time to meditate on the ceremony, which was read from the 1862 Confederate Episcopal Book of Common Prayer.

The 1862 Confederate Prayer book caused all sorts of trouble. Before the War, the American Book of Common Prayer contained a prayer for the president of the United States, which replaced the prayer for the King in the original English Book of Common Prayer. After Louisiana seceded in 1861, Bishop Leonidas Polk noted that it made no sense to pray for the president of what was then a foreign country, and so he substituted a prayer for the governor of Louisiana. When the Southerners set up their own Episcopal province in the South, their 1862 Book of Common Prayer included a prayer for the president of the *Confederate* States. For some reason, this made some northern army officers especially angry, and numerous Southern priests in occupied territory were thrown in jail for refusing to insert the prayer for the *United* States' president.

Shortly after the War ended, the septuagenarian Bishop Richard Hooker Wilmer of Alabama was summoned to Mobile. There a Yankee colonel berated and screamed at him because he had instructed his parishes not to pray for the president of the United States because the Church had not yet officially changed the prayer book. Utterly exasperated by the old man, the colonel finally shouted, "How long are you going to keep doing this?"

Without batting an eyelid, Wilmer shot back, "How long are you going to be here?" The military occupation ordered all Episcopal churches in Alabama closed, and they were only re-opened when President Johnson rescinded the order months later.

I had forgotten how beautiful the wedding ceremony is in the Confederate 1862 Prayer Book:

Wilt thou love her, comfort her, honour and keep her in
sickness and in health; and, forsaking all others, keep
thee only unto her, so long as ye both shall live... I take
thee to my wedded Wife, to have and to hold from this
day forward, for better for worse, for richer for poorer, in
sickness and in health, to love and to cherish, till death do
us part, according to God's holy ordinance.

The mystery of marriage moved me to tears. I was half afraid I'd embarrass Susan.

SOUTHERN BARBECUE
RIGHT AND WRONG

JULY 1996

B est thing about traveling with men (as opposed to wives) is you can stop and eat anything you want, even boiled peanuts.

Early in June I spoke at the Southern League national convention in Montgomery. I drove down with two friends, Mark Denison and Doug Smith. Coming home we left late Saturday afternoon and drove back through Birmingham. By that time we were starving. We all wanted barbecue, but we couldn't find a likely-looking BBQ joint.

When we stopped at a light just east of Jasper, over to our left I spied a fieldstone building with a gigantic sign: "SLICK LIZARD SMOKE-HOUSE—Fill your gizzard at Slick Lizard."

Against their better judgment, I persuaded Mark and Doug that we had probably discovered barbecue heaven. Mark turned left to circle around the Slick Lizard. It was a long narrow building where you could buy only through the take-out window.

We pulled up and out popped one of the cutest, most helpful yellow-haired girls you have ever seen. We ordered three jumbos. My curiosity boiled over.

"Where'd y'all get the name Slick Lizard?"

She never blinked, never batted an eyelid, never even paused. "At Nauvoo."

Ohhhh, yes. Well, that immediately raises *another* question.

"What's Nauvoo?"

"A town up the road a few miles."

I was still baffled. Doug and Mark were starting to snicker uncontrollably.

"But what's the Slick Lizard?"

"*Slick* Lizard (*accent on the first word*) used to be a little town up at Nauvoo."

Our inquiries brought all three ladies working inside to the window to explain. There used to be an elementary school at Slick Lizard, which has now been absorbed as part of suburban Nauvoo. There's a motel there we ought to see, too, with every room decorated differently.

Then one lady said, "Show 'em the tee shirt." Unhappily, they had only *one* "Slick Lizard" tee shirt in stock, and that didn't fit any of us. Then somebody suggested they show us "the cap"—a baseball cap with Slick Lizard and motto.

About that time the ladies gave us our order, and we drove off. It was dark and we were having fun, so I didn't check my barbecue before I bit. Barbecue's barbecue, right? You get coleslaw and hot sauce on it, and maybe, if you're really lucky, old-fashioned vinegar-based sauce—*unlucky*, sweet sauce laced with wretched artificial smoke.

Now I would not, voluntarily, *ever* put ketchup and dill pickles on a barbecue. I wouldn't even imagine such a barbarism, but before I discovered what lurked on my barbecue, I already had a big bite in my mouth.

"What kind of barbecue sauce is that?" I mumbled in bewilderment. It didn't taste bad, mind you, just not quite *familiar*.

"It's *ketchup*," Mark replied in a serious and somewhat wounded tone.

"*Ketchup?!?*"

"And dill pickles."

I couldn't have been more surprised if he had said, "Peanut butter and motor oil." More surprising still, as much as I hate to admit it, it was *delicious*. The classic, succulent pork had been cooked superbly, over a slow fire with steam. The good ladies had loaded up those buns like they expected us to be the last customers that night and it was either give us the meat or throw it to the dogs.

If you ever get near Jasper, Alabama, don't miss the **Slick Lizard Smokehouse No. 2**, 1300 Highway 78 E, Jasper, AL 35501; (205) 221-0811.

CHICKEN CASUALTIES

AUGUST 1996

Jack became a felon.

Our neighbor had a flock of guineas and unusual chicken breeds. For some time he had been trying to cross two rare breeds, and had at last succeeded.

But Jack (and Bear, too) had developed a taste for chicken. Our neighbor caught them red-handed, so to speak. Jack was still in the pen, and had killed about thirty chickens in all, including the cross-bred chicks. Susan was mortified. Our neighbor was extremely kind and understanding (instead of taking a shotgun to Jack, which in his shoes I probably would have done, and only called the neighbors to come drag off the corpse).

I finally had an unassailable reason to shop for chickens. I seized it with both hands. For years I have wanted to go to the giant flea market in Ripley, Mississippi, called "First Monday." The first Monday of the month is Trade Day at Ripley. Dealers are spread over twenty-five acres. As the name implies, it is supposed to take place on the first Monday, but dealers start arriving and setting up the Thursday before.

It's only a little more than an hour from where we are in Memphis. We were supposed to meet friends at the Hardee's on Byhalia Road in Collierville, Tennessee, at seven sharp, but the friends heard "the Hardee's in Byhalia, Mississippi," so by 7:30 a.m. we were already tangled up. They were waiting in Byhalia thinking we were late as usual, and we were waiting in Collierville (with a carload of kids) wondering why they were late for the first time ever. A timely phone call to our answering machine solved the mystery.

The road to Ripley takes you through Potts Camp, Hickory Flat, and Blue Mountain—green, rolling hills under a mild August sky. When we parked at the flea market, I asked the courteous fellow with the missing teeth who collected my parking fee how far the flea market went. It was on flat ground and I couldn't see. "*They's* twenty-five acres," he replied. I despaired of ever bumping into my friend.

First Monday offered something for everyone. Almost every booth had puppies for sale. From 9:00 a.m. to 4:00 p.m., I kept chanting to my kids, "Nothing that eats! You're not taking home anything that eats."

I took along a number of one troy ounce pure silver coins, thinking that if there was any place in the world I could barter with silver, it was a flea market.

Think again. Three times I offered silver or paper, and three times the seller took the paper. Apparently, ordinary people have no idea what silver is, or what it's worth. Nor do they know that the law of this land says silver and gold are money, the paper money being only a *fiat* currency. *Fiat currency*—from the Latin "let there be made"—is created by government decree and double-entry bookkeeping on the accounts of banks and central banks. I feel like the kid pointing out the naked emperor, but the United States Constitution, statutes, and common law all condemn the creation of money in this way, but everybody knows that bankers carry more weight than the law. In this upside down world, most people think of paper as money, rather than gold and silver. Don't despair—the purveyors of phony money haven't won yet. I remember in the great silver and gold rush of 1980, when silver raced to $50 an ounce and gold to $850, how quickly the market learned the value of everything. We were operating a shop buying scrap gold and silver back then. Before silver and gold started rising in 1979, you couldn't have found one person out of a thousand who even knew what a pennyweight was, let alone how many there were to the ounce. Within a few weeks of the rush, however, they could have told you not only what a pennyweight was, but what every shop in town was paying for a pennyweight of 14 karat, 10 karat, and dental gold!

I broke my own rule about bringing home nothing that eats. I came back with seven chickens and four guineas, hoping that perhaps they might ease our neighbor's loss. I had no idea there were so many different types of chickens: hairy-legged chickens, black chickens, white chickens, brown chickens, rumpless Aracuanas, Rhode Island Reds, Domineckers, standard or bantam, Anconias, Anacostas, and a hundred others. Since the children thought they recognized them as our neighbor's now defunct breed, I bought some bantam Golden Seabrights and Silver Seabrights. I also bought two of what I call "Utility Chickens" for a buck apiece to teach Jack to keep his paws off poultry.

When we got home sometime after 6:00 p.m., I still had to build a chicken coop to keep out my low-down, chicken-stealing dogs. Our neighbor was on vacation, and I somehow had to keep these fowl alive until he returned. When we got out of the car Jack thought he had died and gone to snack heaven. "What thoughtful people, to bring me four cages full of chickens!" That impression lasted about four nanoseconds, just long enough for me to smack his prying nose.

A few years ago I spent about a year building a dog house. I will admit I got a bit carried away. It's big enough for two Great Danes to play volley ball in, but that's all right. It is also big enough to hold seven banty chickens and four guineas. I evicted all of Jack's blankets and truck, and started ripping and cutting boards for a fence. Happily, Susan had some chicken wire.

While I was busy building the coop, Susan opened the guinea cage to give them a cup of water. She didn't wire it shut tightly, since she figured we would be opening it soon. Jack sneaked up near the guineas, and they panicked. The cage flew open. One guinea flew due south at slightly less than Mach 1 speed with Jack in *hot* pursuit. One flew north by northeast, disappearing around the house. One flew south by southeast with Bear's hot breath slobbering on his feathers, and one flew into the workshop.

After I had taken all this in but before I had decided which way to run, Susan decided to take up concrete diving. She was standing in the doorway of the workshop, and when she stepped out she tripped on a block of wood and almost broke her elbow. Now I *really* didn't know what to do first: chase the guineas, beat the dogs, or take Susan to the orthopedist. Needless to say, I looked after Susan first. Long after dark Saturday night, Christian (14) and I finished the coop and put the chickens to bed.

Whenever the chickens are out of their house, we tie the dogs up, and that's my problem. I have to figure some way to break them of killing chickens. I bought the Utility Chickens with a training scheme in mind. I plan to stake them out in the yard, put a pinch collar with a long lead on Jack, and every time he dives for the chicken, give him a jerk to remember.

CHICKEN CASUALTIES

Our neighbor didn't even get home from vacation before the chickens took casualties. Somehow the Silver Seabright hen got out, and the dogs nailed her under the clothes line. Although we kept the dogs tied up, Mercy and Zach let them loose not thinking what they were doing, and they got into the pen and gave one guinea a fatal heart attack and ran another into the woods. We got the survivors to our neighbor. I'm still looking for a replacement Silver Seabright.

If any of you has a better way of breaking a chicken stealer, please let me know. My only alternative is to drop Jack off a bridge somewhere, and admit that my thirty-dollar-puppy-turned thousand-dollar-dog has become a habitual and incurable criminal.

SANDERS-STYLE TOURISM

The folks in Gulfport and Biloxi have the "big eye"—as my uncle used to say—calling their shoreline a beach. You have to walk out 300 yards before the water reaches your waist. But my children and I enjoyed it all the same.

Despite a downpour at meeting time that almost washed us all away, the Southern League Chapter was superbly cordial.

We arranged to drive back Saturday by way of Columbus, Mississippi, where General Forrest spent a month of the War recuperating from an illness at Waverley Plantation Mansion, built in 1852. Colonel George Hampton Young, who built Waverley, was originally from Georgia, but he became a crony of Andrew Jackson, Tennessee hero of the 1815 Battle of New Orleans against the British and later United States president. Jackson appointed Young US Land Commissioner for the Mississippi frontier, and you can figure out what happened next. As the man in charge, he cut out a generous helping for himself and built a big house.

Young had ten children, including two sons who served in the Southern army during the War. Those two inherited Waverley but never married, so the house was shut up when the last one died in 1913 and stood empty until the Snows bought it in 1962. Amazingly, the house was nearly perfectly preserved. Waverly is octagonal, and all four floors open onto the central hallway. Todd Childs, who took us through the house, told us that during the War when Waverley hosted balls, the couples would fill up the ground floor dancing, and then spread out to all three upper balconies! Todd lives in Waverley, and sleeps every night in the room where Forrest recovered. If you ever get within 300 miles of Columbus, make it a point to visit Waverley. It *richly* repays the effort.

A WAKE FOR THE LIVING

I took my own advice and ordered a number of books. I thought *Georgia Scenes* (1835) was funny, but Susan threatened to kick me out of bed when I was reading the *Adventures of Captain Simon Suggs* (1845). I was laughing so hard it shook the whole bed and woke her up. These two books are the forebears—along with George Washington Harris's *Sut Lovingood*—of all Southern (and most American) humorous writing.

The greatest treat was Lytle's *A Wake for the Living*. I had already read Lytle's *Bedford Forrest and His Critter Company*, the liveliest Forrest biography in print, but I wasn't prepared for what I found. Lytle knows his people and their history so well that they seem to be right there in the room with you, quirks and all. From Madison Bell's preface to Lytle's last perfectly chiseled sentence of *A Wake for the Living*, his memoir of Southern history as he and his family experienced it was like coming home after years on stormy seas.

OCTOBER 1996

THE ANNUAL FAMILY CAMPING TRIP

This month we made our annual camping trip to Natchez Trace State Park, nearly to the Tennessee River and about two hours from our house. For more than ten years our church has been going camping there at the end of October. Last year we were rained out the first night. This year Susan, Mercy, Zach and I went up early, on Thursday, and for our trouble got rained on again. We went to bed under a clear sky with a gleaming sickle-moon, and woke up in the middle of the night to a powerful thun-

57

derstorm. My head and knee were touching the side of the tent, and as the lightning flashed insistently through my eyelids, I noticed that my knee and head were wet. I kept curling into a tighter and tighter ball, trying to escape the water. Apparently all the water repellent Susan had sprayed on the tent only made it suck up more water.

The morning dawned brilliant, though, and after we had hung everything out to dry, we headed back a short ways west to the next exit on I-40, *Parker's Crossroads*, where I always marvel at General Forrest, who with 2,100 Confederates beat 3,000 Union troops of two armies here. Forrest had his closest brush with disaster at Parker's Crossroads. Caught between two Yankee brigades after his daring raid through west Tennessee on December 31st, 1862, Forrest decided to whip one brigade and then turn and whip the other before they could unite to whip *him*. It would have worked, too, but the detachment Forrest sent to slow down the second army took a wrong turn and missed them. Just as the first Yankee army was raising white flags, the second caught Forrest in the rear. When an adjutant rode up, yelled to him that they had been caught between two battle lines, and asked what to do, Forrest shouted back: "Charge both ways!" He extricated all but 300 men of the 2,100 that were with him, and Yankee General Jeremiah Sullivan was so relieved to see Forrest's back that he didn't bother to chase him down (although he did telegraph Grant to announce his "great victory"). As a result, Forrest was able to cross the Tennessee River at his leisure, carrying captured men, arms, artillery, and supplies back to safety in middle Tennessee. He had entered west Tennessee across the Tennessee River at Clifton with 2,100 inexperienced troops, most of them unarmed. He had led thousands of Union troops on a wild goose chase through west Tennessee all the way to Paducah, Kentucky, and returned with even more men and a fully outfitted brigade.

Unfortunately, the expressway now cuts through the battlefield, but the Parker's Crossroads Battlefield Association has done a great job of erecting markers for a battlefield tour. Seeing it with my own eyes makes it so much easier to understand the battle than just reading about it. If you pass that way on Interstate 40, it's worth the forty-five minutes to tour the battlefield. Be sure to go *south* off the expressway first, and look for the driveway to the log cabin "Information Center." Ask them to tell you about the battle *before* you begin your tour.

They called it "Parker's Crossroads" because Reverend John A. Parker was living there in 1862 when Forrest came through. Parker and his wife Rebecca are buried there at Jones Cemetery. Every grave in the cemetery runs east to west, except those belonging to Parker and his wife, which run north to south. Parker was actually a *Republican* and a Union sympathizer—(even as far west as west Tennessee, loyalties were divided). That is, until the Yankees parked their guns in his front yard and invited Confederate counter-fire on his house. From that day forward, Parker became a staunch Confederate. Before he died in 1864, he left instructions to bury him with his head to the South and his feet to the North, so that when Gabriel blew his trumpet, he could "arise and kick the Yankees back north!"

I enjoy strolling through cemeteries reading the inscriptions and epitaphs. What a world of honor lies in the simple words "Our wife and mother." Upon how many tears rest those tiny tombstones with a sleeping lamb on top, "Asleep in Jesus." One old marker at the Jones Cemetery especially caught my eye: "Walter Cunningham, 1883-1885. Awaiting Resurrection."

As you move forward in time, the inscriptions generally become less eloquent—both our poetry and our realism have weakened. As we left the cemetery, we noticed what looked like a tombstone right next to the portal, but this wasn't a tombstone. It read,

Jones Cemetery 1845
No burying in the driveway

Ennis D. Fesmire

July 1973

Just picture it. The caretakers show up for work, only to find that someone has sneaked into the cemetery during the night. "Thunderation, they done buried another one in the driveway! Ennis is gonna be madder'n a wet wasp. Now we either have to dig 'im up and move 'im, or move the driveway again!"

I *hate* it when they bury people in the driveway.

NATHAN BEDFORD FORREST STATE PARK

On Saturday Susan and I took off by ourselves to visit Nathan Bedford Forrest State Park on the Tennessee River just east of Camden. Pilot Knob there is the highest point in west Tennessee, and right behind a monument to Forrest stands the Tennessee River Folklife Interpretive Center, which, being interpreted, means a museum of how folks live on the river.

They have a musselling boat there, and handmade fish nets and traps. But the best part is the taped interviews with local river people. If you grew up in the city, you probably think that country people are ignorant and stupid because they talk slow and use their own unique, but historical grammar. That would be a *big* mistake, because chances are they are wiser, and harder to fool, than most city folk.

In the Folklife Interpretive Center there is a quote from a local river man, Thomas James ("TJ") Whitfield. In 1944 the Tennessee Valley Authority condemned his farm because it would be flooded when they dammed the Tennessee River and paid him only forty-four dollars an acre for rich farmland. Whitfield comments:

> *A few people down at Pavatt's Cemetery agreed to have some of the graves moved. What they dug up was just a*

*pile of black dirt and then they moved that. I had a child
buried there, and I told that fellow that there was no
way he was moving that child of mine. It's watered-down
communism… that's what TVA is. Now it's based on a
different brand of socialism. But it doesn't matter what
brand it is because communism has failed and the TVA
has failed.*

Like I said, people who live in the country are harder to fool.

They were harder to fool than others about the Tennessee Valley
Authority. In the Thirties, a rural electrification craze swept the minds
of dictators around the world—sort of "keeping up with the Stalinses."
No ruler was a dictator worth his salt unless he had a plan to electrify the
countryside by building huge hydroelectric projects everywhere a river
bed dropped three feet in fifty miles.

Roosevelt wasn't immune to the fad; hence Tennessee Valley Authority
was born in 1934. The grand project would electrify the backwoods and
put chickens and ham on every table. Instead, TVA moved the table, and
the people too, *displacing, disseizing, and dispossessing* thousands of rural
people to make way for huge dams and lakes. Electricity was progress, and
"progress" was the New Deal's product. Uhhh—and a *little* oppression.
Many of those who dwelt in the way of Rooseveltian "progress" did not
go gently into that New Era. Great resentment abides today in Tennessee
toward the Tennessee Valley Authority.

My biggest complaint about what Tennessee Valley Authority did
that day was that it flooded the site of General Forrest's successful raid on
Johnsonville, Tennessee, just across the river on the east bank. Because
the area is all under water now, I can't see the unique lay of the land along
the old riverbank that made victory possible there in October 1864.

Johnsonville was a central supply depot for General Sherman's Union
army. Supplies were brought up the Tennessee River from the North,
dropped there, and then transported to Sherman in Georgia across Tennes-

see by train. Gunboats on the river and gun emplacements above guarded Johnsonville. Forrest grasped that the *west* bank offered a spot where his artillery could lob shells into the mountains of supplies across the river, but neither gunboat nor redoubt artillery could depress their guns low enough to return his fire. Forrest, whose grammar and language were often highly original, was serving as a member of one of the gun crews when he said, "Elevate the breech of that gun a little lower!" Anyway, he destroyed stores worth an estimated $6.7 million ($124.3 million at today's price) and cost the enemy an additional four gunboats, fourteen steamboats, seventeen barges, and 150 prisoners, while Forrest lost only two guns, nine wounded, and two killed.

The riverbanks are all underwater now, so you can't see the gun positions. Unless somebody clues you in, you'll never know what happened here.

THANKSGIVING IN JAIL

B y the time you read this newsletter, I will probably have returned to jail. You're probably curious why I am going to jail. In 1980 I opened my own business selling physical gold and silver. First thing I did when I moved the business here to Tennessee was write the state Attorney General to explain that my understanding was that exchanges of gold and silver money for paper money weren't subject to the sales tax, since they were exchanges of money for money. In Article I, Section 10 of the United States Constitution, it states that "No State shall make any Thing but Gold and Silver Coin a tender in payment of debt." So *only* gold and silver can be money in the United States. Even the Code of the Law of the United States, at Title 12, Section 152, says that "lawful money" means gold and silver coin of the United States. It seemed clear to me that gold and silver was money and therefore changing gold and silver for paper dollars, which were only an approximation or stand-in for real money, would not incur sales tax. To be clear, I wrote the state Attorney General asking what was his official position. He never bothered to answer my certified letter. Or the second. Or the third.

I was thick enough to believe that if the law and the constitution says that silver and gold are money, they really are, so I started a gold and silver bank, to offer people an interface between paper and metallic money. The IRS sent a man to work for the Tennessee Revenue Department with the specific assignment to find charges against me.

At dawn on January 9, 1990, the IRS informed me, with a vicious SWAT team raid, that I was indicted on charges of tax evasion. They charged me with violating a law that had been on the books in Tennessee nineteen years without being used: "delaying and depriving the state of revenue." No one had ever been charged under it.

Thus began my merry pilgrimage through the courts.

About two weeks after I was released from custody after the SWAT attack, I received a card from a dear Christian friend in Germany. Unconscious of these events, she had sent the card as a New Year greeting. It was dated January 9, 1990, the very day we were arrested. She quoted Psalm 68:19-20 (in German): "Gepreisen sei der Herr! Tag fuer Tag traegt er unsere Last, der Gott unseres Heils! Gott ist fuer uns ein Gott von rettender Taten, und der Herr unser Gott hat Auswege aus dem Tod." (I translate this passage from the Lutheran Bible as: "God be praised! Day by day he bears our burden, the God of our salvation! God is for us a God of rescuing [saving] deeds, and the Lord our God has escapes [lit. 'ways out'] from death.")

Since I began fighting the federal government on the money issue, I have been in jail twice. Since I began fighting the state, I have been in jail three times. The prosecution was unconstitutional, but in my case they made an exception. Debtor's prison has been abolished, but not for me.

Surely there is no shame in defeat after fighting so long. I am going to jail, but I have not denied the truth. In the face of injustice and oppression, I have only one weapon: my willingness to stand for the truth and suffer the consequences. I understand that this is a deep and dangerous doctrine that is easily perverted. It certainly doesn't mean that God *always* wants me to suffer, or that my first tactic should always be to throw myself on the enemy's bayonets. God does not willingly afflict the sons of men, and I am not interested in martyrdom.

The conditions of my release from this latest imprisonment are so impossible to perform—six years' probation, $73,000 "restitution" (for what I never took—I never charged sales tax), and a thousand hours of community service—that I have no choice but to go back to jail instead. I have no idea what the judge will do when I appear and voluntarily withdraw from the Community Corrections program that I am now in. I may spend another month in jail, but it could be much, much longer. Don't worry—I've made arrangements to continue *The Moneychanger* newsletter regardless. You may even find it better in my absence!

I probably won't be sending out another newsletter before Thanksgiving. More than likely I'll be having Thanksgiving at the Shelby County Correctional Center, but, Lord willing, I'll be home for Christmas. Please pray for this to end.

The December newsletter will be a bit late going out, hopefully, around the nineteenth.

> *But he had sent a man before them, even Joseph, who was*
> *sold to be a bond-servant; Whose feet they hurt in the*
> *stocks; the iron entered into his soul.*

— Psalm 105:17-18
(Reformed Episcopal Church, Book of Common Prayer)

CAPTIVITY

voluntarily surrendered to serve twenty-six days so that I could get out from under the terrible burden of the alternative sentence. When the twenty-six days came to an end, I wasn't released. Only by living it can you understand the lurking fear that assails your heart once those jail doors close on you: "I'll *never* get out of here." Even when you recognize it as irrational and untrue, it keeps clawing at your mind.

Peter saw Christ walking on the water and jumped out of the boat to walk toward him. Peter kept stepping high and dry *as long as he kept his eyes on Jesus.* When he looked down at his own feet, he began to sink. You and I are no different. As long as we keep our eyes on the *unseen* but almighty God, we can walk on water. When we look at the size of the enemy, the war, and our own strength, we sink.

On my arrest sheet the bailiff wrote "violation of probation" when I had actually *voluntarily* surrendered. Instead of being shipped straight out to the penal farm, therefore, I stayed in the filthy dungeon of the county jail for three days and nights. When I was finally sent upstairs to a cell block, the first question the inmate in charge asked was: "Do you have a shank? You're probably going to need one in here."

MEDIUM SECURITY

When I arrived at the penal farm, a clerical error from the appeals court led them to misclassify me just below "ax-murderer." Instead of being sent to the Red Roof Inn ("Adult Offender Center") I was sent to medium security, the Hotel California ("You can check out any time you like, but you can never leeeeeave!"). There forty men are locked in twenty-three hours a day, with one hour out for exercise and three fifteen-minute trips to eat.

But all these curses turned into blessings, since they brought me together with Christian men who taught me godly hope and patience.

THE CHAINLESS CHAIN GANG

In some miraculous way Susan was able to get me re-classified *quickly* and after another detour I arrived in the Adult Offender Center on November 15, only *eleven days* after I had gone in. First job they set me doing on the chainless chain gang was shoveling mud and broken glass out of concrete ditches for "mosquito control." (It must be working. I never saw a single one.) You may think that sounds like a bad job, but only because you have never been locked up without sunlight, windows, or activity for eleven days. If you had, you'd call it a godsend.

YOU'RE NOT GETTING OUT ON TIME

The day before Thanksgiving Susan learned that I would not be released on November 29—another bureaucratic foul-up.

On December 4, all unexpected, I was told not to go to work because I was going before the work release board. By then I had forgotten about the work release application I had filled in the day I arrived in Adult Offender Center, "just in case" something went wrong. Work release is the West Palm Beach of imprisonment, allowing you to work outside at a regular job during the day, but still returning to prison at night. A friend had already applied to hire me on work release. When I returned to my "dorm" (twelve-man cell) after the hearing, I wrote the following:

And what other way could the iron enter into Joseph's soul? None. Solzhenitsyn spent over two decades in the Gulag, but no other way could God forge the iron into his soul. Countless other times, God has nurtured and tempered his people by oppression.

For the first time, today after ten years of IRS and state investigations and prosecutions, I can see an end to this trial. Even so, I have no inkling how far in the future that end lies.

For the first time, today I can see that the greatest end of this imprisonment for me was not to bring an end to the investigations. It was to restore my hope in Christ, which this weary train of adversity coupled to adversity had eclipsed. In fighting the legal battles, I forgot that the Lord performs great works, that with God, nothing is impossible: to him belong escapes from death. In no other way but by the repeated disappointments of this term of imprisonment could I have recovered my hope. Thus in very faithfulness has God afflicted me.

> *Thou hast ascended on high, thou hast led captivity captive.*
> — Psalm 68:18 (Authorized Version)

What is this change that I find in myself? It is as if for the first time I am reading the Word of God, for the first time seeing, perceiving, accepting, and understanding the love of God. It reminds me of my soul's honeymoon when I was first converted, when I would go to bed every night with my Bible and fall asleep reading it, so hungry was I to know God.

Yesterday it came to me that I ought to read Philippians, so riding in the van to work I opened my bootlegged New Testament and began to read:

That I may know him, and the power of his resurrection, and the fellowship of his sufferings, being made conformable to his death…
— Phil. 3:10 (Authorized Version)

When I saw this, the whole Scripture became one vast, jointed mechanism, and when my finger gently touched the words "the fellowship of his sufferings," all the Scriptures stirred and sighed in sympathy.

What kind of renewal is this? Is it simply self-deception or auto-suggestion? No, because I could not expect or even imagine the change this moment made in me. Surely it was the grace of God renewing and rebuilding me from the ground upwards in my darkest hour.

Without question, this charge is for me, but at the same time not for me, but for those who read these words. The divine economy always works so that not only is one end perfected, but also countless others.

First, the Lord had to clean my wounds, to remove all the dead flesh and trash from my will and mind and heart and desire, before he could give me another work. In my heart, the dam of deadness is broken, washed away in a flood of grace.

— Franklin Sanders
4 December 1996

As we go to the printer with this issue, Franklin is still in jail, but unless some other surprise springs up, he is scheduled to be released on December 20th. He said that I should tell you that December 20, 1996, will be the last day of seven years since the federal government indicted us for exchanging money for money.

— Susan Sanders

AMAZING GRACE

JANUARY 1997

Only thirty years ago this year, the federal government repudiated its last paper note redeemable for actual silver, the Silver Certificate. From then on you could not even get silver from the government in exchange for your Silver Certificates—they had already reneged on the Gold Certificates in 1934. Before then it would have been *unthinkable* to charge anyone criminally for asserting that gold and silver are money. Today, they've been doing exactly that to me for over a decade. "It's dangerous to be right when the government is wrong," warned Voltaire.

July 9, 1991, was the day God delivered Susan and me and fourteen other friends by an acquittal from the IRS charges in federal court. The state, in its own wisdom, managed to convict me. They found a never-before-prosecuted, obscure state law on their books and managed to prosecute me—for failing to charge sales tax on exchanging paper money for gold and silver, most especially Krugerrands, which they were glad to point out were not a United States currency under the Constitution. Krugerrands were why I spent time in the state penal farm. Pardon me if I don't sell them—or anything else—in Tennessee any more.

DOGSAVER

Christian (14) ran in the front door breathless: "Bear was running across the ice and fell into the water and he's in the middle of the lake and can't get out!" The harsh cold spell that struck the rest of the country had hit us, too, but it wasn't quite cold enough to freeze our lake all the way over.

We all ran down to the lake. About five yards from shore there was a ten-foot wide open space, then ice for the next fifty yards or so. Clearly, you couldn't walk on it and survive.

I told the boys to put the johnboat onto the ice and we would push our way out there.

Number one problem: the boat's rope had fallen into the water and was frozen in. We had all run down to the lake so fast, nobody had a knife. Send somebody for a knife! No, Worth has a lighter, he can *burn* through the rope.

We got the boat onto the ice, but with Worth (18 and 180 pounds) and Wright (16) in it, the paddles didn't give enough leverage to push it across the ice. Zach ran up to the house to fetch an axe. He comes running back with a *maul*, which weighs about five times as much as an axe. Worth maneuvered the boat close enough for me to hand him the maul, then with Wright in the back, began to pull the boat across the ice by smashing the maul down ahead of the boat and pulling forward by the handle.

Bear, meanwhile, was sinking again in the open patch about seventy-five yards from shore. Since he was half-Lab and half Australian Shepherd, on this occasion I was thankful he took after his Labrador ancestors, because it was about fifteen degrees and windy, and he was *swimming*.

Worth and Wright got about half way to Bear when I realized what I had done: I was risking two perfectly good boys for one half-breed dog. *Bright.*

With Worth pulling the boat ahead, Wright put my mind at ease by standing straight up in the boat, bending over, and reaching for the seventy-five pound dog. Visions of frozen adolescents danced in my head. "GET DOWN! GET DOWN! Don't stand up!" He crouched and pulled Bear into the boat, took off his thick down parka, and wrapped Bear in it. Alive thus far, Worth and Wright were ready for the trip back to shore.

Worth kept on hollering, but I thought it was just the terrible effort of throwing that maul ahead of the boat from such a bad position in the boat's bow. Then Worth pulled the boat near the shore and I realized *he had no gloves on*.

Boys and dogs survived, and once again Worth proved himself a life-saver—or this time, a *dogsaver*. He can really keep a cool head under pressure. (Of course, at fifteen degrees, that's not hard.)

IN-LAWS

When your daughter marries, one of the great side-blessings is a set of in-laws. John and Suzy Bain are the parents of our new son-in law, Johnny. Right after Christmas we saw the Bains at a party, where Suzy told my Susan this story about a Christmas Day visit to John's mother, Miss Minnie Belle. In March she will be ninety-seven years old, but she's in a nursing home, completely bedridden, and doesn't communicate at all. During their visit Suzy decided to sing to her. I'll let Suzy finish the story:

> "She's always liked to sing a lot, and she really
> responded. I started singing hymns with her—*Amazing
> Grace* and *On Jordan's Stormy Banks*—and she sang
> right along, never missing a word.
>
>> '*On Jordan's stormy banks I stand and cast a
>> wishful eye;
>> To Canaan's fair and happy land where my
>> possessions lie.
>> I'm bound for the promised land, I'm bound for
>> the promised land.
>> O, who will come and go with me? I'm bound for
>> the promised land.*'

"When we finished *On Jordan's Stormy Banks* she lay there and got real quiet for a little while. Then she looked up at me and said,

> 'That's where *I'm* going.'
> I said, 'I know. Isn't it wonderful?'
> 'I want *you* to go with me.'
> 'I'll see you there, Maw-Maw.'
> 'That's good.'

"Then she just closed her eyes and went on back to sleep."

HOMAGE TO THE IRON MOTHER

MARCH 1997

The back door swung open and in walked Zachariah and announced: "I broke my arm, and this time I really did." Susan had sent our ten-year-old and youngest out to feed the horse and bring in the dogs' bowls so he could feed them. I had been working late the night before and had just gotten up and walked into the kitchen.

I turned to see Zach's left arm hanging at his side with two elbows. I felt like someone had just shoved a needle in my head from my eye-tooth down to my innards. Zachie hadn't been able to resist the temptation of walking back from the barn on the fence, about six feet off the ground. He fell and really did break his arm.

Susan has all the compassion a mother should, but after seven children, she is also notorious for ferreting out hypochondriacs of every stripe. She took one look at that arm and headed for her car keys. She knew the ropes.

While she was getting ready, Zachie lay down on the couch. Mercy, our twelve-year-old, was comforting him. Zachie tends to be a worrier. He was scared and in terrible pain, but he wasn't crying or screaming. He had great tears in his eyes, but he never let himself weep or cry out. He was taking it like a man. I was very proud of him.

I heard him whisper something to Mercy about losing his hand. I couldn't let him take that road, so I asked him: So what if the worst happened? What if he did lose his hand? Then he would just get a rubber

75

hand like Woody Harrelson in *Kingpin*—and he had to laugh at that. Yes, I know it probably wasn't a very bright remark, but I was desperate.

Susan took him to the hospital. I couldn't leave. On the way Zachie was struck by remorse for walking the fence instead of doing what he had been told. He looked up at Susan and said, "Oh, Mother, I don't deserve a mother like you!" Susan quickly assured him that was wrong.

Before I could get to the hospital, Susan called from the emergency room. Zachie broke the ulna in his left forearm nearly clean through, and dislocated his radius at the elbow. The doctor wasn't sure if he could set it without opening it up and pinning the bone. In God's good mercy, he was able to reduce the fracture without surgery.

When Zach came out of the surgery that night, some of his friends from church were waiting on him. He came home the next day, sporting a large cast up past his elbow.

MONEYCHANGER INVADES YANKEEDOM

What? Yours truly north of Mason-Dixon's Line? Yes, I spoke at the Wisconsin United States Taxpayer's Party state convention in LaCrosse, Wisconsin. You couldn't miss me. I was the only one there with a Forrest beard and a Confederate flag on my lapel. Pretty ironic, me speaking to a "Taxpayer's" party.

CHEAP HOTHOUSES

My friend Steve M. showed me how to make hothouses out of a few two-by-fours, PVC pipe, and plastic sheeting. Just build a rectangular frame with the two-by-fours, drill ¾" sockets for the PVC pipes, bend the pipes into hoops and insert into sockets, add a PVC ridgepole for stability, and cover with sheeting. Two plastic Quonset military-style huts now inhabit my garden, but that's all right. We can already taste the lettuce and arugula. Soon we'll plant greens.

ZACHARIAH'S ARM

My thanks to all of you for your prayers for Zachariah's broken arm. My own pain is one thing, but my child's pain is much worse. The cast was removed a couple of weeks ago, and Zachie's healing quite well.

SURPRISING SUSAN

Our deep, dark family secret is that Susan is actually *older* than I am. True, she's only forty-two days older, but older still. This April 12 she was facing a milestone birthday. I can't reveal which one, but it's between thirty and seventy (figure the average).

To make this birthday special, I asked our skilled friends, Lloyd and Peggy Bauer, to refinish a silver chest Susan's grandmother had given her. In those days silverware was a highly treasured part of the family estate, and duly guarded under lock and key. It was mahogany, but looked hopeless. The lid was cracked, a hinge was missing, it needed refinishing, the anti-tarnish lining had disintegrated, and the holders underneath the lining were all loose. It was a major reconstruction job.

But a special present wasn't quite enough for this birthday, so I arranged with our friends the Spearmans to throw a surprise birthday party for Susan. Even though all the children knew about it, Susan never had a clue something was cooking. When the day arrived, she was busy packing for our trip to Atlanta. I told her we were meeting friends for dinner. At the last minute Glenda Spearman called Susan with a diversion. Our daughter Mercy, visiting at the Spearmans, had supposedly twisted her ankle on the trampoline. Would we stop by on the way to the restaurant?

I was really fearful Susan would slug me for driving so slow. No, I wouldn't go straight to the restaurant and let her drive by herself to the Spearman's to check on Mercy. No, my foot wasn't broken and the accelerator was working just fine. When we arrived, she was completely surprised. And she loved her silver chest which the Bauers had restored to magnificence.

OLD AND NEW WAYS

Liberty and Johnny accompanied us to Atlanta. On the way back, we arranged to stay Sunday night at the Antebellum Inn in Winchester, Tennessee. It is exactly as you'd picture an antebellum Southern mansion, red brick with white columns. But when we arrived, there were no cars in the parking lot. We walked up to the door to find a note.

> "Susan: Come on in, the door is open, and the key is on the newel post. Be sure to lock up if you go out. There are soft drinks in the refrigerator, just remember what you take so we can charge you for it. Call me if you need anything. Phyllis."

No, we had never met Phyllis. Inside she had left a Sunday paper under the key, and upstairs we had our choice of four huge rooms. The back of the house overlooks pastureland and a lake. We unpacked and settled down to watch TV. Liberty, Susan, and Johnny got hungry, so they went downstairs to the kitchen. Downstairs is also a working restaurant. When they came back upstairs, they had obviously made themselves at home. They brought bowls of the most delicious soup I have ever eaten, brandied mushrooms with scallops. It was worth a trip to Winchester for that alone.

The next morning we met Phyllis Lafferty, who fixed tasty omelettes for breakfast. Most amazingly, we found out that she and her husband are transplants from Ohio. They're Northerners, pardon the phrase. Don't worry, they have done an exceptional job with this 1848 Southern mansion, and have located a chef who could compete with anyone in the world.

If you travel anywhere near Winchester, make sure you stay at the **Antebellum Inn**, 974 Lynchburg Road, Winchester, TN 37398; (931) 967-5550; fax (877) 969-5550.

MAY 1997

For the past month I have been experiencing intermittent computer troubles. The net result was that I ended up reloading all the programs, and for the first time have Windows 95.

Windows 95 has done nothing to soften my iron hatred toward Microsoft and all its Wicked Works and Ways. Their idea of curing a problem with the stove is burning down the house.

Never mind. In the course of all this, I loaded new versions of the programs I use and noticed how fragmented they were. The screen shows twenty or twenty-five boxes and buttons, and there is artwork building this way and that, for five or ten pictures to a page. The Internet is the worst of it.

The hallmark of post-modernism is fragmentation. I wonder how much of that grows from the influence of the cathode ray tube? As we children grew up, watching the picture of the wonderful world in the TV box fragmented our attention span into the time bubbles between commercials. I've read that learning disabilities and attention deficit disorder arise from young children spending too much time in front of a TV. Think about how fast, completely, and widely a TV broadcast changes subjects. My friend Bob Meier tells me the average American attention span today is four seconds, i.e., you have four seconds to rivet someone's attention, or lose it forever.

Computer graphic design has carried the fragmentation to a breaking point. Every program is filled with buttons and boxes and frames, all working and writhing at the same time. Add to this bewildering fragmentation on the screen—a telephone answering machine, a fax machine, a call identifier, and whatever else may be running in your office—and all ingredients for a nervous breakdown are close at hand.

REPUTATION IS VALUABLE, EVEN TO A MULE

Last month we took our Magic Road, Highway 64, to the Atlanta Investment Conference. My daughter Liberty and her husband Johnny went with us. It was a beautiful day, and just as we crossed over from Hardin to Wayne County, I looked off down in a broad field next to a creek bottom, and there were two men working a pair of Belgian mules.

Belgian mules are huge Palomino beasts bred out of Belgian draft horses. Johnny was driving, so I had him slam on the brakes and turn back around. We pulled up on the shoulder to watch these men work their mules.

The mules were pulling logs out of the underbrush next to the creek, about fifty yards from us. The men used no reins or control other than their voices. Very softly they would talk to the mules, or whistle or cluck, standing with their arms folded over their chests. With infinite care and perfect control the mules disappeared into the brush where the younger man would hitch them up to a log. Then a soft sound from the older man would send them straining out with the log.

It was beautiful to watch. I think I'd have given half of everything I owned (wife and children excepted) to be able to work a mule like that.

Suddenly one of the mules bolted out of the brush and ran about twenty-five yards, and then stood still. The younger man walked over to him, and reached up to stroke the mule's nose and forehead with his hand.

The older man looked up at us sheepishly. "She stepped on a branch, and it popped up and scared her," he explained. I reckon he wanted to maintain his mule's reputation.

SONIC BLOOM SPRING

This is a tough time of year for me. The air is filled with the scent of clover, willow, and honeysuckle, and across the road frogs sing all night in the lake. The days are crisp and sunny, and all I want to do is get to my garden, but work keeps getting in my way. We sprayed everything with Sonic Bloom this spring and for the first time our apple trees are setting fruit. Just wait until I get tomatoes in the ground.

Sonic Bloom is another discovery from the dark world of unpublicized discoveries. It's a "foliar feed," that is, you spray it onto the plants. Then you play—I am not kidding—classical music to them. Apparently the music pleases the plants so much that the mouths ("stoma") in their leaves open up and drink in the Sonic Bloom. That, at least, is the theory.

COMBUSTION ENGINES ARE
THE WORK OF THE DEVIL

Around newsletter deadline time I get wound a little tight. Not too tight, just about as tight as the mainspring in the famous Munich *Glockenspiel* tower. This month we're also trying to get the yard ready for a church picnic (we live on five acres east of Memphis) and plant a garden, but every time it almost dries out, the rain starts again.

We didn't have any operational lawn mowers anyway. We had to borrow a trailer to take in the forty-eight-inch lawnmower, and the smaller one goes to a repairman in another direction. We retrieved the smaller one, resuscitated after only two trips to the repairman, but it literally disintegrated in my hands—only *after* I had spent forty-five minutes repairing the pull cord. The whole front half of the housing fell off. Really. And the front wheels.

Then the *other* repair shop called. The forty-eight-inch mower was ready, but it rained and we didn't have the trailer to pick it up. By last Sunday my back was to the wall, and the grass was thirty-six inches high. Sunday night I made the forty-five-minute trip in our 1980 Ford pick-up (some call it a "put-down") to borrow the trailer. I could just make a gigantic round of errands Monday morning *and* get back to work if everything worked perfectly.

It didn't.

Susan's station wagon needed a new muffler, or we the passengers were going to have to buy a better burial insurance policy. The truck and trailer was too bulky for sixteen-year-old Wright to drive, so I sent him off to the muffler shop (twenty-five minutes one way) in the station wagon, windows down, and I followed in the truck, pulling the trailer. We dropped off the station wagon, picked up the forty-eight-inch mower, picked up the mail, bought a bottle of black strap molasses, and headed home, merely an hour behind schedule.

Nearly home, I hit a bump. The heavy trailer bounced, jerking the truck up and down, and I heard a loud noise. A fleeting rear-view mirror inspection revealed a long cylindrical object bouncing off the road into the weeds.

It was my muffler.

At this point I have spent a half day's time and $236 to get at least one working mower home. To this you must now add $110.79 for a new truck muffler, and the $42 to fix the small mower that is now parted like the Red Sea. I drove home, unloaded the big mower, returned the trailer, and Wright spent the rest of the day shuttling vehicles back and forth to the muffler shop.

Dawned Tuesday. The sun appeared. Wright and Christian attacked the yard, mower and weed eater blazing. They hadn't been working five minutes before Christian appeared to inform me that the mower wouldn't run. It just died.

I tried cranking, then took off the air filter cover and sent Christian for some starter spray. No small engine on my place starts without it.

We didn't have any. Then go back and get the WD-40. We had about two sprays of that, but after thirty or forty cranks and an injury probably necessitating back surgery, it was obvious the mower wouldn't start. I growled at Wright to hop in the car and make the forty-five minute trip to get some starter spray. I stomped back thirty yards to the house, climbed the porch, and then calmly exploded. I turned to the boys. Raising my hand shoulder high, I pointed to the mower and yelled, "Internal combustion engines are *the work of the Devil!*"

They weren't sure whether to laugh or to run. I'm not sure I was kidding.

AT HOME IN SOUTH CAROLINA

Late in May I learned about a great opportunity to send Wright and Christian to a week-long Christian worldview seminar in Norfolk, Virginia, sponsored by Calvary Reformed Presbyterian Church. The only hitch? I was committed to attend the Southern League Summer Institute near Charleston, South Carolina, which is nowhere near Norfolk. I wheedled at Susan all through June to convince her to take them and spend the week at nearby Williamsburg with relatives. She dredged up every excuse, but I finally cornered her.

Well… They were scheduled to return home on Saturday after the seminar. Before I left the Institute on Friday, I called Susan. "There's just so much to see," she purred, "I've decided to stay till *Wednesday.*"

They saw Jamestown's restored first successful English settlement in Virginia; colonial Williamsburg fully restored to its 1760 glory and packed with actors in period dress making everything from barrels to bread; Carter's Grove, the Carter Plantation built in 1755; and the 1864 Wilderness Battleground, site of the first battle between General Ulysses S. Grant and Robert E. Lee, all within easy driving distance, not to mention Virginia Beach—and they loved it all. If you have children, think about vacationing there next year.

Speaking of vacations, don't sell Charleston short. No city in the United States looks quite like Charleston. The historic area on the peninsula has all been restored, and it is a great cultural treasure. The Southern League Summer Institute was about an hour away on Seabrook Island, but we made several field trips to Charleston.

Since I didn't have to hurry home, Worth and I accepted Dr. Jim Kibler's gracious invitation to spend the night at his plantation home near Whitmire, South Carolina, built in 1804. Jim has done a superb job of restoring the place. It is one of those rare spots on earth where you immediately feel at peace and welcome, as if there were benign spirits hovering about. We thoroughly enjoyed ourselves, even though we didn't get to see or hear the resident ghosts.

THE BEST FRIED FISH YOU EVER ATE

Jim took us out to eat, and on the way we rounded a bend and there stood five huge wild turkeys in the middle of the road, *the first I've ever seen*. We drove to the Carlisle Fish Camp. That night the special was all the flounder you could eat for $4.99, including French fries, slaw, and strange oblong hush puppies. Worth and I agreed: it was the best fried fish we ever ate. It has a gymnasium-sized room with homemade plywood booths and friendly, eager waitresses. If you get *anywhere* near Carlisle, South Carolina, don't miss the Carlisle Fish Camp. Best of all, there's no "No Smoking" section. **Carlisle Fish Camp**, 4024 Carlisle-Santuck Road, Carlisle, SC 29031; (864) 427-7703.

FIRST GRANDCHILD

One night not too long ago Susan and I had already retired when the phone rang. I groggily woke up to the news that my daughter Liberty is going to have a baby. How do you go back to sleep after *that*? If I had stayed in bed I would have choked on my own tears anyway.

Children are an unspeakable blessing, but *grandchildren*!

All I could think about was that passage when the prophet Nathan announces to David that God would establish his house on the throne of Israel forever. Stunned by the grace of God, David prays: "Who am I, O Lord God, and what is my house, that You have brought me this far?" 2 Samuel 7:18 (New American Standard Bible)

Maybe more traits are inherited than we think. I never saw a woman take more joy in pregnancy than my daughter Liberty. Every time I see her she lectures me about the importance of salt for pregnant mothers or the latest refinements in natural childbirth or why pregnant mothers should eat ten eggs a day.

I think she inherited it from Susan. Liberty was born in Little Rock, where we became the third couple since the discovery of ether to try natural childbirth. When Susan first approached me about it, I told her that was only for people who eat nuts and berries, and she could count me out. She sneaked around and got a copy of Bradley's *Husband-Coached Childbirth*. Once I picked it up, I couldn't stop reading. I'd still recommend it as indispensable for *any* expectant father. It was hilarious and instructive, and I was converted.

But the obstetrician was not. Naturally, when Liberty arrived, our sympathetic obstetrician wasn't on duty. After I had coached Susan all the way through labor, delivery time came, and they whisked Susan out in the bed, and the obstetrician shut the door in my face. Momentarily I pondered my choices: pound the obstetrician into the concrete with a chair leg, or persuade humbly. As a first shot, I chose persuasion, and was admitted to the delivery room for the *denouement*.

I don't know of any event in the lives of a married couple that can bind their hearts together like natural (actually *prepared*) childbirth.

The delivery room personnel didn't know what to do with a mother undrugged, awake, and co-operating. When it was all over, one of them said, "It's time to go!" and the Iron Woman sat up and swung her legs over the side of the bed, ready to *walk* out of the room. They like to *fainted*.

That was only the preview. They should have seen what she did with the rest of them.

Now, we are proud to announce that with the addition of son-in-law *and* baby, we have exceeded the maximum allowable group size of ten people at Olan Mills photo studio. "You're too many," they informed us.

BREAKING GROUND

Our congregation has been saving for thirteen years for a home of our own, and on September 20th we're going to hold a ground-breaking ceremony.

Saving for a building has been doubly hard because in 1988 the IRS started investigating our church. I don't understand much that government agents do. The IRS was investigating me, but decided to jump to my church—Presbyterians, who have been resisting government control of the church for, oh, 500 years. The IRS demanded all the records, not just financial records, but everything including counseling records. The church session told them they would be glad to answer any specific request, but—in nice words— they weren't going to open the bride of Christ up to a government fishing expedition, not that there was anything to find anyway. Only one member of the church left.

That attack by the IRS cost the church heavily, but only proved how stupid the government agents were, because the church turned out all along to be "conspiring" only to obey the Scriptures.

KROGER-BACKED CURRENCY

I've been amazed at the number of ways people can raise money when they put their minds to it. Our church has done really well with garage sales, believe it or not. Also, the giant grocery chain Kroger will sell your organization "Kroger coupons," twenty-five-dollar certificates that are good at any Kroger store, just like Federal Reserve notes. For every $100 the church sells in Kroger coupons, Kroger rebates us five dollars. It's like free money, since it's a fairly safe bet you're going to buy groceries anyway. Frankly, I'd rather have Kroger coupons, backed by bananas, toilet paper, and cans of tuna fish than Federal Reserve notes backed by debt any day.

PEPPER PLAGUE

Something attacked and killed nearly all the varieties of hot and sweet peppers I ordered from the seed catalog. The leaves never developed spots or holes, in fact the plants appeared completely healthy, but they just *wilted*, as if they could not get water. No, I didn't forget to water them. Nothing seemed to help. Do any of you have any idea what killed my pepper plants? (Assuming somebody didn't sneak in at night and play acid rock to them.)

I DON'T GET IT

A friend from New Jersey visited not long ago and commented upon how much more modestly our scantily-clad women dress than *their* scantily-clad women. You could have fooled me. At Kroger I see women in short, short shorts who shouldn't leave home without wearing a lead-lined muumuu, just in case Superman is in the neighborhood using his x-ray vision.

I don't get it. Don't women realize that what you conceal is always more enchanting than what you reveal? Even a poker player knows that. Is there a conspiracy to suppress the wondrous air of mysterious femininity that dresses give a woman? (Okay, my secret is out; write me all the angry letters you want.)

OCTOBER 1997

GARAGE SALE DOG

Maybe I just lost my mind. At the church garage salc I was supposed to be selling stuff, not buying it. There was a four-month-old puppy up for adoption. Maybe I got hooked because he was a Labrador cross, like Jack the Dalmador and Bear the Labrador Shepherd. This dog is half Lab, half German short-haired pointer. He's only half the size of the other two, but barks like a St. Bernard and growls like a Tasmanian devil. I now have a *three-dog security system*. No border collie, yet.

Unfortunately, none of the dogs likes the horse. Nor does the horse like dogs, but he loves dog *food*. A few nights after we got the new dog, Susan woke me up about 2:00 a.m. "There's something out on the deck!"

The deck runs on two sides of the house. Every dog was barking and it sounded like somebody was dragging a whiskey barrel over the deck. I ran through the house to the kitchen, threw open the door to find… the *horse*, clomping across the deck, trying to glean the dogs' bowls.

I ran him off the porch and he disappeared out into the yard. Last time I looked out the bedroom window, there was a Labradorian stand-off. Everyone was perfectly still. About twenty-five yards off the deck stood the horse, waiting to make his move. Facing him from the deck near their bowls stood all three dogs, motionless in the moonlight, daring him to try. I went to bed.

CANADA GEESE RETURN

Last Sunday morning was clear with a high blue sky. I was up early, rebuilding the fire in Susan's smoker. Three dogs, feigning intense inattention, watched innocently as I pulled out the half-done chickens. A loud honking made me look up, and just brushing the tops of the pines above was a huge "V" of Canada geese, circling to land on the lake across the road. I could have reached up and touched them. When I looked down our driveway, I could see them splashing down on the lake. They come in late in the evenings, too, just at sundown or right after dark. You can hear them overhead, honking down to the lake for landing instructions, and somebody on the lake usually answers back. No matter how black the night, their honking fills it with company and warm hospitality.

ANOTHER MOUTH TO FEED

Liberty was in labor fifty-six hours before Tucker Lee Sanders Bain finally arrived on October 15. We had planned to leave on our annual camping trip that day, but Tucker put that on hold.

Tuesday night at midnight I woke up to find Susan and all my children all dressed.

"What are you doing?" I asked.

"Liberty's at the hospital, and we're all going." First grandbaby.

"No, you're not. That baby won't be here for hours. Go back to bed."

Around 5:00 a.m. Susan woke me up flashing the light on her 400-candlepower wristwatch. "I've got to get over to that hospital! It's five o'clock." Yes, I thought, five o'clock happens twice a day, but I silently threw in the towel, and we all went to the hospital, where Susan immediately started back-seat driving—a *delivery*, no less. Talk about *bossy*.

A little before nine that evening the doctor recommended a Caesarean section, and at 9:06 p.m. Tucker arrived, somewhat bruised from that long labor.

They don't do this labor business the way they used to. Anybody and everybody can come into the labor room. When they brought back Liberty with Tucker, there were twenty-two (22) people by actual headcount, counting Tucker.

Now actually I am a fair judge of baby-flesh, having seen a number of them and been present when seven were born, and I must admit, this one *is* a keeper. We got to go on our camping trip—after one last trip to the hospital to see the baby. However, as soon as we got back, Susan had to move in with Liberty and Johnny, "Just to help her train that baby to sleep through the night." I never bothered to mention that not even Olympic trainers sleep with their charges. Still, that's how I found her when I sneaked in early Tuesday morning, sleeping with Tucker crooked in her arm. Women are sure something. You'd think Susan would have had *enough* of babies by now, but I guess not.

Liberty and Tucker (and Johnny) are all fine now, and Tucker's raising his head and trying to do push-ups.

WILD FOOD

Unlike modern agriculture, the produce of the woods is unpredictable. You have to enjoy it when it is pleased to produce, in its own time. Funny, some years the wild cherries, possum grapes, or persimmons are astonishingly delicious and profuse, other years just so-so. This year the possum grapes are hanging in huge, full clusters, like I've never seen. Two years ago the persimmons were a spiritual journey, sweet, floral, hiding mysterious flavors hinting of something else. This year, they're a little thin, almost watery.

One perfect hot, ripe fall day Zachariah and I went for a walk. Zach found persimmons at the trees we know, and we stopped and stooped. Even though these are not the grandest persimmons I have ever eaten, their delights rival any sophisticated dinner I have ever eaten, *and* they have another benefit the expensive dinner lacks. You can square off and spit persimmon pits about twenty-five feet.

TREE MANAGEMENT

DECEMBER 1997

We have two wood-burning stoves, and if you've ever paid a winter electric bill for an all-electric home, you know why. They burn six or seven cords a winter, so I cut a lot of firewood. My friend Ron's neighbor had a big red oak that was hit by lightning, and Ron graciously volunteered to help us cut it.

Ron is a machinist extraordinaire, one of those people who can do anything with machinery or metal. He has meticulously restored an ancient International Harvester Farm-All tractor, complete down to the decals on the gas tank. Ron pulled his big trailer over with his tractor. Christian and Wright rode on the trailer and Justin, Worth, and I followed in our old Ford pickup.

The tree was in Ron's neighbor's pasture, and it must have been four feet through at the very base, but it branched into three trunks. We downed the first two without much trouble, and quickly cut it into splittable lengths. Ron and I worked the chain saws while the boys split or loaded.

The remaining trunk was nearly clean of limbs, except for one large limb pointing the way the trunk was leaning. Ron was cutting and didn't want to drop it into the nearby trees. He cut a wedge out of one side, and then cut into the other, but the tree wouldn't drop. We got Worth to bring the steel wedges. He hammered first one, then another, then a third into the cut, and it still wouldn't budge.

About that time we noticed Ron's tractor, sitting exactly 180 degrees from the direction that tree should fall, and about thirty feet back. Although it seemed impossible that the tree could fall on his tractor, Ron went over to move it. He had no sooner climbed into the seat and turned on the key than the tree began to quiver. It spun 180 degrees. All together, the boys and I shouted to him to get away, because the tree—*how could it?*—was dropping directly toward the tractor.

I still don't know how Ron did it, but he must have jumped off the back of that tractor about twenty-five feet at one leap. One nanosecond he was there, the next he wasn't, and the next that tree came crashing down right across the middle of where Ron had just been sitting.

It broke the tractor clean in half.

For a minute, all you could hear was the gasoline pouring out of the tractor's crushed gas tank. We were all stunned—not the least Ron. All I could think was that if he hadn't moved fast enough, we'd be hauling him home instead of the firewood. After breaking our stunned silence, we thanked God for sparing Ron's life.

CHRISTMAS IS COMING . . .

. . . and I am slow catching the spirit of the season. We still haven't got a Christmas tree. Our tradition is to cut our own cedar tree, and over the years they have gotten larger and larger—about fifteen feet. Susan complains about the size, but I think she secretly likes having a tree large enough to display all the ornaments she has collected for herself and the children.

I remember Justin's second Christmas. He was thirteen months old, and Liberty was just over three. I left them in the living room staring at the Christmas tree, and went back into the kitchen. After a few minutes I heard what sounded like a muffled cat meowing. I followed the sound into the living room, where to my astonishment I saw the tree pulled over at an angle, and both children standing under it. Justin had been tugging on it and when it came crashing down on them, Liberty reached up and grabbed the trunk. She just stood there holding the tree off of Justin until one of us came to help.

This was not, by the way, a fifteen-foot tree, but a falling tree is a falling tree.

PUTTING OURSELVES IN
THE WAY OF LAND

JANUARY 1998

S usan and I have been driving to and fro along the Magic Road, scour-
ing middle Tennessee for a homestead to weather out Y2K.

Maybe Y2K will be the end of the world as we know it, maybe not.
Maybe all the computers and embedded chips in the depths of the ocean
can handle the switch to 2000; maybe not. Maybe this won't be when
the system goes down—yet. We've always wanted to live in the country
anyway. A subscriber in Lawrence County invited us back to visit middle
Tennessee—and we took her up on it. So Monday and Tuesday before
New Year's we drove back along the Magic Road to look for land and a
place to move.

Susan thinks I'm crazy looking for land when I have not the money
to pay for it. "Well, maybe so," I said, "but if I don't put myself *in the way*
of land, I'll never find any."

All our children (except Liberty and Johnny Ray Bain and *grandson*
Tucker B.) went along, so we had to caravan in two cars. On the way it
started snowing—not spitting daintily, but flopping down in great wet
globs. We plowed through, but by the time we arrived, there were about
four inches on the ground.

Even without snow, our friends' place is extraordinarily charming: a wooden house next to a pond, chimney smoking. It sits in a valley between two ridges, on the high side of a creek bottom, maybe 500 feet from the creek. Add snow, and it's so beautiful you have to rub your eyes to make sure you're not seeing things.

Neither the children nor I could resist the temptation, so we left our friends' house and climbed to the top of the ridge, four hundred feet or more above the valley floor. When we reached the pasture at the top (they were all huffing and puffing behind me) we found cows crowding around a huge round bale of hay, but there was ample room to play. A general snowball fight broke out among the children (I call them children although they range from twenty-one down to eleven).

The wet snow was perfect to roll up giant balls of snow for snowmen. While Christian (14), Ellen Robinson (Justin's fiancée), Justin (21), Worth (19), Wright (17), Mercy (13), and Zachariah (11) were playing, I just looked out over the valley trying to fix the moment and the place in my heart. Some secret lay hidden in these hills, utterly silent and asleep under a thick blanket of snow.

Tuesday afternoon Susan and I were waiting with our gracious hosts for the children to come back from town. Toasty warm in the kitchen, we ate spicy soup and gazed out a broad window. The snow began to fall again in huge lumps.

Susan looked out the window and sighed, "I think I've gone to heaven." Our hearts have been captured.

On a recent outing to Lawrence County, we came across a log barn that must be over a hundred years old. Although it was all hand-hewn logs, hand fitted together piece by piece, the wall was *perfectly plumb and square!* The logs are fitted together in a complicated pattern that both locks them in and slants off the water so the log ends won't rot. Try that with an axe, an adze, and a piece of string with a rock tied to it for a plumb line!

We are decided. We are definitely moving to middle Tennessee, and that right soon, so I may not get to plant a garden this year. Even though we have had a little snow, it still hasn't frozen out my winter greens and cabbage in our current lot. If this is global warming, keep it up!

FEBRUARY 1998

OH, TO BE AT HOME IN LAWRENCE COUNTY

We plan to be far gone from our house here in Eads just outside Memphis by the June before Y2K strikes, but we are not waiting till then to move. In January it became apparent that we needed to move quickly so the house we rent could be sold. It occurred to us that it made more sense to move directly to Lawrence County than to move, wait six months, then have to move again. Susan went over to Lawrenceburg to scout out some rental houses, and found a newish four-bedroom to rent for $500 a month (rentals in Lawrence County are apparently a whole lot cheaper than in Memphis).

Middle Tennessee is where we are headed, come fair or foul weather, and definitely come Y2K. Eastern Wayne County and western Lawrence County are all "hills and hollers," with springs everywhere. The hills only rise three or four hundred feet above the hollers to 900 feet or so above sea level, but they seem higher when you climb them personally. Creeks and branches and springs are *everywhere*, so water is not a problem. There are places on top of those hills where you break out of the trees and look across the valley. You could swear the hills across the valley are calling your name. Leastways, I can hear them calling *my* name.

Lawrence County lies three hours east of Memphis, three hours west of Chattanooga, and two hours south of Nashville. The nearest city of any size is Florence, Alabama. Population is only 32,000, with 15,000 in Lawrenceburg. In the 1940s the Amish moved into the northeastern part of the county. Wayne County to the west boasts 15,000 souls. The people I have met are just plain, friendly country people. While she was shopping for a house, Susan and a friend of ours stopped by the square to check out the shops. I suppose the lady waiting on them heard their discussion, because just as Susan left she inquired, "Have you decided on a church yet?"

But I hadn't reckoned with a lot of things, not the least of which was what to do with four boys still in school, one a senior in high school, and one about to get married in July. There was also the matter of leaving at such a distance Liberty and Johnny and Tucker, who were still living (and working) in Memphis. Nor had I thought through leaving our church in Memphis in the middle of building a sanctuary.

We thought it over, and it just became *impossible* to move as quickly as we had planned. Providentially, we found a place about five minutes east of where we live in Eads (it's no small job finding a place big enough when you have six children at home), and were able to negotiate a six-month lease. So we remain in Shelby County for the time being. But middle Tennessee already has our hearts.

The move eastward into the country is still on, just delayed somewhat. I still believe that a Y2K problem would make life impossible in urban areas. Living in the country is the big goal here. Y2K just offers a timely excuse.

MARCH 1998

On March 14, 1998, my father, C. Franklin Sanders, Senior, passed peacefully away. He was born in Michie, Tennessee, on October 21, 1910. He was an apt student, but had to spend two years in the tenth grade waiting for his little country high school to add the last two grades. From there he went to West Tennessee Normal School in Memphis (now Memphis State University), and lettered in four sports, one (football) he'd never played before. Later he became a football and basketball coach, and then a school principal and superintendent.

My father professed faith in Jesus Christ and was baptized as a young boy, and was always an enthusiastic Christian and a good and loving father. He leaves two sisters, a brother, two sons, two daughters, fifteen grandchildren, and two great-grandchildren. "Precious in the Lord is the death of his saints!" The funeral was in Memphis on Tuesday, March 17, and we buried my father at the Palestine Baptist Church Cemetery in Pearson, Arkansas, where my mother's parents are buried.

For the past several years he had suffered from senile dementia and recently had declined rapidly. It was difficult for him to communicate, but it seemed that as life became harder for him, his nature became sweeter. Join with me in rejoicing in the kindness of our loving heavenly Father, for whom every father in heaven and earth is named, that he has taken my father to be with Jesus and so relieved his suffering and wiped every tear away from his eye.

Glory be to the Father, the Son, and the Holy Ghost, now and forever, hidden in glory and mystery, Amen.

MOVING WOES

This month we moved—from a house with over 4,000 square feet to about 2,200 square feet. In the rain. But the move didn't stop there. It just kept on and kept on, and we're still cleaning up over there—not to mention unpacking here.

Susan began to calculate the cost of renting storage space, and ended up buying herself a forty-five-foot trailer. By the time we had to pay for storage, then load, unload, load again, and unload again, she calculated we would be better off buying the trailer, using it for storage and hauling, and selling it later. My wife is a genius—and beautiful, too. I'm thinking about setting her up in the moving business.

Right now, it seems like I've been moving all my life. I have abandoned all hope of finding anything in these boxes. Gypsies live better than this. If it hadn't been for my boys to help, Susan and I would both have just quit and hitchhiked to Texas. We may end up doing that anyway. Still no sign of a permanent home.

RIDING WITH SUSAN

S usan and I hadn't visited Clarksville since I was stationed at Fort Campbell in 1970 and 71.

Don't get excited—I wasn't Airborne. The 101st wasn't even stationed there then. I was a Remington Ranger with a garrison Combat Engineer battalion. You know—I flew a typewriter.

We were so poor I had to borrow fifty cents to pay attention. The first month I was in the army I got paid $46 [sic]. I didn't know which to hit first, the paymaster or the floor. Once we got to Clarksville, Susan found out we could rent a johnboat on Post for $5 a day—another $5 rented a ten-horse motor.

Clarksville was settled in the 1790s and the whole area is filled with fascinating historical sites and laced with small rivers and creeks. Saturdays Susan would fry up some chicken and we'd launch our yacht into a river or creek and float down to the Cumberland River. Sometimes we'd launch out on the Cumberland's wide bosom, and *putt-putt* upriver toward Nashville. The army was not my choice of careers, but Saturdays in the johnboat helped ease the pain.

When I was stationed at Fort Campbell, I never guessed we might come back one day with seven children.

The weekend of March 23rd we drove up to Clarksville with seven children, a son-in-law, and a grandson—a logistical problem similar to

Napoleon's withdrawal from Moscow. We met friends there for the Tennessee State Fiddlers' Championship. Fiddlers' contests are gatherings where folks who play mostly "Old Time" music compete in performance. "Old Time" music is Southern music before Nashville got to it with production symphonies and drums. Generally an Old Time band comprises only stringed instruments—fiddle, banjo, guitar, mandolin, maybe a bass (wash-tub or manufactured)—and occasionally somebody playing spoons or harmonica. Around Clarksville and to the south also thrives a *hotbed* of cloggers, so the occasion included a clogging competition.

The Fiddlers' Championship was *great*. I met some old-time banjo players and even got a personal lesson. They also staged a clogging contest—not as in arteries, but dancing. I never knew humans could move their feet so fast. Clogging must be seen to be grasped. Think of Irish step dancing, but without the Irish and faster. The body is held still and straight, while all the motion takes place in the ankles. Feet move too fast to see. The man who came in second also had two little boys—they couldn't have been more than six and nine—who competed, too. I was sitting where I could watch him as his boys danced. I never saw such delight on a man's face as he watched his sons.

The best part of these gatherings often takes place *outside*, where people come together in little groups and jam. If you have never been to a fiddler's convention or old-time music festival, *go!* The granddaddy of them all is held at Galax, Virginia, the second weekend in August. You'll remember it forever.

On the way back from Clarksville we stopped at Fort Donelson battlefield, where I always have to brood and mourn over the stupidity of the Confederate generals who let themselves get locked up and lost a 15,000 man army. But I also get to remember Bedford Forrest again, who broke out here at night with most of his cavalry intact. "Boys," he said, "these fellers are talking about surrendering, but I'm going out of here or bust hell wide open trying."

MAGIC ROAD BARBECUE

Past Fort Donelson along the Magic Road lies Paris, which ought to appear on every world map as the home of Trolinger's Old Fashioned Butcher Shoppe. Their barbecue ranks among the finest in the South, and they still make the same old-fashioned vinegar-based barbecue sauce they've made since "since 1917." What a weekend. **Trolinger's Old Fashioned Butcher Shoppe**, 2305 East Wood St., Paris, TN 38242; (731) 642-8667.

SUSAN ON THE ROAD

On April 1 I packed up Susan about 6 p.m. and we headed to Gary North's Y2K seminar in Springdale, Arkansas. It's a 5½-hour trip. Susan drove. She averaged seventy-four miles an hour, even though the last fifty miles lie over mountains with a twenty mph speed limit. All I can do is climb in the car, pray, and pull down my blindfold.

The seminar was nearly completely sold out. Four hundred or more came from all over the United States. We arrived a bit late (been up late the night before), and Gary was saying that some demographer friend of his was predicting that the Grayheads would lead the next population move to rural areas. We're a bit too young to be classed with the Grayheads, but we are headed to the country anyway. I want land.

Maybe Gary was thinking about his own neighborhood. On the way to Springdale, near Fayetteville, I saw the first billboard I ever saw for *dentures*. "You bet they fit."

MAY 1998

SUSAN GETS FREE GRANITE

We drove down to visit Jim Kibler in Abbeville, South Carolina. Abbeville was the scene of the first mass meeting for secession in the South after Lincoln's election in 1860, just a year before the War broke out. The organizers expected fifty people, but three thousand showed up. To accommodate the crowd, they moved the meeting from the town square to a nearby hill, which has since been renamed "Secession Hill." Yes, I dug up some "secesh" dirt to take home to Tennessee. Who knows what soil like that will grow? Jim wore a cap made like the first Secession Flag, in "turkey red" with the South Carolina crescent and star—not the blue flag with one star on it known as The Bonnie Blue Flag. That came later. First came the "turkey red" flag.

If you're planning a vacation this year, forget Disneyworld and take the family to South Carolina. Little towns like Abbeville and Newberry have been sprucing up their town squares, stripping off all the junky over-laid facades back to the original building faces. The result is charming. Newberry has a French Gothic opera house built in 1885, and there are historic buildings, homes, and churches everywhere.

SUSAN THINKS FAST

If you *ever* get within 200 miles of Abbeville and fail to eat at the Veranda Café there, kick yourself. But be careful—you can *hurt yourself* eating there. We had been tipped off to order the spoon bread and sweet potato soufflé, and were not disappointed. The spoon bread was a sort of corn meal casserole with chopped turnip greens, onions, peppers, and tomatoes that leapt off the plate into your mouth. The soufflé was feathery whipped sweet potatoes topped with pecans.

Susan said no to dessert until she found out they had *homemade* co-conut meringue pie *and* Robert E. Lee orange cake. Poor Susan, she was in a fix then, but quick-wittedly ordered a piece of the pie to eat there and a slice of cake to go. You can talk about French cuisine and fancy food, but heaven comes no nearer than a truck-stop-thick slab of coconut me-ringue pie, yellow custard chunky with coconut and little drops of honey standing on the mile-high meringue. Best of all, the waitress was as much fun as the food. **The Veranda Café**, 102 Trinity St., Abbeville, SC 29620; (864) 459-2224.

ROADSIDE SHOPPING WITH SUSAN

Jim knows all the local attractions. At Ninety-Six, South Carolina, we stopped at the Ninety-Six Fabric Store. I thought I might have to physically restrain Susan, whose father nicknamed her "Hot Needle Hattie." Jim also knows all the antique stores, and Susan wanted to stop at every one. We did. I was astounded at the prices, which were in some cases very reasonable and in others ridiculously low. Unfortunately (or fortunately) we were in a Camry, not much suited to hauling wardrobes. That didn't stop Susan, however, from making me stop at Elberton, Georgia, "Granite Capital of the World." There are 155 monument makers in Elberton, and they all pitch their scrap in the same ravine, where we were bound to stop. ("Honey, I know it's free, but what are you going to do with *granite*?") Believe me: it doesn't take many slabs of scrap granite to make a load, either for me or for the Camry. We looked like the Jukes and Kallikaks, or at least Okies and Arkies on their way to California, *circa* 1936. We were piled in that poor Camry, lurching down the road hauling granite and piles of *stuff* and the three of us packed in there with our noses pressed to the windows for air. I got an urge to stop at a junk pile and retrieve an old mattress to tie down on the top just to round out the picture, but Susan wouldn't let me.

Jim survived until we got him home to Athens, Georgia, but the quest wasn't over. Susan had fallen in love with a bush called Grancy Graybeard that has festoons of feathery white blooms. Jim gave us directions to the Pottery Barn in Commerce, about twenty miles away. Nothing he said had prepared us for the reality. The place must be a mile long. We literally got lost in the bush and tree division looking for a Grancy Graybeard. Unfortunately for the Camry and our image, before we found Grancy we also found assorted annuals, two rhododendrons and a sweet olive (some people call them tea olives. It's a lovely bush like cherry laurel with tiny white blooms that fill the air with a faint smell of apricots.) We had lost Jim, but gained a botanical garden. Chain stores open and close so quickly, this one has now vanished. They are not permanent landmarks or permanent sources of prosperity.

We didn't want to get hung up on Atlanta's freeways, so we cut across through Gainesville and Dawsonville. When we passed through Marblehill and I looked over and saw a whole mountain of marble next to the road, I was some kind of glad it was dark and Susan was napping.

I've been writing too long and now don't have space to tell about spending the night at South Pittsburg, Tennessee, in a motel behind the Tennessee-Alabama Fireworks store. We bought Zachariah a whole *brick* of Black Cats and rockets galore and then went to the Lodge Cast Iron Outlet. Just in case the Camry's springs hadn't been demolished already, we picked up a dozen cast iron skillets and Dutch ovens to finish off the job. "They make *great* wedding presents even if Y2K doesn't happen!" Shopper's Logic if I've ever heard it.

Why would anyone go to Disneyworld when you can go riding with Susan?

BEAUTIFUL

Lately I went shopping with Susan for her new glasses. A well-mannered, friendly lady was helping us, and in the course of the conversation it came out that Susan had seven children.

"You don't look like a woman with seven children!" she said.

Because that wasn't the first time I had heard that, I got to thinking about it. Turned out her mother-in-law also had seven children. When the lady had finished writing up Susan's frames, I said, "Tell me what a woman with seven children should look like."

A little bewildered, she returned, "Well, I'm not sure."

"What does your mother-in-law look like?"

With enthusiasm and evident affection, she began to describe her mother-in-law. She had a master's degree in chemistry, and now she spent a lot of time doing volunteer work, etc., etc.

I was left in a quandary. She had described a woman who sounded much like Susan—charming, lively, energetic. What is a woman with seven children supposed to look like? Beautiful.

Motherhood gives us all, men and women, a lesson in Christian living. When the angel Gabriel announced to Mary that she would become the mother of our Lord Jesus, she must have been dismayed. "How can this be? I have never known a man." But Mary did not argue or alibi. She said, "Be it done to me according to the Lord's will."

Of course, a single woman or a woman without children can just as well serve God fruitfully, but motherhood gives us a unique example of Christian service. By submitting to motherhood completely, a woman is completed. She faces the terrors of death itself in childbirth, and afterward demands so great they seem utterly impossible, but God gives her grace upon grace as she needs it. The greater her burdens, the greater his grace, and the greater her completion.

This is a mystery beyond me, that God gives us the grace to submit to our own perfection.

NEW TENANTS

We only moved ten minutes from our old five acres, but we're still in boxes. Right now, if I can find underwear, pants, and socks, I count myself blessed for the day.

BREAKING NEWS

Before I forget it, the famous Tucker Lee Sanders Bain cut his first tooth on Easter day. It is a very fine tooth, and I would tell you about it but you might not thank me and I've run out of room, anyway.

HIGH SPRING

It's high spring and the value of inside work dwindles to invisibility. Privet and honeysuckle fill the air with dusty perfume. Last night I worked late, and when I finally got to bed about 2:00 a.m., I lay there listening to a whippoorwill and several other birds—day birds—singing. I recalled Chaucer's tender description of spring's heart-stirring madness. You probably had to memorize it in high school, like I did:

> *And smale fowles maken melodye,*
> *That slepen all the night with open eye*
> *So priketh hem natur in hir corages.*

(And little birds make melody,
That sleep all night with open eye,
So Nature pricks them in their tiny hearts.)

— "General Prologue," *Canterbury Tales*, lines 9-11

Springtime we keep all the windows open to enjoy the air and the fragrance. I noticed that an awfully large number of bees seem to be clustered on one of the screens, but didn't think anything about it. That evening I was working late, barefoot as usual (I'm from Tennessee, aren't I?), and something pricked my foot. I looked down to see a dying honeybee that had left his stinger in my foot. Reminds me of me with the government. Game, but not much judgment.

Next day the room was filled with bees. Pleasant, well-mannered bees, mind you, but bees nonetheless. Susan bought sticky fly strips to place at the window screen. When I went to bed I had to step like a tango dancer to dodge all the bees *hors de combat* on the floor.

I asked my landlord to de-bee the house, and he located a beekeeper who promised to entice them out. We went on a weekend family trip Saturday, but the beekeeper refused to come because the barometer was dropping and the sky lowering. Swarming bees, normally very mild tempered, get grouchy in bad weather. Meanwhile they seem to have disappeared. Maybe they moved out on their own?

LIVING IN THE COUNTRY CHANGES YOU

CHICKEN CENTRAL

If you don't get things done and Y2K turns into an emergency, you're going to have trouble. I've seen a grocery store buying-panic before a hurricane, and you don't want to get caught in one. Trying to prepare can overwhelm you, so you have to take it one step at a time. An Alabama friend of mine remarked, "I try to do something every day toward Y2K." That strikes me as sensible. Even if you only buy a cast iron frying pan, an axe, an extra box of .22 shells or canned tobacco next time you're in Walmart, do something every day.

For us, chickens are part of that something. When I visited Nicaragua in 1989, I noticed that almost every household in that war-impoverished country had a chicken coop. Chickens furnish eggs and meat and they eat scraps. The chickens in Nicaragua were so poorly fed then that scrambled eggs were *white*—the chickens didn't get enough proteins to form yellow yolks.

On Valentine's Day I gave Susan some money for something she had long desired: *piano lessons*. Later she told me she felt foolish spending money on something so frivolous with Y2K staring us in the face. "Are you kidding?" I asked. "If Y2K gets bad, you're going to need music *more than ever.*" Me, I'm practicing the banjo. Computers or no computers, my world won't end—not unless music ends.

Susan can read my mind. I know this, and have come to accept the humiliation over the years. Friday evening she says to me, "Now let's not bring anything back from First Monday that eats." She says this all general-like, as if to nobody in particular, but I'm the only one in the room, and she knows I have chickens on the brain.

Imagine my surprise Saturday morning when she says, "You know, I'd really like to have a little Banty rooster around to wake me up in the morning." I say nothing, but I start calculating.

If you're looking for chickens, First Monday in Ripley, Mississippi, is *Chicken Central*: furry-footed chickens, Golden Seabright or Silver Seabright banties, Barred Rocks, Domineckers, Buff Orpingtons, not to mention rheas, emus, ostriches, ducks and geese, pot-bellied pigs, goats, and of course, dogs. I wanted to make a bee-line for the Chicken Man from Alabama. He has the very best selection of exotic chickens, pigeons, ducks, doves, and much more. No, Susan had to drag me on a long detour rooster shopping. Some boys were selling a yellow headed, green-black banty rooster with a jaunty red comb for two bucks, but a cage cost three bucks and Susan had to shop first.

When we shop for chickens, "dog-resistance" is our first concern. Our dogs are what you might call *chicken fanciers*. They never met a chicken they didn't like. Hence Susan immediately ruled out the giant rooster with the bass voice. Not only was his crow too low, he wouldn't last two nano-seconds around those dogs—too big and slow. At our house, any chicken with a life expectancy greater than a quark needs both supersonic speed and a profound mastery of evasive tactics.

Finally we got to the Chicken Man. He had a pair of banties that took your breath away—BB ("Black Breasted") Reds. The rooster had a mane of flowing bright red feathers, just about the prettiest thing I had ever seen, but my heart fell when I asked him how much they were: twelve bucks. I knew Susan wouldn't spring for that, not when she knew she could buy a perfectly good rooster for two bucks elsewhere. We wandered through the chicken sellers. Somebody ought to report them to the federal government for price fixing. *Every* pair of banties cost twelve bucks.

I knew we had bought a rooster, but I had to make sure our two dollar rooster didn't die of loneliness. This became a fairly easy sell when we found two green-black banty hens for three bucks apiece. Cage, three bucks; rooster, two bucks; then two hens, three bucks each. Susan was bursting with pride—three chickens and a cage for eleven bucks. Any way you looked at it, we had beaten the market by one dollar and a hen. I traded in my three dollar cage for a ten dollar cage big enough for the chickens to walk around in until we can build a coop.

Experience hath shown that our new rooster, *Two Dollar*, exactly fits our requirements. Not only is he an indefatigable crower, but he is also a turbo-super-charged runner. He got out on Sunday and it took eight of us to catch him. We'd never have caught him even then if I hadn't distracted him while Justin sneaked up from behind with a fish net. Never give a chicken an even break, especially not a fast one.

VACATION

I've been running like a scalded dog trying to keep up with business day to day. On top of that we've travelled much more than usual, so your newsletter is late again this month.

I had been promising a friend that I would write a short book about community organizing for Y2K, but the last six months have been some of the busiest I have ever known. Between caring for the gold and silver business and writing a newsletter every month, it was all I could do to squeeze in breakfast, and some mornings I didn't get that.

My wonderful friend offered us use of his family's place on one of the San Juan Islands in Puget Sound for us to take a necessary vacation. That was just the first hurdle. The greatest hurdle was talking Susan into a vacation. Not that she didn't need the rest—she's just, well, *frugal*. After substantial jockeying, cajoling, and wheedling, I convinced her I had to go or die—and that really wasn't far from the mark. I work the same way unsuccessful drunks drink whiskey: too much, all at once, for too long. We packed up Christian, Mercy, and Zach and flew to Seattle.

Seattle is *some different* from Tennessee, but our friends showed us superb hospitality. While we were there I got to visit and meet face to face for the first time Dr. Tom Dorman and Dr. Jonathan Wright of Tahoma Clinic in Kent, Washington. What an amazing operation! It was the very first doctor's office I have ever seen where the personnel genuinely respected your time. They were solicitous to a fault.

I tried to pack too much into our trip. For years I have wanted to visit a friend in Eugene, Oregon, so we drove there, almost five hours from Seattle through some of the worst traffic I have ever experienced. But the warm welcome from our friends in Eugene made it all worthwhile, not to mention a visit to one of the best flea markets I have ever seen. It was a bit short in the chicken department, but they made up for that lack with a huge selection of aging hippies.

They raise all sorts of stuff out there we never see, especially in the berry line. In fact, I showed my ignorance at supper when one of my friends mentioned that he loved the Marion Berry cobbler. I thought it was a joke. I asked if that was the cobbler sprinkled with cocaine in memory of the famous Washington, DC, mayor. Whoops—there really is a berry called a "Marion" berry, and now everybody knew I really was a hick.

After an all too short visit in Eugene, we drove to the Oregon coast, and then up the coast from Florence to Lincoln City. Breathtaking is hardly the word to describe the vistas. If you *ever* have a chance to make this trip, take it, and don't miss the sea lion cave.

From the coast we headed back to Portland, through some of the best tended farm land I have ever seen. After a grueling ride through unrelenting traffic, we finally arrived at our friends' house in Washington, a stone's throw from Canada. My children, especially Zachariah, seemed to get along awfully well with our hosts' children. He and their daughter Victoria seemed to pay a lot of attention to each other, for children of that age. After a short visit and more gracious hospitality, we left for the San Juan Islands.

Apparently the Confederate Secret Service has agents even in Washington State. On the way to pick up the ferry at Anacortes, we passed a house on Highway 20 flying a Mississippi State flag. When we passed the same house on the way back, our agent had run up the Confederate battle flag, the St. Andrew's Cross that so many people mis-call the "Stars and

Bars." It was the *first* national flag that was called "the Stars and Bars," not the Confederate battle flag.

On Orcas Island we had use of a place right on the beach, totally private with a view of the round hills of islands rising out of the water. It was a scene of rest and peace to treasure up in your heart for years. Orcas is wonderful—not a fast-food restaurant on the island. I worked a little on the book about preparing for Y2K, and Susan took the children exploring. The time passed all too soon.

When we got back to Memphis, I only had three days to pack again and travel to Harrisonburg, Virginia, where I was to speak four times at the Great Revival in the Southern Armies conference sponsored by Parkview Baptist Church and Sprinkle Publications. I have no idea how I measured up, but the other speakers offered a spiritual feast. Susan and I got to see the beautiful Shenandoah Valley and wonder at the vast imagination of God, who could create such diverse beauty as Oregon and Washington and Virginia on the same globe, totally different but all totally charming.

JUSTIN GETS MARRIED

Susan was in a push to get back to Memphis at the end of the week because our eldest son Justin was getting married on July 11. Now I've run out of space, and can't tell you about the sweet joy of that celebration. I thought I was pretty stolid, but found that when the wedding service began, the stately words from the Book of Common Prayer were so moving that tears filled *my* eyes. I had brought an extra handkerchief thinking that Susan might need it, but I had to loan one to Charley Robinson, the bride's father, while I wore out the other. What a profound mystery is this union we call marriage! Even after nearly thirty-two years and seven children, I barely comprehend it.

THINKING CHICKEN AGAIN

Early in the morning when the light is gray and seems to drizzle out of the heavens, even from a cloudless sky, is *not* a good time to peer into the future. One morning way too early I was riding down the road musing on Y2K when the thought hit me: who will need fifty-one-year-old newsletter writers when there isn't any news? Exactly what would I do if suddenly our prosperous world disappeared?

I quickly ran through the copious list of my talents. How about killing hogs? Nope, no good at that. Driving mules? No, not enough mule-learning. Cruise director? No ships. Lemonade stand operator? No lemons. Dance instructor? Two left feet. Basketball trainer? Two left hands. Hurdy-gurdy player? No monkey, no hurdy-gurdy. I went on like this for quite a while, with like unsatisfying results.

Friends, what would *you* do if suddenly the area of your expertise and livelihood evaporated? It's not a joke. What talents do you have that you can trade for a living in a world without electricity? How would you and your family eat?

You'd better ask yourself this question, and you'd better find some reasonable answer.

A VISIT TO GOOSE POND FARM

"I want there to be no peasant so poor in all my realm
that he will not have a chicken in his pot every Sunday."

— Henri IV (1553-1610), King of France

Thus I got thinking about chickens again.

In early August Susan and I visited our friends Charlie and Laura Ritch on Goose Pond Farm near Hartselle, Alabama. We knew Charlie was raising range-fed chickens, lamb, and beef, and we were dying to see his operation. You have to see it to believe it, and to understand how it works.

Charlie buys about 1,000 day-old chicks. He raises them in a barn for the first four weeks, until they're fledged ("grow feathers"). Then he moves them into pens on his pasture. The pens are ten feet by twelve feet, about two feet high, and hold about a hundred chickens. They're mostly covered with tin, with chicken wire on the sides. Once a day, he moves the pens exactly one pen length, so that the chickens stay on the same ground only one day.

The chickens do what chickens naturally do, scratch around in the grass and eat bugs. Charlie also feeds them grain. In four weeks (eight weeks from day-old chicks) they are ready to slaughter at four-and-a-half to five pounds.

Don't miss what the chickens do for the soil. There's no stench of manure, because the manure doesn't pile up in the same place. The chickens are scratching around in the grass and leaving manure on the pasture. After the chickens are moved, Charlie puts first sheep, then cattle on the pasture. His pastures are lush and green. He told me that in a recent drought, neighboring farmers were forced to feed their cattle hay five weeks before he ever found it necessary.

The slaughtering, Charlie tells me, is where most people drop out of the chicken business. It is *very* hard to learn how to take a chicken from feathered bird to clean, attractive, well-dressed carcass. It is hot, tiring, exacting, smelly work. Charlie has persevered, and has found the equipment (including an electric chicken plucker) to do the job. He, his wife, his two girls, and a couple of helpers can now slaughter and dress about three hundred chickens in a half a day.

His customers are local folk who don't want to eat commercial chickens fed on estrogens, arsenic, and who knows what else. They love his chickens and pay a premium price. Laura served us a delicious chicken gumbo, so I know why. Charlie's chickens most assuredly do not taste like grocery store chickens.

"What do you do with all the offal from slaughtering the chickens?" I asked Charlie.

"No problem," he said, "I cover it up with wood chips and compost it. Whenever I see maintenance workers chipping brush by the road, I invite them to dump their chips on my farm."

"Doesn't that compost pile stink?" I asked.

"Nope," he said, "if it stinks, you put more wood chips on it. After eight or nine months, it's compost, like black gold."

A GYPSY WAGON FOR CHICKENS

Charlie's operation does not stop with range-fed chickens for meat. He raises eggs, too. We walked out into his pasture toward what looked like a gypsy wagon. I found out it was a cotton wagon, on which Charlie has built a chicken house. Along one side are laying boxes, so the eggs can be gathered from outside. The floor is wire, and a mounted fifty-five gallon drum provides a mobile water supply.

Charlie usually locates the chickens near the cattle. In the morning he lets the chickens out to roam free. At night, most all of them voluntarily climb back into the wagon to roost, and he gathers in the stragglers and shuts them up. Staying near the cattle, the chickens scratch through the manure and help keep the cattle free of parasites. Once a week or so Charlie hitches up his tractor to the Gypsy Chicken Wagon, and tows it over the hill, out of sight. If you don't get it out of sight of the previous location, at night the chickens will return to the former site to roost. As with the chickens Charlie raises for meat, the constant moving avoids heaps of manure and the health problems that concentration breeds.

How many eggs can you gather from eighty-five to a hundred chickens? A whole lot. A sea of eggs. Free-range eggs do not resemble store-bought eggs, except that they both have shells. The yolk stands up about a quarter inch higher, and is a deep yellow. Talk about taste! As my friend Kit says, "You can hurt yourself eating them, they're so good." As long as you keep them cool, about the temperature of your air-conditioned house, they'll keep three weeks or more. We're still eating on the eggs Charlie and Laura sold my wife. (Our car looked like an egg wagon coming home.) Of course, finding folks who are willing to buy free-range eggs is not much trouble, once they learn you have them for sale.

CHICKENS ARE COOL

What I like about Charlie's operation is that it does not depend on complicated technology, electricity, or drugs. Certainly he uses electricity, but the same thing could be done on a much smaller scale with or without power. If you can grow or buy feed grain nearby, and raise your own chicks, this operation can be practically self-sufficient. At the very least, it would be a very good way to add plenty of meat to your diet.

You may be thinking, "Sure, that's okay for somebody who grew up on a farm, but what about me?" Well, I don't know if Charlie and Laura grew up on farms, but I do know Charlie was a successful businessman before he went to raising chickens. I think that any diligent person of reasonable intelligence and ambition could learn to do this. Best of all, it doesn't take a 500-acre farm to do it. Charlie and Laura have eighty acres, but an acre or less could raise quite a few chickens. Joel Salatin points out that "a couple working fifty hours a week for six months a year on 20 acres can NET $25,000-$30,000" using these same techniques.

Salatin explains the whole system in *Pastured Poultry Profits*. Charlie and Laura Ritch's address is: **Goose Pond Farm**, 298 Goose Pond Road, Hartselle, AL 35640; (256) 751-0987; raisedonpasture.com.

You may not be looking for a career in poultry, but some experience and education might come in handy just in case Y2K problems don't blow over by the end of the first week of 2000.

A DAY WITHOUT SUSAN

Saturday a week ago was one of the strangest days I've ever known, like a dream when crazy things keep happening. That morning Two Dollar rooster disappeared. We searched around the pen and found a mess of shiny green-black feathers. Our dog Bear sat off to one side with a look of pained innocence.

Susan disappeared early in the morning, and J. Edgar Hoover himself couldn't find her once she leaves to "run errands." She's just gone till she comes back. The children were scattered hither and yon, and I was left alone to work. About 2:00 p.m. Justin dragooned Worth and me into driving to Smithville, south of Tupelo, to check out a truck.

What *was* I thinking? The man had told Justin that Smithville was "only about forty-five minutes from Memphis," but Tupelo is 105 miles, and Smithville lies beyond that another twenty miles. It's all the way across Mississippi. From Smithville you can spit into Alabama without drawing a deep breath.

Then the rain came—gully-washing, frog-strangling, eighteen-wheeler-floating rain. Blowing sideways.

We didn't get back until after six. There was a cryptic note from Susan on the back door: "Look at Jack." He had two huge gashes on his bottom left leg, clean down to the knuckles. Justin, Worth, and I opened a methyl sulfonyl methane (MSM) capsule and poured it on the wounds, then bound them up as best we could.

At the latest First Monday I had bought two pairs of mallards to turn loose on the lake with Zach's canvasback pair, but all six ducks were still in cages because I hadn't clipped their wings. Worth and Justin helped me clip them, and then we carried them (in the cage) the six hundred yards over the hill to the lake and threw them in one at a time.

What a sight! All you could see was weeds trembling and duck tails popping up. They chattered and fussed and chased each other and enjoyed themselves so it was a joy to watch them.

We left the ducks on the lake, but we hadn't been back at the house ten minutes when Worth motioned toward the window. There were all six ducks, standing in a knot by their cages. The lake was just too scary. They were used to those cages, like inmates crowding around a prison entrance.

Justin was late for supper with his new bride, so he left and I went back to my office downstairs. Before long the phone rang. About ten minutes from our house a deer had jumped in front of Justin's car. The front was trashed and the radiator knocked loose.

Their meeting sure hadn't done the deer any good, either. It was small, about as big as a medium sized dog. Right where the woods met the road's edge he had jumped in front of Justin. I shivered. Jim Kibler had been right. I should have put deer whistles on all the cars. The wind blowing through them creates an ultra high pitched whistle that scares off the deer. You can't hear it but the deer sure can.

While Justin was waiting for the police to arrive, a fellow pulled up towing a fishing boat. He struck up a conversation with Justin, and after considerable verbal jockeying, asked what Justin was going to do with the deer. Nothing, came the surprised reply. Oh, then would you mind if I have it? Sure.

That fellow waited about forty-five minutes just to take that road-killed deer home. I reckon some people love venison.

By now it was way past dark and my Disappearing Wife had still not re-materialized. I began to wonder if I had been trapped inside a Salvador

Dali painting. Nothing seemed to quite make sense. She finally arrived, and as usual, looked at me like I was crazy to worry about her.

I was really *glad* to get out of that day.

IMPULSE BUYS

Never let a chicken-fancying husband make the trip to First Monday by himself. I took the big cage, and came back with six Old English black banty pullets, two plain mallards, two crested mallards, and a handsome little yellow banty rooster with two yellow hens. That's not as much poultry as it sounds like, though. Banties are small, compact chickens, the Mickey Rooneys of chickendom. (Charlie Ritch just snorts contemptuously when I mention them. I am not even chicken feed next to Charlie.) Besides, I really was quite self-disciplined. A man at the flea market overheard me inquiring about banties and pulled me off to the side.

"I've got over 200 banties, all kinds—a dollar and a half apiece," he whispered. Heaven help me, he started ticking off the varieties.

I squirmed, I twisted, I scowled, I coveted, I teetered on the brink, but sanity triumphed.

"No," I said, "my wife would kill me."

Like I said, what I bought wasn't near as much poultry as it sounds like.

SEPTEMBER 1998

I promise this will be the last chicken buying story. We drove down to First Monday again, escorted by Susan, so I could replace Two Dollar rooster with another Old English Black bantam. Mercy, it was hot, but I finally found a man who had a whole cage full of the type I wanted. I bought a couple of extra black hens, just in case. Then I saw an Old English "BB"

(Black Breasted) rooster with two hens. With his deep gold mane and red trim I couldn't resist. As I was putting them in the cage, I made the fatal mistake of asking about a yellow rooster in a cage with two hens.

He was a hefty rascal, pale yellow with a big tail of curly feathers that looked like he'd backed up too close to a window fan. The man made me a special price: five bucks for the rooster and both hens. I must have had "sucker" written all over my face.

I stuck the Yellow Dog rooster and the two hens in the cage with the others. The cage was about four feet long, so Zachariah grabbed one end and I grabbed the other and we walked off down the street to look at shotguns.

All of a sudden that cage commenced bucking and pitching. I looked down and that Yellow Dog rooster had my Old English BB rooster's comb in his beak, trying to bash his brains out on the floor. "Slap that thing!" I shouted to Zach, "I'll run get another cage."

We got all our business done and as we were about to drive away, I realized I wanted to get another t-shirt for a friend. (It had a picture of Nathan Bedford Forrest on the back and the legend: "No damned man kills me and lives.") Just as I was stepping out of the car Zach and Christian raised the hitherto unmentioned idea of buying a rat terrier puppy.

This outlandish thought had never crossed my mind. Why would I want a little yappy, nippy feist dog? Then again, why not? They catch rats and mice, and in the country rodents are a problem.

These kids must read me as easily as chicken dealers do.

We walked over to The Chicken Man from Alabama. He had a cage full of rat terrier pups. Heaven help me, I lost my mind momentarily. I bought one. We named him Bull.

Whoa! We were driving away from the First Monday when I spotted a portable sawmill. Susan pulled over and we got out and talked to the gentleman and got him to demonstrate for us. When he told her she could make money with it, I thought I'd lost her for sure.

WHERE'S THE MUSIC

OCTOBER 1998

recently read *Tabletalk Magazine*'s issue about Johann Sebastian Bach.

Speaking of the thorough bass, which is the harmonic accompaniment in baroque music, [Bach] said this:

The thorough bass is the most perfect foundation of music, being played with both hands in such a manner that the left hand plays the notes written down while the right hand adds consonances and dissonances, in order to make a well-sounding harmony to the glory of God and the permissible delectation of the spirit; and the aim and final reason, as of all music, so of the thorough bass, should be none else but the glory of God and the recreation of the mind. Where this is not observed, there will be no real music, but only a devilish hubbub.

— *Tabletalk*, Ligonier Ministries, 400 Technology Park, Lake Mary, FL 32746; (800) 435-4343

Things percolate in your mind while you're not consciously thinking of them. It must have been so with this, because Bach's words struck me a few days later when I was driving down a road through my beloved Tennessee countryside. It was a glorious Indian summer day. The sun was bright, but not too hot, and I was driving down one of those roads where the trees spread their protecting branches over the road like cherubim's wings over the mercy seat. The radio was playing Beethoven's Pastoral Symphony, which I don't remember ever consciously hearing before. The music seemed to reach into my breast and explode in that very glory of God Bach spoke of. By the end of the symphony I was in tears.

On the other hand, music doesn't seem tied to technical excellence or intellectual exercise. What I know of music could be put in a boxcar and leave plenty of room for a full load, but I love the banjo, which I play with great fervor if little success.

So when I heard that Bela Fleck, one of the world's top banjoists, was coming to town, I sprang for tickets for Susan and me, as well as some of my grown kids and their spouses. Fleck was touring with bassist Edgar Myers and mandolin player Mike Marshall. It should have been a great evening, but it was terribly disappointing. Fleck came from bluegrass, but has progressed to what I have to describe as jazz. All three musicians were technically brilliant and intellectually challenging, but there was no *music*. Susan's leg started twitching, a sure sign the evening had gone on too long, so we left quickly after the last piece. We missed the encore, which my children assured me later was the best part of the evening, being pure bluegrass.

All this had passed out of my mind by the next Saturday morning when I tuned into the bluegrass show on my car radio. I wasn't paying much attention when they started playing Alison Krauss' *In the Palm of Your Hand* (Alison Krauss and the Cox Family, *I Know Who Holds Tomorrow*). Now I am not comparing this simple bluegrass song to Bach, but Krauss' pure voice and the perfect lyrics evoked that same glory of God, and although I've heard that same song a thousand times, I found myself again in tears.

It's obvious I don't understand music.

TUCKER'S ONE

Has it been just a year since Tucker Lee Sanders Bain, our first grandchild, arrived? On October 15th we celebrated his first birthday. What did we do with ourselves before we had Tucker? Much to my surprise, he has survived a year without my children tearing him apart in their eagerness to hold him. He acts about like the Prince of Wales, bestowing his favor on whom he pleases. Most of all he likes the concrete pig on the edge of our patio. Not long ago we bought one of those green glass gazing balls country people used to put out in their yards. Tucker saw that and thought it was just like his ball. He pulled it off the stand, and bounced it. Once.

There may be something better than being a grandfather, but I haven't yet figured out what that might be.

TEOTWAWKI

Whoops, in all this fun I forgot about Y2K. As if the wild stock markets of the last few years weren't enough trouble, computers make not only the money economy's financial abstractions possible, but also the electronic payment and banking system which undergirds them—i.e., most modern financial transactions. If Y2K pulls the plug on our computers, the financial system will simply cease to exist.

Now my crystal ball is broken, so I can't tell you whether Y2K will be only a momentary glitch or TEOTWAWKI (The End of the World as We Know It). My research leads me to conclude that it will be very bad indeed if the power and communications go down, bad enough to demand thorough and careful preparation. But if people prepare individually, if local churches and communities prepare, then at least the worst effects of a Y2K situation (violence, starvation, and pestilence) can be turned aside. If local communities learn *now* how to deal with each other in local markets and encourage local producers with real money, well, maybe TEOTWAWKI won't be such a bad thing after all.

It might just be a return to peaceful reality.

MONEYCHANGER GOES TO VEGAS

Last month we travelled to Reno, Nevada, then drove down via Las Vegas across the angle of Nevada to meet Liberty and Johnny at the Grand Canyon. Nevada's beauty takes your breath away, but it sure isn't Tennessee. Compared to that dry air out there, I live in a terrarium. The country is so dramatic, so wild that everything built by man looks out of place—imposed, contrived. "Untameable" comes to mind, and there's a *lot* of it to drive across.

For all those who buy the globalists' and Chamber of Commerce assurances that services and tourism will make us all rich, I suggest a trip to Nevada. It's a land where the local industries that actually produce something, largely mining and ranching, are being run off the land in favor of tourism, chiefly gambling.

Nevada legalized gambling in the 1930s. For those who believe gambling is the cure-all for state budgets (as our neighbors in Mississippi do), I suggest a trip to Nevada. The cure doesn't costless come. The newest, best built buildings are the casinos. Most every other building (in Tonopah, for example) looks abandoned.

If gambling can save, Nevada must be getting closer to heaven. There are slot machines and video poker everywhere. They greet you when you get off your plane, they're in Safeway, K-Mart, everywhere. If gambling could bring prosperity, why hasn't it? It's had nearly sixty years in Nevada.

Nevada's biggest headache is that the federal government controls eighty-five per cent of the land. Development is not a problem, or over-development, but government "ownership" which keeps out the sort of development—ranching, farming, and mining—that might form the foundation of permanent prosperity. The environmentalists' cries that private owners will rape the land are simply misinformed. No sane person fouls his own nest. Rather, it's the *lack* of local ownership, a lack of incentive to preserve, which encourages, indeed, guarantees, overuse.

I must be wrong. I read an article in the Reno *Gazette Journal* which claimed that Nevada "leads the nation in population and job growth." Yeah, but what kind of jobs? The same paper had one-and-a-half pages of ads for jobs in "casino/gambling" out of four pages, and maybe a third of a page for "skilled trades." If that's true, the state doesn't show prosperity in people or place—except in the casinos and other tourist attractions.

Then there is that other tourist attraction, legalized prostitution. There are lonely brothels out in the desert, just clusters of trailers—"Cottontail Ranch," "Shady Lady Ranch," "Angel's Ladies"—some complete with their own *airstrips* and signs that promise "Free all night parking for trucks."

By all means, visit Nevada if you ever have the chance. It's a land of great beauty, and strange contradictions.

From Reno we drove to Las Vegas, stopped long enough for Susan to watch some circus acts at the Circus Circus Casino and to let her win fourteen dollars on a slot machine the size of a panel truck. Then we went to that miracle of New Deal Engineering, Hoover Dam. Truly a stupendous sight and accomplishment—decorated with all the trappings and statues

of 1930s American Fascist Building Style. I know we fought a war with the Nazis, but it sure wasn't over architecture. Hoover Dam's decorations would fit unnoticed among Berlin's few remnants of the Hitler-time.

We left Hoover Dam after dark, and drove about a hundred hours on to Grand Canyon in Arizona. I know it took a hundred hours, because I was driving. I was behind the wheel so long I began to look like Chevy Chase.

It was worth the risk. The first glance of Grand Canyon will drop your jaw down on your chest. The scenery is amazing enough, but more amazing is where they put the six million tourists who pass through there every year.

CHRISTMAS IS COMING . . .

. . . and we just got the best present parents could get—an announcement from Justin and Ellen that we will soon be grandparents again in June.

I'm so proud of myself. I've written almost a whole letter, and never used the word "chicken" once.

I made it. Didn't I?

A CURE FOR BELLYACHE

This is our first Christmas in the last twelve years in a new house. I have forfeited my reputation for outlandishly tall Christmas trees. In our old house I could ram a fifteen-foot cedar through the front door. That was the only tree big enough to display all the ornaments we've collected over now thirty-one years of marriage. We still have the ornaments we bought in Germany in 1972, hand made in the Erzgebirge, little angels on stars and moons playing violins and harps. Everything on that tree, even the clumsy construction paper ones laboriously cut out by six-year-old hands, holds a sweet memory to be savored at Christmas time. But when we moved, the ornaments got packed at the front of Susan's fifty-two-foot trailer, hopelessly out of reach now.

In response to my gentle bellyaching, Susan decorated the house with pine rope and tiny lights over the doorways, and even secured a midget tree someplace. When the 16th arrived, our thirty-first wedding anniversary, we were too tired to go out to dinner.

I reckon the cheer of Christmas is where you find it. Travelling too much and way too busy, I have failed wretchedly at Christmas shopping, yet again. Justin, Ellen, Worth, and a friend took a well-deserved vacation in Colorado, only to get caught out there in the ice storms. They may not make it back for Christmas. The printer called this afternoon and warned us that ice storms were predicted tomorrow, so late tonight we'll have to drive down to Mississippi and spend the night so we can be sure to get the newsletter printed tomorrow. Maybe Susan and I won't make it back for Christmas either.

In the midst of this worriment comes the church year calendar to our rescue. Advent Sunday reminds us to remember something greater than our present circumstances. Then Sunday after Sunday our anticipation is fed on the promised Immanuel. To fight the gloom of my Christmas failure while I work, I play over and over *An American Christmas* by the Boston Camerata (Erato), American carols, hymns, and spirituals from 1770–1870. About the time I forget what joy Christmas brings, I hear:

> *Methinks I see a heav'nly host*
> *Of angels on the wing;*
> *Methinks I hear their cheerful notes,*
> *So merrily they sing.*
> *Let all your fears be banished hence;*
> *Glad tidings we proclaim,*
> *For there's a Savior born today,*
> *And Jesus is his name.*
> *Lord! And shall Angels have their songs,*
> *And Men no Tunes to raise?*
> *O may we lose these useless Tongues*
> *When they forget to praise!*
> *Glory to God that reigns above,*
> *That pitied us forlorn.*
> *We join to sing our Maker's Love,*
> *For there's a Savior born.*

> — William Billings, *The Suffolk Harmony*, 1786

Some of my Christian friends refuse to celebrate Christmas. Alas, I cannot join their misplaced zeal. My weak mortality is too forgetful, and must be reminded week by week, month by month, and year by year of that merry angel song. My own feet start tapping, my throat humming, and I think I can even hear the stars singing. The temptation to join the cosmic merriment is not to be withstood—nor should it be. Like David, I will rejoice to be called a fool and worse while I dance that dance.

BUILDING A LIFE

I try to keep one delicious book going all the time. I hold it back and savor it late at night, when the world cannot bother. I bought James I. Robertson's *Stonewall Jackson: The Man, The Soldier, The Legend* back in the summer, but could only read it by fits and starts. Recently I neared the end, and night after night couldn't escape its call.

When I think of monuments stone and bronze, Percy Shelley's words from his poem *Ozymandias* come to mind:

> *And on the pedestal these words appear:*
> *'My name is Ozymandias, King of Kings:*
> *Look on my works, ye mighty, and despair!'*
> *Nothing beside remains. Round the decay*
> *Of that colossal wreck, boundless and bare,*
> *The lone and level sands stretch far away.*

For all their arrogant claim to permanence, stone and bronze monuments announce themselves only to the empty spaces of oblivion. They are the most impermanent of memorials, a sacrifice to human vanity. The only imperishable monument we can build is *a life*. We don't normally think of life that way, but if any man ever did, it was Thomas Jonathan "Stonewall" Jackson. Not that Jackson set out to build a monument to himself—the thought is laughable!—but rather that he consciously strained every nerve to build a life of obedience to God. His memory stands like Ebenezer, a stone raised up in the Bible to remind all who follow of who came before (1 Samuel 7:12). Jackson set out to do his duty and to follow God, and every step of his life he marched in the same direction, not dragging, not sorrowfully, but with all his heart. Long after the bronze and stone statue of Jackson in Lexington Cemetery has crumbled to dust, the monument of his life will last.

Despite other biographers' attempts to mask it, Jackson was *quirky*. What a service Robertson has rendered us, to paint Jackson with all his quirks and queerness! I cannot remember another book that so richly brings to life not merely a man, but also his times. It reads like current newspaper reports from the front, as if we knew and enjoyed the companionship of the actors.

The picture of Jackson the cold and unapproachable Christian which other biographers have painted does not entice us to imitation. That Jackson is too high, too angelic to hearten mere mortals bogged down in contrary clay. Rather, it is Robertson's Jackson, the Christian struggling daily against the world, the flesh, and the devil (familiar from our own experience) who encourages us to excellence and more perfect piety. It is the Jackson who is so self-conscious and shy that when he is called on to pray in church mumbles and locks up in confused embarrassment. Yet when his pastor stopped calling on him to pray, he went to him and gently reprimanded him, reminding him that because it was his duty to pray, he must learn to do it. It is the Jackson who cannot stop mourning after his first wife's death.

The last two chapters of the book detail Jackson's tragic wounding by friendly fire, his death, and then his burial. I confess, they wrung steady tears from my eyes. The most moving incident occurred when Jackson's body lay in state in the Virginia Capitol in 1863:

During the remainder of the day . . . an estimated
20,000 people filed by the casket for a final look.
Finally, Governor Letcher ordered the doors closed.
A few minutes later, a loud voice demanded admittance.
When soldiers opened the door, a one-armed veteran
pointed to his stump and, with tears spilling from his
eyes, shouted: 'By this arm which I lost for my country,
I demand the privilege of seeing [my] General once
more!' Governor Letcher put his arm around the man's
shoulder and ushered him to the coffin.

AT HOME

In 1990 Guido Koehler came from Germany to spend his sixteenth
summer with us, and became a member of the family. He's studying medicine in San Diego now, and this Christmas brought his mother to visit us.
They arrived at our house on New Year's Eve while we were struggling with
huge business demands and trying to leave for our annual New Year's trip
to Wall Doxey State Park down at Holly Springs, Mississippi. I was in my
office frantically fielding phone calls about 4:00 p.m. when Mercy came
down the stairs and announced like the butler at a banquet, "Christian has
broken his wrist." Enter Christian, with two wrists where one ought to be.

We were still trying to get ready for a week-long trip. Susan looked at
me, and I looked at her, then she said calmly, "You take him to the hospital
and I'll go to Kroger. We'll meet you at Wall Doxey." Now if you don't
have seven children and house guests, that may sound cold, but I guess
we've just gotten used to perpetual crises and doing what has to be done
when crisis hollers. I took Christian to Methodist Hospital, where the
news was good and the wrist was set, and he and I drove to Wall Doxey.
By firecracker time he had recovered most of his enthusiasm.

January 1999. Clock is ticking. Y2K is less than twelve months away
and we're still in suburban Memphis.

THE GREAT CHICKEN SLAUGHTER

Somehow we have become the favorite meeting place for neighborhood dogs. We have three of our own and two others have taken up quasi-permanent residence. Every so often a dead chicken shows up. I look at the dogs, the dogs look at me. "Chicken? What chicken?" I glare at the dogs. Butter wouldn't melt in their mouths. Given enough time, though, the chickens will outbreed them. They're bantams, and bantams are good setters. The recent warm weather has them thinking spring is here, so they're laying and setting.

I'm just waiting. One of these days the chicken killer is going to slip up.

FEBRUARY 1999

A CHICKENLESS WORLD

I spoke too soon. After a particularly frustrating weekend out of town, we returned home to find that the blasted dogs had run amok among the chickens. Killed all but two, and it was all I could do to keep from killing me a couple of dogs.

I was holding my breath about it, but when my mother, who lives with us now, started crying as she put up the eggs we had salvaged, I nearly cried as well. Strange, how attached I'd gotten to those chickens. I loved to hear all those roosters crowing at each other, and watch them all scratching in the yard. No matter how many times they worked over a spot, they would scour the ground again and again with tireless hope. No matter

142

how chickenless the world appeared, just step outside with a handful of grain and holler "Chick! Chick!" and here they came running.

Before I go back to First Monday to re-chicken my yard, I intend to investigate *dog-proofing*.

CULLMAN AND ATLANTA

Last fall I had to travel so much that Susan threatened me with bodily harm if I took another speaking engagement after the first of the year. I had to wheedle for all I was worth, but she relented to let me go down to Cullman, Alabama, on April 8. I'll be speaking at the Cullman Civic Center about preparing for Y2K. It's hard to explain living on the slope of a volcano. Over one shoulder you see the smoky plume arising from the funnel. Over the other, you see your vineyard. Which will shape your life, fear or faith?

God gives us means, and expects us to use them, I don't deny that, but the means alone won't save us. Everybody remembers the old story about the fellow trapped on his roof by a flood. A canoe comes by and offers him a ride, but he waves him off, "No, I have prayed and God will save me." A bigger boat comes by, the crew begs him to get on, warns him the water is rising. "No, I have prayed and God will save me." Finally a helicopter hovers overhead, lowers a ladder to him, but he waves them away, "No, I have prayed and God will save me." The waters rise, and he drowns.

When he gets to heaven he complains to St. Peter, "I don't understand it. I prayed and prayed, why didn't God save me?"

"Well," St. Peter said, "He sent a canoe, a boat, and a helicopter. What were you waiting for?"

THE GREAT REVIVAL IN THE SOUTHERN ARMIES

I will be speaking at the Fifth Annual Great Revival in the Southern Armies conference here at our own Immanuel Reformed Episcopal Church on "The Life and Conversion of Nathan Bedford Forrest." I spoke at this conference last year in Harrisonburg, Virginia, and was treated to a banquet of excellent speakers.

The Conversion of Nathan Bedford Forrest was a strange case. His mother was such a strict Sabbath-keeper that she wouldn't even cook on Sundays. He was always respectful of Christianity and preachers, inviting them to dine with him and his officers when he was in the field. Neither drink nor other vices tempted him. Yet it was late in his life, after the war, that he heard a sermon in a Cumberland Presbyterian Church that deeply affected him with repentance. The lion became a lamb.

I don't think conversion is so much a one-off experience as it is a set of stair-steps in our lives, and at each point God opens to us a new light so bright that everything in the past seems like darkness, even though it had its dim light.

THE JOYS OF ORTHODOXY

I was honored when my bishop asked me to help team-teach a Sunday school class on the Thirty-Nine Articles, the 1562 Anglican statement of faith found in the Book of Common Prayer. I know that some people consider theology the world's most exciting subject, second only to collecting string, but they never suspect how they are cheating themselves.

It fell my lot to elucidate Article IV, *Of the Resurrection of Christ.* "Christ did truly rise again from death, and took again his body, with flesh, bones, and all things appertaining to the perfection of Man's nature; wherewith he ascended into Heaven, and there sitteth, until he return to judge all Men at the last day."

Teaching is hard work, and surprising. I spent hours refreshing my memory and understanding before I could presume to approach the task. I had to return all the way to the history of the early church, which spent centuries hammering out its understanding of God's revelation. I had to make a long detour into the dual nature of Christ. What astounding mystery, that the perfect God would unite his nature with the perfect man in one person!

A wonderful surprise waited for me. The more I pondered this mystery, the more my confidence and hope in Christ glowed. I returned to my favorite book, Hebrews, to find there on every page the reiteration of Christ's dual nature. How secure is our hope, because this perfect God-man had accomplished for us what we could not do! What confidence we have because he, the perfect man, was tempted as we are in all things but was without sin, and now sits at the right hand of God to plead for poor sinners.

In our arrogant and provincial age every self-appointed expert wants to reinvent the church and reinterpret Christianity. What joy they would find if only they walked the old paths the saints have always walked!

MARCH 1999

FLU

Well, the flu got us. Last newsletter (as usual) I stayed up way too late and lost too much sleep. Susan was already feeling bad on Wednesday. For so many years that memory runneth not to the contrary, Susan has always left about 6:30 a.m. to take the newsletter to the printer. She got up as usual, got dressed, and then as we were about to leave, she looked at me and announced flatly, "I'm not going."

I was flabbergasted. I fiddled around grabbing everything I needed, and by the time I was finished she had printed a sign and hung it on the bedroom door: "Sick and dying person inside. Do not disturb."

By the time I got back at noon she rallied enough to help label and stamp the newsletters. On the way home from the printer I had felt a scratchiness in *my* throat. By that night, I was down, too. We spent the next five days in bed. On Saturday I woke up and tried to comb my hair, but couldn't. Every hair on my head hurt. We were supposed to take a trip with my children, and they went without us. They all came home early—sick. Then my mother got it. And once you get it, you can't get over it. Three weeks later Susan had another relapse.

So I'm warning you, don't get too tired. From the west coast to the east, I have friends who have come down with this flu, and it is deadly.

RE-CHICKENING

All that's left of my chickens is one lone black rooster. I call him "Supersonic" because he must be the world's fastest chicken—he's still alive, so he can obviously outrun a dog.

But the tragedy of losing his whole chicken community has, I am afraid, driven him crazy. Do you remember Patty Hearst, the heiress who was kidnapped by the Symbionese Liberation Army in the 1970s? They kept her so long she began identifying with them.

I think that's happened to Supersonic. He now thinks he's a dog. When the dogs lie around sleeping in the sunshine, there is Supersonic, strolling amongst them. When we call the dogs to feed them, here comes Supersonic, running like the chow bell is for him alone. I haven't yet witnessed it, but I'm pretty sure somebody is eating the dogs' food, too.

Supersonic may be crazy, but he's not suicidal. We have two tall cedar trees next to our garage, and at night Supersonic climbs up about twenty-five feet above the ground. Obviously, he believes in jumping dogs. This has made parking somewhat of a problem, but, look, a chicken's gotta do what a chicken's gotta do. So far, he's survived.

Next Saturday is the flea market down at Ripley, Mississippi. I know the Chicken Man will be there, so I will replenish my flock. I'm thinking about throwing in a surprise for the dogs, too. I may buy a gamecock. Next time the dogs come for chicken dinner, they might get a surprise.

Then too, I might just buy an *emu*. I'll just hide that monster around the corner of the house, and call Jack and Bear, just to see the look on their faces when they round that corner and behold that six-foot chicken.

Do emus eat dogs?

NOT WORTH KILLING

It's springtime, and I'm not worth killing. You're lucky you got a newsletter at all this month. That sun starts shining, redbuds and azaleas blooming, fescue greening up, blue jays playing—all I can think about is getting outside and staying there. I feel like that anonymous medieval English poet who wrote, "Sumer is icumen in/Lhude sing *cuccu*!" Once it starts raining next fall, I'll be okay again.

Rejoice in Easter!

APRIL 1999

PRAYERS, PLEASE

This afternoon as I was finishing this newsletter Susan came into the room with terrible news. Our beloved bishop and pastor and brother in Christ, Dan Morse, was in a car wreck. His car ran off the road and hit a tree, no one knows why. When the medics reached him he apparently had been without oxygen. They airlifted him to the hospital, where they put him on a ventilator. His second cervical vertebra is broken. The last news we had was that he was in a state of low level consciousness and was responding to stimuli in his feet and legs, a good sign although he remains in critical condition.

Truly Dan has been our "father in Christ," ever faithful with a warm and merry heart filled with the grace of God above measure. If you have ever been blessed by anything I have written, you can thank God for Dan Morse. For the past fifteen years he has been my teacher and counselor in every perplexity, leading me into the grace of God and out of the cramped straits of my own soul. As I sit here staring at this computer screen, it seems that the world has stopped, but above all I know that the greatest honor I can show my brother is to carry on after his faithful example.

Would you please pray that God would heal our beloved Dan, and comfort his family with the knowledge that he is safe in the hands of our loving God?

WEDDING MODE

Long-time readers know that Susan and I have seven children. In 1996 we entered the wedding mode when Liberty, our eldest, married. Last summer Justin married Ellen. This summer, on June 19, our next child, Worth, will marry Shawn O'Rourke in Nashville. What a blessing it is to witness God carrying on his covenant in the lives of our children!

One of the biggest blessings of the wedding mode is that you get *two for one*. Where before you only had one son or daughter, now you have two. As if that weren't enough, then they start having *grandchildren*.

MAY 1999

SPEAKING

I flew to Washington, DC, to speak for The Conservative Caucus for an all-day conference, "Y2K and the Presidency." Sunday I caught the red-eye flight back to Memphis and landed about 8:00 a.m. Driving to church, the incense of honeysuckle, privet, and rambling roses lifted me up to heaven. That's why I love the spring. Before you can get tired of one delicious smell, another comes right behind it—except for chestnut trees, which smell like an Exxon Valdez chlorine spill.

RE-CHICKENING

The Ripley flea market was *hot for chickens* in April, and prices were high. Nothing deterred, I succumbed to every temptation. I got a full-sized gamecock and three game hens. Bantams were everywhere. I got a pair of white Chinese Silkies, a Black-Breasted old English game pair, a quail-breasted same, and silver Seabrights, a rooster and two hens. And I didn't forget my black Japanese rooster, Supersonic, the only survivor of the Great Chicken Slaughter. I bought him two hens.

Then I saw the ducks. Call ducks are the duck equivalent of bantams, and I couldn't resist a mallard pair. Then I saw two India Green ducks, the prettiest things I ever saw. They're iridescent black green, and the drake has deep peacock blue feathers as well. On top of all this, a friend gave me three BB old English roosters.

Sadly, one BB red rooster died, as did one of the Chinese silkies. First chickens I ever lost to anything but dogs.

But that gamecock isn't worth a hoot. Oh, he looks good, but Zachariah let out all the chickens one day, and I heard Ellen screaming. I ran outside to find that gamecock cold-cocked on the ground. One of the BB reds had knocked him out. I was disgusted. This is *not* a dog-beating rooster.

On top of that, one of the ducks thinks he's a rooster. Climbs up on the water pot and tries to crow.

Now Zachariah has chicken fever. We got the Murray McMurray Hatchery catalog—(800) 456-3280—and Zachariah went crazy. He's made a long list of fowl he intends to purchase. I have to admit, those peacocks do look nice.

AT HOME IN THE MONEY PIT

JUNE 1999

We're moving east again. This time all the way to middle Tennessee. We've found our homestead. Time is running out. We have yet to learn to farm, but we do have chickens now.

We've already started moving, but it will be a while before everything gets to middle Tennessee. It's a long ways from eastern Shelby County to Wayne County, nearly three hours. I intend to *try* to mail the next newsletter on June 14, but that's a slippery schedule—remember tolerance. Think, too, charitably about a man whose wife bought a fifty-two-foot trailer to store things upon our last move in April 1998, then filled up a twenty-four-foot truck last week, leaving behind another 24-foot truckload to be moved. I am thinking about making a large pile in our new pasture and setting fire to it.

Susan likes moving so much she's decided to stretch it out over twelve weeks instead of doing it all at once. Most of the time now Susan is three hours away from me.

This is a train wreck. I don't mean the moving, I mean me. I must be the most helplessly uxorious man in the world. I'm never quite at peace when Susan's out of the room. You'd think that after thirty-two years of marriage that some of the "new" would have worn off.

Moving is easy, just like jogging through molasses up to your hips. Nobody moves fast enough, and whatever was taken care of months ago pops up from the dead to haunt you.

The whole family is moving. Worth left several months ago to build a house for Shawn, his wife-to-be. We are moving into two places, a cabin in the woods and a farmhouse in a field. The farmhouse sits on a high ridge, and it makes you feel like you're on the ocean with the fields like waves billowing away from you. When the hay is knee-high, the wind blows through it so that the ground almost moves beneath you.

The first weekend here Susan was like a ten-year-old, dancing and clapping her hands. When she woke up in the morning she would just sit next to the window and listen to the birds.

Then we got a firsthand experience of The Money Pit. You remember the movie. The couple buys a house to renovate and everything has to be replaced, including the stairs. The contractors are carnivorous and cantankerous. We got a dose of the same. Susan wanted to install propane heaters, a cookstove, and a run-through hot water heater. That sent a workman under the house, who reported the joists needed jacking up. When the workman went under to jack up the joists, he found out that some of the cast iron drainage pipe had been replaced with PVC and welded with—duct tape. The resulting sewage leak had caused the piers to sink and the floor to sag. Then all the drainage pipes on one end of the house died. Then we found out termites had been exercising in the main floor joist. Oh, yes, and when the repairman took up the linoleum in the back bathroom he promptly fell through the rotten floor—so then we had to replace the bathroom floor. We bought a new kitchen counter because all the wood under the sink had rotted out, and when we tried to fit it in, the new counter proved only five inches too long. Whoops—don't forget a new kitchen sink, too.

After we install a new pressure tank for the well.

WEDDING

As if moving weren't enough to keep everyone busy, our son Worth is getting married this weekend. Worth's bride is from Nashville, so Susan has had to make all arrangements long distance. Warning to men: do not mess with women preparing for a wedding. This is none of your business. Just write the checks and keep your mouth shut.

Worth's flexibility has made me very proud. Not only is he building a house, a job similar to herding cats (all contractors are cantankerous), but he has also become a farmer. They now have three milch cows, unknown numbers of beef cattle, and myriad chickens. Maybe they didn't quite understand what they were undertaking with the milch cow discipline—twice a day, every day.

Let us charitably and with due reticence remark that in growing up, Worth was not always our most enthusiastic worker. I was therefore amused to hear him complaining, "You just don't know how hard it is to get somebody to work a reasonable twelve hour day." He was dead serious. I didn't say a word.

We would covet your prayers for our final move on July 3, 1999. Let this be our final move. When I say final, I mean final. I intend to put down roots.

PRAYERS

Just as I was leaving my dentist's office on Thursday, June 3, the receptionist handed me the phone. "It's for you. It's your son Justin."

"Ellen's obstetrician wants to induce her labor this afternoon, and we have to leave in just a little while."

"Whoa! Wait a minute!" I countered. "She's not due until the twentieth. Call your mother first." Susan was over in Wayne County, three hours away. After seven of her own, she's our resident expert on labor and delivery.

By the time I got there, they were heading out the door to the hospital. I headed back to work. Susan had hopped in the car, and by the time I went up to the hospital that evening, she met us there, and of course Ellen's parents came. Our daughter Liberty was already there, coaching away. She's as bossy as her mother, but Justin and Ellen had everything well in hand. They'd already finished their Lamaze course.

Ellen labored on through the night, but it was slow going. Friday evening we stopped off at Liberty's house on the way to the hospital, when we got a call from Justin. "The baby's about to be born!"

We all hopped in our cars and raced to the hospital. Shortly after 8:00 p.m., Elijah Ward Otey Sanders made his entry into the world. They named him Elijah, which means "Jehovah is God;" Ward, a family name that means "guardian," and Otey, after the first Episcopal bishop of Tennessee, Ellen's great-great-great-grandfather and a saintly man—yes, the same bishop who rode through Tennessee on horseback, planting churches along the way.

Things seemed orderly enough for me to leave for the weekend to go back over to Wayne County and help Susan with our never-ending move. When I came back Monday morning, June 7, the news wasn't good. Elijah's lung had collapsed, a common danger with premature babies. I was stunned.

There are some times when everything is taken out of your hands and all you can do is pray, so pray we did. We called the church prayer chain, and then I cranked up my e-mail. I already had a list of people to whom I was sending updates on my pastor, Dan Morse, who was injured in a car wreck in April. I sent them all an e-mail asking them to pray for Elijah. There was nothing else to do.

The first time I could get to the hospital to see him, Elijah was covered with tubes, including a drainage/suction tube in an incision in his chest, a feeding tube, IV in his scalp and navel, and an endotracheal tube for the respirator. I know rationally that all these are evidences of tender care, but this does not inspire confidence. He looked terrible. As soon as I could, I went back to my computer and emailed everyone what news I had.

Their response was wonderfully comforting. Justin and Ellen—and Elijah—got e-mails from all over the country, no, all over the *world*, assuring them that people were praying for Elijah.

Something certainly worked, and I lay it at the door of those faithful brothers and sisters who prayed for Elijah. (Of course, those faithful doctors and nurses who cared for him deserve credit, too.) Day after day Elijah made great progress. On Friday he pulled out his feeding tube himself, and that evening Ellen got to breast feed him for the first time.

On Monday, June 14, Elijah came home.

Please accept our deepest thanks for your prayers. Join with us, too, in praising God for his faithfulness generation after generation, in thanking him for his deliverance, and for this beautiful new child of the covenant, Elijah Ward Otey Sanders.

JULY 1999

Our pastor and bishop, Dan Morse, who broke his neck in a car wreck on April 21 has come home from the hospital, and is making great improvements. He still has a long recuperation and rehabilitation before him, but last Sunday by the grace of God he walked to communion. He still has little feeling and strength in his hands, and experiences some pain from back muscle spasms.

Thank you for your continuing prayers on his behalf. Little by little our gracious God is restoring Dan to full health and strength.

> *Thou, O God, hast taught me from my youth up until now;*
> *therefore will I tell of thy wondrous works. Forsake me*
> *not, O God, in mine old age, when I am gray-headed, until*
> *I have showed thy strength unto this generation, and thy*
> *power to all them that are yet to come. Thy righteousness,*
> *O God, is very high, and great things are they that thou*
> *hast done: O God, who is like unto thee!*

> — Psalm 71:16-18
> (Reformed Episcopal Church, Book of Common Prayer)

MOVING DAY

Moving day came and went, and came back, but we survived. Susan rented a twenty-five-foot truck. At 7:00 p.m. on moving day she pulled me off the truck and said, "These people have been working all day. They need food."

I cast my eye despairingly on what remained. There was at least another truckload. But everybody in America moves on July Fourth, so Susan was afraid she couldn't rent another truck. She found one somehow, and by 6:00 p.m. the next day we had crammed it full, and loaded another fourteen-foot open trailer.

Where did all this *stuff* come from? Remember Susan bought a fifty-two-foot trailer a year and a half ago when we made the first move, and we filled *that* up, too. I've been without that stuff so long I'm beginning to wonder if I need it. Frankly, the idea of backing the thing into the pasture, unloading it, and starting a large bonfire is beginning to look reasonable to me. I'm ready to start all over.

FREE THE CHICKENS

We had moved the chickens the weekend before, but had still kept them separated in their cages. Some animal rights activist made the decision to free the chickens. At least, that is the only plausible explanation other than some child forgetting to lock a cage door. Remember that we had six roosters.

The chickens were loosed, whereupon began a titanic struggle for domination. You would think a standard sized gamecock would more than overmatch five bantam roosters, even if they all ganged up on him at once. They didn't, but he has more fight than smarts. Every one of them must have beaten him up, because by the end of the day his head was covered with blood, and except for one banty, the others showed ne'er a scratch. The lone banty whom the gamecock managed to best has exiled himself across the road to the barn. The rest have come to an uneasy truce. My hens have started laying again, but have chosen to lay under one of the garbage cans. This makes egg gathering inconvenient and surprising.

ZACHARIAH BUYS A DOG

You'd think that two no-good Labrador half-breeds and an impulse-buy rat terrier would be enough dogs for anybody.

Zachariah decided he must have a dog. I asked a veterinarian friend what sort of dog he would recommend for the country (with the coyotes in mind), and he recommended a Great Pyrenees. They are big gentle dogs, and bond to whatever animals they live with, making them excellent guard dogs. Zachariah decided he needed a Great Pyrenees.

He had discovered a lady in Corinth, Mississippi, who had some pups for sale, and had been calling her for weeks. When you're twelve, buying a dog deserves such expense. After we moved, I finally had time to take him down there, and spent a long, *hot* day in the car.

These are *not* small dogs. They stand about hip high, and weigh ninety to a hundred and twenty pounds, sixty of which are fur. They are very affable and gentle, and will guard any animals they are raised with (at about eight weeks old, they bond to whatever they are around). This one was raised with chickens. Zach bought him thinking about all the coyotes in our neighborhood, most of whom are chicken lovers. Such a magnificent dog had to have a grand name. Zach settled on "Kaiser." Kaiser is big and friendly. He looks like a thirty-pound Q-tip without the stick. Justin started working with him and is astonished at how tractable and eager to please he is. His greatest sin is chasing chickens, but since he has been raised around them there is no danger he'll bother them other than stirring up a little fun.

Jack, our Dalmador, was a little anxious about his alpha-dog status, and was grouchy for days. Apparently that has now all been sorted out, and the dogs have gone back to their favorite pastime, barking all night. The coyotes are not impressed.

WORTH GOT MARRIED

On June 18, Worth was married in Nashville to Shawn O'Rourke. It truly was a beautiful wedding, with attendants enough to fill a 747. I must be getting old. Two handkerchiefs were not enough.

Worth and Shawn are building a log house. He has finally found someone who will work hard enough and long enough to suit him: *Amish*. There is a large Amish community in his part of the county. They drive their buggies to work and tether their horses in the woods. On Sundays you can see them everywhere on the roads, families in their buggies with what seems like dozens of tow-headed children hanging on. The Walmart in Lawrenceburg has a special part of the parking lot with hitching rails reserved for horse-drawn vehicles.

The Amish use splendid, huge Belgian horses—they weigh, literally, a ton. I saw them plowing earlier in the spring. I promise you, there was a boy who looked no older than eight driving a three-horse team. If they start them that early, no wonder they can work.

Could there be anything in the world more glorious than working horses? The Amish don't seem to notice.

ELIJAH THRIVES

Justin and Ellen's baby Elijah is thriving, after the initial scare he gave us. He has a shrill scream just like his daddy, paying Justin back for his raising. Until the work on the cabin is finished we are all living together in a *very* small farmhouse—Justin, Ellen, and Elijah, Susan, four children, and me. It may be 1,200 square feet. We call the farmhouse "The Top," because standing outside it feels like The Top of the World. Not many people understand why we named the other place (the cabin) "The Shoe." However, if you ever heard the nursery rhyme, and you recall that Susan and I have seven children, you'll work it out.

WAYNE COUNTY FAST FOOD

Early one morning my son Justin and I were driving down the gravel road from our cabin to the farm. There is no traffic, so I just stopped the car in the middle of the road, opened my door, and climbed out, somewhat to Justin's astonishment.

There by the side of the road were loops and streamers of blackberry bushes, bent down with flashes of black and red fruit. My childhood memory of the hateful business of picking blackberries (my mother made me go with my grandmother) wasn't just the thorns pricking your hands, but worse yet, crowding into the blackberry thickets as a living chigger collector. It wasn't that I didn't like blackberries. I love them. I just can't stand chiggers.

But here was a whole supermarket of unchiggered blackberries, spilling over the road from the fencerows, begging to be picked. Justin and I held out full hands, cupped them off the vines, and scooped them into our mouths. After a few minutes we climbed back into the car, and as we were driving off, I turned to Justin and smiled, "Wayne County fast food."

About a week later I stopped at a wild cherry tree. I had been noticing the big patch of fallen wild cherries underneath the tree on the road, so I stopped, got out of the car, and scooped off a handful. I handed them to Justin, who had never eaten them before. They were perfectly ripe.

"Did you ever think about the way God makes these things for our delight?" I asked him.

"Yeah," he answered, "it's like all the trees have fruit hanging down, prepared just for us."

"Yes, but you do have to reach up and grab it," I said. "It is Paradise Restored."

A HORSE POINTS THE WAY

We wouldn't have noticed the house where we are now living if it hadn't been for a horse. In fact, we were lost. It was late 1998. In the pasture down the road we spotted a coyote as big as a German shepherd, studying the calves in the pasture on the other side. We stopped, but he paid us no attention. He stared as long as he wanted, then loped off.

We finally came to a fork in the road. There at the fence corner stood a magnificent white Arabian, hanging his head over the fence, staring at us. Weird as it sounds, he seemed to be welcoming us, as if he was saying, "Well! There you are! What's kept you so long?" I mentioned it to Susan, shook my head, and drove on. Later my son Wright got lost again, and found out that the house there was for sale. One thing led to another, and we ended up there. The horse was for sale, too.

Everybody has their gifts, and Justin's gift is handling horses. Mysteriously, they recognize they have to obey him. The horse, General, was fairly old, but in good shape and inexpensive, so I bought him as a present for Justin.

We moved in over the weekend of July Fourth. Things remain in a near-perfect mess, but we're up and operating, and just for my physical situation, I'm about as happy as I can ever remember.

Personally I am happy, but when I think about American society at large, I am astonished. I recently drove south down through western Alabama to Tuscaloosa, about a four-hour drive, then east across Alabama, Georgia, and South Carolina to Charleston. From here to Tuscaloosa I spotted one, count 'em, one roadside fruit stand. Our country has been deeply, thoroughly homogenized. Every little town boasts a Walmart, and BP, Texaco, Exxon, and Chevron stations, a chain grocery store, and the same battery of chain eateries: McDonald's, Burger King, Hardee's, Pizza Inn—you know the names. We went to a restaurant in a small town near here and they didn't even have fresh, home-grown vegetables on the menus! Calzone and pizza, but no vegetables. Not even Swiss steak.

For some, the assurance of the bland sameness of a Big Mac from coast to coast may lend a certain homeyness to foreign climes. For me, however, the words "poverty of choice" and "loss of local identity" spring to mind. You can drive across the South, indeed, across America, and you'll hardly be able to tell Charleston from Dallas unless you venture far, far off the expressway. The malls and shopping centers and subdivisions are all identical. It may be success, but it sure is boring.

WHAT HAPPENED TO THE PEOPLE?

Driving around this rural area you can't help but notice the decline of the agricultural population. Where have they all gone? To Walmart? Barns and outbuildings are there, but they are closed and abandoned. There are not even many people sitting on porches in the evenings. I guess it's cooler inside.

I dread to always make government the goat, but since the government took over the direction of agriculture back in the 1930s, the farming population has declined from about half of the population to a number so low that they dropped the category from the census in 1990. People just can't make a living at farming, so they take a job at a factory. They may raise a few cattle, but most just live there out of habit. Old people don't farm any more, because the government pays them social security not to work.

When I look at the abandoned farmland side by side with strip malls, I think of what George Fitzhugh observed over a hundred years ago in *Cannibals All!*, that the great danger to a free-labor economy is over-population. Ending serfdom creates a surplus of labor, which inevitably ends in wage-slavery and chronic poverty for workers. Because capital has so much more economic power than labor, labor's weakness forces it to bid down wages to starvation levels, which eventually creates that restive, unemployed proletariat that has nothing to lose by revolution. Stability—for the rulers—demands the reduction of the labor force with minimum wage laws, licensing, mandatory retirement, and population control. The Great Depression brought the New Deal, which was in fact industrial capitalism shucking off the expense of supporting people in infancy, infirmity, and old age onto the taxpayers' backs. Peace is bought with welfare for the unemployables, abortion, and devices like the Full Employment Act of 1948.

Sorry, I have no grand solution to modernism's cultural poverty. I trot down to Walmart like everyone else, as much for convenience as for lack of choice. For the little good it seems to do, I try to patronize locally-owned establishments, and ferret out those little places that delight me with the good things of my own neighbors—and I like to share that goodness with you, my readers by telling you about these places. The trouble generously repays itself, like scooping blackberries off the vines next to the road. We joke about our little "milk co-op" with four or five families in our neighborhood. Some of us pay ($32 a month), and some of us milk, but we all enjoy fresh, creamy non-pasteurized, non-homogenized milk. Next week the peaches will start coming in at Duck River Orchards, and I will gladly drive over the hot, dusty roads to enjoy them. And I'll keep on wondering if there isn't something more to the economics of living than just the bottom line.

Last Sunday Susan and I were sitting out in our yard, watching the sunset with our neighbors. The martins were busy scooping their supper out of the air. "Surely," I thought, "surely if the birds can make a living here, I can, too."

Over the field the martins fly
And scoop their supper from the sky!
Content with food their only pay
It doesn't look like work, but play.
If I, like them, could toil and sing

Then surely work would lose its sting.
A swooping bird, I'd spend my days
And join the martins' hymn of praise
To that good God who martins feeds
And 'ere I ask, supplies my needs.
O, from my blinded eyes remove
The fretful scales that hide that Love—
O, let me live beneath that Grace
And breathe my last in its embrace.

— Franklin Sanders, July 1999

"STRAINGIN' BOB WAR"

Zachariah went to Chicken Killing Camp. At least, that's what I call his stay at my friend Charlie Ritch's Goose Pond Farm. When Zachariah was invited to help with the chicken killing and dressing, he couldn't volunteer fast enough.

It's not easy work. Zach went down on Monday with a friend whose dad graciously gave Zach a ride. On Wednesday our pastor, Chuck (ineluctably nicknamed "Friar Chuck"), and I drove down to watch the action. Charlie gets the boys up early to bring in the chickens from their pens in the pasture. I wasn't sure how long it would take to drive down there, so Chuck and I left Lawrenceburg, Tennessee, about 4:30 a.m. in the stone dark. By the time we passed the Burger King in Hartselle, Alabama, the sun was just peeking over the trees. At 6:00 a.m. it was magical dawn at Goose Pond Farm. The air was thick with hazy mist ("ghost fog"), and the pasture was filled with cattle, sheep, and, yes, those are two pigs. Laura told us that Charlie was down in the pasture with the boys, bringing up the chickens, so we walked back down the drive to find them.

By the time we got there, they had a long trailer stacked high with chicken coops. While we were standing there, I noticed a big red hawk sitting high up in a tree. I pointed him out to Charlie, and he nodded. "Thanks to them I only have half of my egg-laying flock left. And there's

165

a $5,000 federal fine for shooting them." Ain't the Yankee government great? I thought.

We rode the trailer back up to the house, where Laura had a memorable breakfast waiting on us. She performs some magic on grits with cheese and garlic. And unless you have seen and eaten them, you'd think I was eggs-aggerating about the superb taste and utter yellowness of free range eggs.

After breakfast Friar Chuck and I followed the crew outside to watch them process chickens. The operation is quick, efficient, and scrupulously clean. They take the chickens out of the coops and place them headfirst in sheet metal cones, then slit their throats.

Charlie sells his Goose Pond chickens almost by subscription. He sends his customers post cards and they arrive on processing day to pick them up. I felt lucky to coax three frozen chickens out of him, and grandly generous to sell one to Friar Chuck. Although the hawks have halved her egg-laying flock, Laura found three dozen eggs to sell us. I am proud to report that I also shared these with Chuck. I had to. He saw Laura giving them to me.

Now Zach has chicken fever. Wilber has loaned him several chicken catalogs, and he's agitating to order chickens. Next Monday we're heading down to the flea market at Ardmore, Tennessee/Alabama (it sits astride the line) to see what we can find. Susan has already bought a dozen month-old, black, sex-linked chicks. "Egg Laying Muh-sheens," Susan calls them, her eyes glazing over with hope.

Speaking of which, one of our game hens is setting a clutch of eggs. At least, we hope that's what she's setting. Susan put three nest-egg gourds in the box to trick the hens into laying, and now the hen is setting on— something. Whether she hatches out chickens or the Sasquatch Gourd Beast remains to be seen.

Besides Zachariah, everybody else is working at something. When you call us you can hear hammering and pounding in the background as three of the boys work under their Leader (not me) to finish fixing up the Shoe. Evenings Justin is learning Elementary Barbed Wire Management, a.k.a., "straingin' bob war." Susan keeps the highways hot driving to Lawrenceburg, Waynesboro, Florence, and elsewhere to keep the whole undertaking supplied. Ellen stays busy taking care of Elijah, and I'm not sure exactly what Mercy is doing, but she always turns up in time to go swimming with the boys in the evening. A neighbor down the road graciously allows them into his Chisholm Creek swimming hole, which is about seven feet deep. A tree hangs over the creek, sporting a rope whereupon they launch themselves into space and strategically drop into the deepest place. I wish I were as fearless as they are.

SEPTEMBER 1999

Zachariah and Christian are getting hunting fever. The country here is full of turkeys and deer—and coyotes. Zach got hold of the Cabela's catalog and went wild. He ordered a deer stand and enough camouflage for a battalion of Rangers. He even got a crossbow. Maybe he thinks he'll be hunting knights and varlets, I don't know.

SUCCESS!

The hen that was hatching the nest egg gourd is still sitting. Another of our banties made a nest under the big lawn mower. The dogs started annoying her day before yesterday, so we figured it was time to move her. When we did we found four little chicks! We moved her and the rest of her eggs into a safe pen with a nest box. Today there were six chicks. These are not the only additions. Susan got some guineas (over protests about their noise) and Zach bought a turkey, positively the ugliest, ungainliest animal alive. His taste in pets runs to the omnivorous.

ONE DISASTER AT A TIME

THE FATEFUL JARS

Every month Susan and I drive down to New Albany, Mississippi, to take the newsletter to the printer. Last month as usual, while we were waiting we went shopping at Walmart. Susan found two pallets of quart canning jars at about half the price they were selling for up here. We bought them all, some for us and some for our friends here, and made arrangements to pick them up Saturday.

That was Thursday. On Friday Susan and I again yielded to Zachariah's importuning, this time for pigs. Our Y2K preparations wouldn't be complete, Zach argued, without pigs. He knew my weak spot. The long and short of his importuning was that at next First Friday we ended up with two pigs, one turkey and six guineas. There was an old dog pen in the pasture where we kept General, so we put the pigs over there. Zach had bought fifty pounds of pig mash, and we put that in a galvanized garbage can with a lid near the pigpen.

Saturday was a busy day for all of us. Susan and Zach drove to New Albany for the jars while Justin and I spent most of the day helping Friar Chuck move. When we came back we took a tour of the back side of the far pasture looking for springs. When we got back to the house, we spied two pigs in our front yard!

Forget chasing pigs. They can run forty-five miles an hour and turn on a dime. How can you hold them? No handles on a pig. After Justin and

I had thoroughly exhausted ourselves out in the field, Susan drove up in the truck, pulling a trailer load of jars.

THAT SUDDENLY

She backed the truck into the tractor shed and Justin unhitched the trailer. I was in the truck in the next stall, getting ready to pull out when Susan climbed in her truck and pulled away. She couldn't see that Kaiser had lain down in front of her truck wheel. Justin and I watched helplessly as the truck wheel rolled over him.

He was killed almost instantly.

Susan was horrified, weeping inconsolably. Justin and I stood stock-still, shocked clueless. I pulled up my truck and let down the back gate by Kaiser. I told Justin I would go get some shovels and asked him to put Kaiser in the back of the truck. Justin just looked at me. "I can't," he said.

I reached down to pick him up as quickly as I could. I didn't want Susan to have to see him. Zachariah stood by in shocked disbelief. I asked him where he wanted us to bury him, and he pointed over to a hill at the back of the property, beneath a line of trees where his grave can be seen every morning from the bathroom window.

After I herded Susan into the house, Justin and I got shovels. Zach climbed up on the back of the trailer next to Kaiser. We drove over the pasture to the hill and started digging.

The dirt was so hard we couldn't dig. We had to use the shovels like picks, pecking out a grave. Zach and Justin said nothing, and I was grateful not to have to speak. I was doing all right until I realized that the grave wasn't big enough. "It won't do," I said, "he's such a big dog."

Zach went back to the house to check on Susan and get something. Justin and I drove over to the other pasture to pick up some big rocks to cover the grave. I couldn't bear to think about the coyotes digging him up. It was almost dark.

We had no more gotten back than I saw the lights of the other truck bumping across the pasture. Susan pulled up and frantically yelled, "You've got to come over to the barn. General's down and his legs are stiff and he is all swollen."

"One disaster at a time," was all I could think. We drove over to the barn and there was General, lying on his side, stiff-legged and swollen. I ran and called our friend Arnold Threatt. I knew General was foundering but didn't know what to do. Where could he have gotten into grain? Then it hit me: the pig feed.

Arnold, bless him, said he would come right over. We drove back out to the pasture to finish burying Kaiser. I laid him in the grave and Justin and I covered him with dirt and then covered the grave with rocks. Zach had taken off his collar and choker. From somewhere he had gotten a little Slim Jim sausage to put on the grave, a treat too late. All these I laid on the rocks, and then we four prayed. Through it all Jack and Bear and Bull, our other dogs, sat quietly by the grave. Impassive and noble, Jack sat staring into the distance, as if he understood better than we did.

No sooner did we get back to the barn than Arnold and his wife Pam pulled up with Billy Willett, who raises Belgian horses. Shortly, Arnold's daughter Angela and her husband James arrived. We all pulled and pushed to get General up, filled him with as much vegetable oil as we could, and walked him. Around and around, stop for more oil, down he goes, wrestle him up again, do it all over. The stars watched while we fought. The time crept by until morning was bare hours away. Finally only Justin and Arnold and I were still awake. General was on his feet by himself. Someone had to make a decision whether to keep it up or not. Justin decided General was well enough to leave, and we agreed.

Sunday morning I dreaded to get out of bed. I looked out the window, and there lay General. What we'd done wasn't enough, but it had been all we could do. We all went to church.

Foolish woman? Shall we accept good from God and not evil? The LORD gave, and the LORD hath taken away. Blessed be the name of the LORD.

— Job 2:9-10 (Authorized Version in my own words)

FACING GOD

My friend Charlie Ritch called Monday after that terrible Saturday. "On a farm," he said, "you are around life and death daily." Death is not sanitized, not clinical, but *personal*. When something dies, you must dig the hole and put it away, just as our forebears did with their own family members, on their own property. On a farm, you can't hide from death. And to say that you can't hide from death is to say you can't hide from God, for every time you face death, you face God.

City-dwellers live in a bubble where everything is controlled and controllable—virtual reality. Think of that wry scene in the movie *Being There*, where Chance the gardener (Peter Sellers) hits the street for the first time in his life. His entire adult life has been spent in a bubble, confined within the walls of an urban garden, seeing only the old man who owned the house and his maid. Of the world, this idiot savant knew only what he saw on TV, which he watched every minute he didn't spend in the garden. He puts on one of the old man's fine suits and walks out into the streets of the urban slum which had long ago surrounded his garden oasis. Several thugs accost him. By chance he had slipped the TV remote control into his pocket as he left his room for the last time. When the thieves threaten him, he stands rigidly unmoved. Without any hint of fear (or any other emotion), he slips his hand into his pocket, pulls out the remote control, and starts snicking it at the thugs. Virtual reality.

When you let animals into your life, you open yourself to an uncontrolled and uncontrollable reality. You meet God in person, so to speak. But the same is all the more true of making friends, or marrying, or having children. You give up all claim to undisturbed, selfish existence and

171

make yourself vulnerable. You give your love in pawn—a pawn liable to reclaiming at any time.

So you climb out of the bubble. You open yourself to love. And with love comes not only the possibility of pain, but also the certainty. You open yourself to the unrestrained mercy of God—for unrestrained blessing.

What choice have we? To stay in the climate-controlled bubble of self-absorption, cut off from the world, where the prospect of pain is diminished but the possibility of joy annihilated?

> *Return to your rest, O my soul,*
> *For the* LORD *has dealt bountifully with you.*
> *For You have rescued my soul from death,*
> *My eyes from tears,*
> *My feet from stumbling.*

> — Psalm 116:7-8 (New American Standard Bible)

Return, O my soul, return to love's Original, shining so intensely that we cannot view it. God is the origin of love. And love always returns to love, seeks love, and finds that love in the love of the Father, Son, and Holy Ghost. Our love for each other returns to God.

Who are we, that God has made us in his image, and he is love? So are we.

PIGS GONE WILD

Six people are no match for two pigs. For about a week, just as I was about to leave for work at the Shoe, the cry of "Pig out!" would go up, and everyone would rush outside to corral them. The dogs inevitably got into the act, thinking it a great game to run the pigs through the woods, over the hills, and down the hollers. Pigs are pests.

Then one morning the pigs showed up hurt. The male, whom I called "Pork," had a big gash on his scrotum, and the female had cuts all over her. The boys corralled Pork, and then we together managed to catch Chop. Foolishly thinking she was exhausted, I put her into the truck, and she promptly hopped out. Last I saw of her was two hams winking at me down the road.

A week passed and Susan changed Pork's name to "Houdini" for his ability to escape any confinement. Once we stopped chasing him, he settled down to rooting in the flowerbeds. Then suddenly one morning, Chop reappeared, slimmed down considerably. Susan coaxed up both pigs with food, and as they ate she crooned "Old MacDonald" to them and scratched their backs.

Leave it to a woman to make peace with all creation. The pigs, now styled Houdini and Princess, come up every day about 3:00 p.m. to eat, then disappear again. I hope they can run faster than coyotes.

Who would name a pig "Princess"? I named them "Pork" and "Chop" to give everybody a hint that their residence with us was not a permanent arrangement. I'm not supporting a petting zoo.

BISHOP DAN MORSE

Many of y'all have asked how Bishop Dan Morse is doing. He has physical therapy every day for one and a half hours, and occupational therapy. The physical therapy deals with problems of walking, balance, and his lower body. Occupational therapy deals with his upper body, especially the use of his arms and hands. His right hand has been the slowest to recover.

Dan's accident occurred April 19, 1999. A little over four months later, God is answering your prayers and ours. Dan has not only survived, but he also retains his cheerful spirit and his trust in God, and little by little his healing is going forward.

Would you please keep on praying for Bishop Dan Morse, that God would grant him a full and complete recovery? Would you also pray for his wife, Marianne, as she cares for him? Pray, too, for Dan's family as they handle all the difficulties of his long-term recovery.

A ROYAL PATH

From nowhere along the dirt road we drive to work every morning, orange-eyed yellow daisies have suddenly bloomed. Out of the dust and terrible dryness, daisies have turned our road into a royal path.

OCTOBER 1999

ENTER Y2K

Business and government spokesmen fill the air with comforting words, but no facts. Rumors fly everywhere. Every day the hugeness of preparing weighs down on me. The big rally in gold and silver caught a lot of people flatfooted as they were waiting to do something "a little later in the year." Then today I received Jim Lord's latest newsletter on Y2K preparedness in which he enclosed a special flyer about rumors of the Fed limiting cash withdrawals beginning this month. Very little would surprise me.

If you haven't yet prepared, you'd better get in high gear. Think about your family, and act.

MORE SAD NEWS—AND GLAD

Justin and Ellen were looking for a dog of their own, and they had got a little Labrador-Shepherd puppy, Dixie. Unhappily, she developed a hernia and had to be put to sleep. We buried her on the hill next to Kaiser.

But Justin wasn't to be stymied. He searched and searched and found a beautiful Great Pyrenees pup they have named Cleopatra—Cleo for short. This is a great dog. "Dogs on valium" I call them. Sleep in the yard all day, bark at coyotes all night.

A few Sundays ago Susan and I climbed on the four-wheeler for a long drive. We got pretty far down an abandoned road and looked back to see Bull, our rat terrier, running sixty miles an hour behind us. Well, shoot, you've got to stop and pick him up. He sat contentedly in my lap, enjoying the breeze. Then we looked back again, and there was Jack, our Dalmador. He's so stupid/courageous he'll follow you down the road until he wears the pads off his feet, then lie around on his back with his feet in the air for a week. I'm not picking him up. I'm not.

Needless to say in a little while we are riding down the road with me driving, Bull in my lap, Susan's head over one of my shoulders, and Jack beside her slobbering on my other shoulder. I thought when my children started moving out I wouldn't have to do this stuff anymore.

Then came dogs.

TUCKER'S BIRTHDAY

My grandson Tucker celebrates his second birthday on October 15, Elijah is getting fat and singing, and Liberty is expecting her second baby December 8. Last weekend we drove the whole mob to Ripley for First Monday. We came away with some great buys, but for the first time, no animals. I will not ride two and a half hours with chickens or pigs. I'd sooner tie a mattress and wringer washer to the roof of my car.

The leaves are turning, but the county took a notion to clip the road-sides and mowed down all our yellow daisies. What are these people thinking?

PREHISTORIC COWS

Justin decided he wanted to raise cattle, but not just *any* cattle. *Highland Cattle*. We found a small herd in east Tennessee.

These cows are *very* rugged, with long hair and great curving horns. They're much more docile than they look. Generally they're raised for beef, but they can also be milked. My friend Randy calls them "prehistoric cows."

Lately, however, they're a problem. Just to give them a once-over every day, Justin began feeding them a tiny bit of sweet feed. Problem is nine cattle, only four feeders, and there is nothing more rambunctious than a thousand pounds of long-horned cow that thinks it is about to be shortchanged a snack. This has occasioned manifold ruses to draw them off while someone sneaks into the pasture with the feed. The pied piper takes a bucket and bangs it along the fence, moving *away* from the feeders, cows following. Despite a multitude of disappointments, they never seem to catch on. Anyway, Pilgrim, the three-year old bull who's pushing a ton, always gets first choice. Belle, the lead cow, is the only one who will push him aside—or try to. The cows have a very rigid hierarchy. Whoever gets out of line quickly gets a horn in the side.

Speaking of animals, we got yet another Great Pyrenees pup. Mercy and Ellen named this one Orion, because he has stars in his eyes.

Something has been killing our chickens (and some of the new male turkeys Zachariah bought to keep company with Bob, Zach's first turkey, a hen). We thought it was the dogs as usual, but last week we finally moved into our re-furbished cabin, taking the suspect dogs with us, and chickens still disappeared. The Great Pyrenees are not suspects, because about the time they are six to eight weeks old, they *imprint* on whatever is around them: goats, sheep, cats, chickens, grandchildren—and spend the rest of their lives *defending* those creatures.

Suspicion's jaundiced eye is beginning to look again dog-ward.

FALLING AWAY

I may be imagining it, but it seems like something is falling away from me every day I spend here on our own land out in middle Tennessee, like some lizard shedding his skin. When I go back to a city, the press of people and traffic attacks me. No wonder urbanites are sick so much. All that stress and emotion and speed is bound to affect you.

THIRD TIME LUCKY

We've been moving since April of 1998. It's now November 1999. I used to say that I was thankful if I could find socks and underwear in the morning. I'm past that now. I just buy new ones once a week. No point looking. You can't find them anyway. We're also moving the office once more. I am ready to be rooted in place.

Since we bought this farm in July of this year, we've been living in its 1,200-square-foot house with no running water—Susan, me, three and sometimes four children, plus Justin and Ellen and their baby Elijah. I am really tired of sleeping on a trundle bed. We are moving for the last time, a whisker before Y2K hits. We are finally moving into the Shoe. This is the last move. God willing, this will be my place on the earth from now on, the place where I will be buried.

OLD CARS

I drive old cars. I do this because I like them, of course, but mostly because they are cheap. I got in the habit when all my seven children lived at home. Children make new cars look old very quickly, so why waste the money? When you've got kids, that's all you've got. I try never to drive a car made in the current decade. I am what the folks at AAA call a "heavy user of roadside services."

So I was in Nashville, and our 1984 LTD station wagon broke down. (Look, it rides *great*, and it's *big*.) It wouldn't start, even though Walmart had replaced the battery a week before. *New battery.*

Friends gave me a jump, the car started, then I went into a building to use the phone, and left Christian waiting in the car. Six minutes later he came in, held up the keys, and announced, "Car's dead." I called Triple A.

Truck came out, fellow jumped off the car, I pulled out of the parking place, and it died again, permanently. I had him tow me to a Ford dealership.

I am *not* a heavy user of dealership "services." Susan and I favor the Underground Economy in mechanics, a.k.a., shade-tree mechanics. Something about the smell of old motor oil on the ground gets my blood running. I like the way it shines and changes color when the sun hits it. Besides, how can you trust a mechanic with all his digits intact? Really, it's the *game* I love—did I *really* need a complete engine overhaul, or did he just con me?

So we pull into the dealership, and a perky attendant steps out. Clean fingernails. Clean clothes. All ten fingers. "What's wrong?"

I quickly congratulate myself on not remarking, "Oh, nothing, I just thought it would be a fine day to have my car towed." I did *not* say that. I was *polite*.

"It won't start. Dead, but a new battery."

"Well, I don't know," he says cheerfully, "we don't usually work on cars over ten years old."

I didn't know which to hit first, him or the pavement. "You know: hard to get parts, bolts twist off." He smiled. I didn't. "But we'll see what we can do."

We wait in the spotless waiting room while they prepare my car for a complete walletectomy. Thirty minutes later they call my name over the *loudspeaker*, and I go out into the service area. Mr. We-Don't-Work-On-Old-Cars tells me I had a cable loose. I go to the cashier, mentally enumerating the friends I can call for a loan.

The cashier hands me the bill. Sixty-five bucks for the work (must have been a *very* loose cable) and $6.50 for an "environment fee." "What's this?" I ask, manfully suppressing the volcanic anger and acid vituperation coruscating up my throat.

"I don't know. I just add them up. Ask one of the guys outside."

I buttonhole one of the servicemeisters outside. "What's this?"

"Oh, that's a charge for disposing of the fluids and oil we use when we work on cars."

"Who did that," I ask cheerfully, "the communists in Washington or the local soviet in Nashville?"

He never batted an eyelash. "I think it was the local soviet."

GRANDSONS

To the praise and glory of God on December 8, 1999, at 11:55 a.m. Wallace Bedford Bain, a child of God's everlasting covenant, entered into this world. His mother, Liberty Sanders Bain, is recovering well from her c-section. His father, Johnny Ray Bain, is exhausted. Pray that Bedford might live up to the lives of the great heroes whose name he bears. As you might have guessed, he is named for William Wallace and Bedford Forrest.

Join us in giving thanks and praise to God for the great blessing of this wonderful delivery, and pray that God might graciously make this child his faithful soldier and servant throughout his whole life.

This is our third grandchild. Just one thing I still don't understand. Why do my children always roll their eyes when I say, "Three down, forty-six to go"?

HEY, GOD!

Our daughter Liberty, her husband Johnny, and their sons Tucker (2) and Bedford (three weeks) came to spend the holidays. Under normal circumstances Tucker is a character, but he never lets circumstances remain normal for long.

For some kids, Sunday brings an agony of restriction. When I was a little older than Tucker, I knew that every Sunday that dawned, I would be taken to church where my daddy would instruct me to sit still. I knew also that every Sunday that dawned I would fail to sit still, and be taken out into the foyer for my regular Sunday whipping.

Tucker, on the other hand, loves worship service. He longs to make up part of the procession; he longs to preach. In fact, if the preacher stops even a nanosecond, Tucker will stand up and boldly pick up the preaching ball. Since he doesn't yet speak complete English, the product is loud, if not intelligible—not unlike many sermons I've heard from grown men.

Tucker wants to participate in the procession so badly that his mamma and daddy have to restrain him. One Sunday as the procession was leaving, he slipped away, and next thing anybody knew Tucker was leading it out of the church, strutting all the way.

He also loves to light and snuff candles. He will turn any handy instrument into a candlesnuffer, and wear you out lighting candles so he can snuff them.

Tucker doesn't leave his zeal at church. He has created a shortage of prayer books and Bibles at our house. The minute you lay one down, Tucker spies it, opens it, and begins marching around the house. He even found a box under the Christmas tree that he appropriated as a Tucker-size *priedieu* (kneeler). Whether kneeling or processing, he fixes his countenance in a look of utter seriousness and loudly proclaims, "GodGodGod GOD GodGod GODGODGOD!" This continues for hours on end. He never tires of it. I think that's what Paul meant when he wrote about "praying without ceasing."

Tucker was walking up the driveway in the sun with his daddy one day. Suddenly he closed his eyes, threw up his arms, and shouted, "Hey, God! Hey, God! Hey, God!"

THE END OF THE WORLD
COMES AND GOES

Y2K has been looming at us for a long time, and that will soon end. Maybe I'm just obtuse, but I intend to keep working along, writing these newsletters, and come hell or Y2K, mailing them out to you. My fervent prayer is that God will keep and protect you, whatever the outcome, and that all our work in the last two and a half years has benefited you.

Whatever happens, the world will not end. God will still control all things, and will continue to work out his gracious will in the affairs of men. Psalm 68:19-20 declares: "Blessed be the Lord, who daily loadeth us with benefits, even the God of our salvation. He that is our God is the God of salvation; and unto GOD the Lord belong the issues from death." (Authorized Version)

I like Luther's translation of the same passage: "Gepreisen sei der Herr! Tag fuer Tag traegt er unsere Last," "Blessed be the Lord, who daily bears our burden," and "und der Herr unser Gott hat Auswege aus dem Tod," "and to the Lord our God belong escapes from death." Which translation is the truth? God bears our burdens or loads us up with benefits? God grants us new beginnings out of death or grants us escapes from death? Apparently, the Hebrew allows for *both*. In the mysterious providence of God, those things which seem to us at first to be burdens (which he bears for us!) turn into blessings. What we thought was the ending becomes a beginning. To him belong, in this world and the next, our escapes from death.

JANUARY 2000

Y2K came and went. Some folks seemed disappointed the world didn't collapse, but I was just as happy it didn't. My world has threatened to collapse for too long.

After fighting in court six years and appealing up to the Tennessee Supreme Court, I went to jail twice in 1996. While I was in jail, my attorney filed a federal *habeas corpus*, but the judge just sat on it till 1998. That is when the 6th Circuit agreed to hear the case. It's the year 2000 now, and we are still waiting on the court to hear the appeal and to know if they will allow oral argument. My attorney thinks this may happen in June.

Sunday, January 9, my phone rang. It was a friend from Memphis.

"Do you know what today is!" she asked breathlessly.

I thought for a minute. "No, I don't."

"Ten years ago today they arrested you and Susan!"

I suppose my ability to overlook such a momentous anniversary testifies to the grace of God. Our enemies gathered together, intent on destroying us, but God delivered us all. It's a longer story than that, but I've told it before.

HORSE-DRAWN

TWIN PILLARS

Justin has bought a pair of huge black Percheron draft horses. We named them Jachin and Boaz after the two pillars in front of the first temple: "He will establish" on the right and "Strength" on the left. Actually, as it turned out, Boaz is the slightly smaller, and therefore the off, or right, horse. Jachin is the taller and lead, left horse. They are only about a year and a half old, but already huge. I can peer over their backs, but I'm nearly six foot three.

These are the gentlest, friendliest horses I've ever seen. They're like big puppies. We had been thinking about buying mules, but a friend counseled against it. Unlike the palomino-colored Belgian draft horses, Percherons are usually black or sometimes gray. They were originally bred as war horses in France, and have much more spirit than Belgians. They are also more economical—less hay, same work. When horses furnished the main motive power in the United States, eighty percent of the equine population was Percheron.

Although the horses have never been broken to saddles, Justin threw one up on Boaz to test him. He acted like he'd been saddled all his life. Never stirred a peg. Bear in mind these Percherons are still *colts*.

If they ever learn how big they are, we're all in trouble. They'll take over the farm.

PIG-HERDING COWS

The first time Justin and I witnessed it, I thought it was a fluke. The pigs escaped their sty and ran down the pasture where our Highland cattle were grazing. The whole herd turned and, for all I could tell, began herding the pigs back towards us. Then a couple of weeks ago we were feeding the pigs and Houdini got out. The cows were way over by the barn, 250 yards away. Bonnie, the Highland cow that we are milking, came running up to investigate. While she was standing there I hollered, "Bonnie, herd that pig!"

Bonnie stared at the pig in disgust, then began lowing and lowing. Once she had alerted the rest of the herd, she began circling that pig.

I'm telling you, these cows herd pigs. Maybe I ought to take them on the road?

Today is January 12 and Susan planted 140 bulbs in sixty-degree weather. Hope springs eternal. Spring doesn't always keep up.

FEBRUARY 2000

MY MISTAKE

All right, I made a mistake last month about Jachin and Boaz. Now hear the correction, as seen from *behind* (riding on the wagon seat): The *lead* horse is always on the *right*, and is always the taller of the pair. The *off* horse is always on the *left*. So . . . as you look at Jachin and Boaz *from behind*, they are in the same order as the Temple pillars, with Jachin on the right and Boaz on the left. However, just to complicate matters more, Boaz has grown so much that he is now somewhat taller than Jachin, the right horse.

I can't keep up with animals anyhow.

My attorney, Dr. Edwin Vieira, Jr., just informed me that the US 6th Circuit Court of Appeals in Cincinnati has granted oral argument in my appeal from the Tennessee conviction. Of course, they only granted 15 minutes.

JACK MEETS HIS MATCH

Our daughter Liberty and her husband Johnny were planning to spend a couple of weeks with us at Christmas, so I volunteered to drive Memphis-ward to pick up their dogs, Rex and Molly. Molly is a good-natured golden retriever. Rex is a jolly dog, part-pit bull, part-velociraptor. Johnny picked him up in the middle of the road when he was a puppy. At least, that's the story Johnny tells.

So I came rolling in one night with Rex and Molly, and left them outside to get acquainted with Jack the Dalmador, Bear the Labrador shepherd, and Bull the rat terrier.

That was The Night of the Long Dog Fights. You never saw so much hair-raising and anatomy sniffing and stiff-legging in your life. They would low-rumble growl for minutes on end, never moving a hair, then the fight would break out—Jack and Rex mostly, with Bull nipping at Rex's heels. At last Rex caught on to Bull and chased him (alone) around the house. At that point we learned that Bull could run just a little shy of the speed of sound. Rex took to hiding out under the porch.

After a couple of days it was obvious no peace was possible. We took Rex and Molly over to Justin's house and left them there with the Great Pyrenees pups, Cleo and Orion. No problem. Nothing bothers a Great Pyrenees. Peace ruled.

Until one day Justin rode the four-wheeler over to our cabin, the Shoe. Jack followed him back over the several-mile drive and arrived winded. I am working peacefully inside when the snarling, barking, slobbering, and screaming erupts. I race out there with Justin, and in spite of broomsticks, kicks, and cold water, it's nearly impossible to tear Jack and Rex apart. Jack would fight a circle saw. *Guts* he has—brains, none.

Justin took Jack to the vet, who had to staple up his nose and bind up his foot and ear. As if this weren't enough to satisfy George Foreman, heavyweight champ of the world, a few days later Jack followed our pickup back from the Shoe again to the Top. Once again, Jack obliged Rex, but Rex only got a mouthful of adhesive tape for his trouble.

TRANSPORT

I love driving the horse-drawn wagon. Every now and then Justin lets me drive. Now all this may appear pure crazy to you, but only if you have never handled horses. Justin is headed for a four-day draft horse school next month. Who knows? One day he may end up driving a beer wagon!

If any of y'all know where we could pick up some horse-drawn implements, let us know. Also, Susan asked a question I can't answer, and maybe one of y'all knows: How do they water cattle in North Dakota in the winter?

MARCH 2000

A CONFEDERATE SIGHTING

In February Justin and I journeyed to Eugene, Oregon, on business. It is *beautiful*.

Oregon's state motto is, "We know what's best for you." Their old state motto was, "We never met a rule we didn't like." I almost got thrown out of the Oregon Coast Aquarium for absent-mindedly chewing gum. As it was explained to me, it might strangle the birds [*sic*].

As far as I know, Oregon is the only state where you can be arrested for *pumping your own gasoline*! Eugene serves as the retirement haven for an entire generation of hippies. Odd, isn't it—the apostles of license become the apostles of control in their dotage? "*Yeah*, man, *cool*, smoke all the dope you want, just don't throw the butt on the ground. That's like, you know, *littering*. Bummer."

But we didn't even notice all that, thanks to both the superb graciousness of our host and Oregon's breathtaking scenery. One day our host drove us up the McKenzie River for a taste of the Cascade Mountains. Justin and I sneaked away two days and drove over the Coast Range to the coast. A landslide had closed the highway just on the other side of Sea Lion Caves, but we got to see the caves and then drove south past the Oregon dunes to Coos Bay. Another day we drove up the Willamette Valley to Corvallis, then across to Newport.

Like other Oregon coast cities, Newport has a splendid arched bridge in the High Thirties style (American Fascist Massif).

I wholeheartedly recommend you take your family for a vacation in Oregon. The people are hospitable and the scenery extraordinary. Just don't break the rules.

On the way at a tiny village called Eddyville, I almost ran off the road. *Somebody was flying a Confederate flag right on the road.* (Apparently that isn't yet against the law.)

FIFTEEN YEARS

On March 7, 2000, the United States 6th Circuit Court of Appeals heard oral arguments in my appeal from my 1996 Tennessee conviction for refusing to collect sales tax on exchanges of gold and silver money for paper money. We had brought this all the way to federal court. When we met my attorney, Dr. Edwin Vieira, Jr., at the court, he asked how long it had taken us to get there.

"Fifteen years," I replied.

That's how long I've been fighting this. No one in the country knows more about United States monetary law than Edwin. In oral argument each side gets fifteen minutes to present its case, but can reserve three minutes of that for rebuttal. Edwin began like a Browning .50 caliber machine gun, mowing down everything in front of him, answering the most detailed questions without a blink. He reserved three minutes for rebuttal.

The woman lawyer for the state of Tennessee stood up and argued for only six minutes. Basically her argument was, "Franklin Sanders is a bad person. He was a bad person in Arkansas, and he skipped across the river to Tennessee and he was a bad person there." I expected this, but was astonished when the (federal) judge asked her if it was the state of Tennessee's position that when gold and silver coin are used as money they are not subject to the sales tax. She answered, "Yes."

Hmm, I thought, If that's the case, *what in the world are we doing here?* That's what I've been arguing for fifteen years!

EGG EATERS

APRIL 2000

Over a week had passed without our finding any eggs. Finally, Susan went climbing through the hayloft, and found not only three and a half dozen eggs, but also a setting hen. The children had been sticking eggs under her, and *thirteen* had hatched.

For some time they've been living in the big barn.

Yesterday Susan moved the hen and the chicks down from the loft, because she was afraid the chicks would fall through the cracks in the loft floor. She had an old chicken cage downstairs. It's just a five foot square wooden frame, with PVC pipe bent into half hoops. The pipes fit into sockets on the frame, and over the frame there is chicken wire. Susan arranged a nest in a box, and moved all the chicks and the setting hen into the cage.

This morning we had a 10:30 a.m. appointment for family pictures. Our daughter-in-law Shawn, Worth's wife, brought Katie and Caroline, her two little sisters, with her, so Susan invited them to come back with us to see the new chicks.

Susan and I came into the house to finish off this installment of the newsletter. She sent Zachariah with the girls to show them the chicks. Shortly Zachariah returned with the news that within the cage he could find no hen and no chicks. Every one had disappeared. Susan was heartbroken. I'll be doing good to get her to finish laying out this newsletter.

Suspicion has fallen on Cleo and Orion, the Great Pyrenees. We already know they are egg eaters, and they were certainly suspects last fall in the Great Serial Chicken Disappearance. Somebody tried to lay the blame on Rex, Johnny and Liberty's dog who is still over here visiting, but Liberty came vigorously to his defense. To Susan it doesn't really matter who did it. All her little chicks, some black, some yellow, have disappeared. I feel so sorry for her.

Of course, it might have been a snake.

The lesson here might be: "Chicken knows best—don't move the chicks."

JUSTIN'S RIDE

Justin went to draft horse school in Poplarville, Mississippi. He sat with the instructor, Kenny, on a forecart, a sort of chariot that you hook up in front of large implements, learning to drive a pair of Belgian draft horses. Christian (kicking and screaming and heel-digging—he's seventeen) went with Justin, and enjoyed it every bit as much. The school started from the most basic things—how to harness up a team—and progressed to driving various sized teams pulling different implements.

Justin's Percherons are still colts, not quite two years old. They're not too big yet, about up to my shoulder. By the time they're full grown, I probably won't be able to see over their backs, and I'm six foot three inches. If Justin had his way, he'd spend all his time with those horses.

MULE DAYS

Up in Columbia, Tennessee, forty-five minutes north of where we live, they celebrate Mule Days the first weekend of April every year. People bring mules and horses from all over and there's a big show and competition. Susan, Justin, and I went up Friday afternoon for the mule auction, which was a bit disappointing. On Saturday the whole family went back to watch the mule-pulling competition and the show.

Mules compete in five or six classes. A pair of mules is hitched to a big metal sled. They have to pull it at least ten feet. Catch is, they keep loading it with fifty-pound concrete blocks until the teams that can't move it ten feet are eliminated. They start with tiny "pony" mules about the size of Shetland ponies. They may not weigh much, but they sure have a heart for digging in and pulling. Those little mules made the sand *fly* digging for traction. After all the entries but one team have been eliminated, the next class starts pulling.

While that was taking place a fellow pulled up behind us on a miniature flat-bed wagon about eight feet long, pulled by a pair of *miniature* horses. I had heard about them, but that hadn't prepared me for the reality. One horse was a charcoal gray stallion with a black mane. He stood there and neighed just like he was fifteen feet tall. The man wanted $4,000 for the rig and both horses, and if I'd had it on me, I would have bought 'em in a New York minute.

COUNTRY LIVING

MAY 2000

Last year the swallows built a nest in the corner of the carport where we were *all* living. By "all" I mean Justin, Ellen, Elijah, Wright, Christian, Zachariah, Mercy, Susan, and Franklin. In 1,200 square feet in the farmhouse at the Top.

Back to the swallows. A swallow would *swoop* in under the carport up to the nest. I believe the little birds (Swallowlings? Swallowettes?) could *hear* their parents flying in because they set up such a ruckus to be fed. In due wonderment we watched those swallows most of the summer.

Now they're back, although not to exactly the same nest in the same corner. Another pair has staked that one out. The others had to build a new nest. As the couple builds, they chitter-chatter and gossip to each other. They look like they are dressed in tails. The male wears an orange shirt front, the female white with an orange throat—elegant birds.

TULIP POPLARS BLOOM

The circle of our driveway is lined with tulip poplars, and I have been eagerly waiting for them to bloom. These are not "tulip trees." The bloom on tulip poplars begins with pale green petals that quickly turn to ivory. Around the inside of the bloom is a wide orange stripe. At the center the pistil is an elongated yellow cone, surrounded by a multitude of yellow stamens. The tulip blossom smells faintly like cake baking, and when they bloom the whole tree comes alive.

Last night came a terrible storm. Reading in bed before I went to sleep, at one point I thought a tornado was blowing up. (Three years ago one laid waste a huge swath not a mile from our cabin—blew down thirty-foot pines in a path a hundred feet wide.) Yesterday was fairly hot, about eighty-five degrees, but this morning was about sixty. The sky is full of fluffy white clouds and the sky is intensely blue. The air is filled with a sweet but sharp smell, too tart for honeysuckle but almost too sweet for roses. Clover? This is the kind of day you'd wait fifty years for, just to live through one time.

RISEN INDEED!

The trees aren't fully leafed out yet, so you can now see the blooming dogwoods through the woods, like they're floating in the air. How is it that dogwoods always know to bloom in time for Easter, no matter when Easter falls?

In the early church on Easter morning believers greeted each other with the cry, "He is risen!" The others answered back, "He is risen indeed!"

The dogwoods remember.

MOWER TROUBLES

The weather has been perfect for grass, so the cattle are grazing up to their shoulders in it. Farmers are starting to bale the first cutting of hay, which leaves me anxious. Why? Well, Justin bought an International Harvester New Idea horse-drawn mower. I don't know how old it is, but it works like a charm. That is, it *did* work, until I got hold of it.

Justin hooked Jachin and Boaz up to it the first time, and although it sounds like somebody beating handfuls of tin cans together, they settled down and pulled like champs. I couldn't resist asking Justin to let me take them for a round. The first one was fine, but on the second the mower lost the bolts that hold on the driving arm, the one that transfers force from the gear box to the blade.

From Justin's place it's a half hour drive to town, so you don't just run in to pick up a bolt. It took several days and an energetic argument about what size bolt actually fit the hole, but I finally rounded up bolts and got them replaced. Justin hitched up the team again, and the mower was working just fine.

Once again, I couldn't resist, but my pride caught up with me. I wanted to cut just as *close* as I could get to the fence. I caught a fence post with the tip end of the mower blade.

Now at this point, put your high school physics to work. The mower is shaped like an "L," with the mower tongue as the upright part of the L and the blade as the horizontal stroke. A force of almost 4,000 pounds of horsemeat relentlessly impels the tongue forward. Suddenly, at a right angle the blade catches on the fence post and stops. The horses don't. This pivots the mower clockwise, and all the force is exerted on the tongue where it connects to the mower. At which point, you'd better have a stout tongue.

We didn't. Somebody had replaced the original tongue with (I soon discovered) a *cedar* pole. Cedar, as compared to white or red oak, has approximately the same tensile strength as wet toilet paper or dry egg yolk. The tongue cracked at the socket.

Now we have a real mess, fixable only in two stages. First, remove the remains of the tongue from the mower. Second, take the tongue to the Amish to have a replacement made. Before we ever started, I could have predicted that it was an all day job. Taking out the seven bolts took us about three hours, including the time spent looking for tools and the time to hacksaw through one bolt. Finally we took it to the same Amish shop where we had bought our Hochstettler wagon. We asked how much a new white oak tongue would cost.

"We get twenty dollars for a wagon tongue," he told us. Fine, I said, this one is a little different. As long as it doesn't cost over thirty, that will be fine.

We got into the car and drove away. Justin turned to me and said, "Do you feel like you just cheated somebody?"

I shrugged my shoulders. "I know what you mean, but he named his own price."

CHICKEN CATHEDRAL

For one reason or another, the projected chicken coop has not been built for the last year (note passive voice, which obscures the actor). Susan took matters into her own hands. She got out her old *Country Living* magazine for plans for a *mobile* chicken house and, with the help of several boys, started building.

When I finally got up nerve enough to walk out to the barn, I was astonished. What she had built was not a chicken *coop*, but a chicken *cathedral*. She has painted the whole thing, and plans to paint a sign on the back, "Home of the Dixie Chicks." The "X" will be, of course, a Confederate flag.

Last Monday we went down to the flea market at Ardmore, Tennessee/Alabama. I had called the Chicken Man and arranged for him to bring some German Morans (five hens and two roosters, in case one of them had a weak heart) and a black-green East Indian drake to replace the one the varmints/dogs got, the mate for my little hen. Susan also had to buy six guineas, to keep the ticks out of the yard, and Zach bought three Khaki Campbell ducklings.

NO GREEN ACRES

JUNE 2000

Getting in the hay just about killed us.

Nothing went right. We didn't have a tractor or a baler, but we did have two big Percheron horses, a horse-drawn mower, and a Hochstettler wagon that's eight feet wide and sixteen feet long. We started mowing and finally got the horses used to the mower.

THE FIRST CASUALTY

Then the horses, who love to spook the cows by running up on them, were put out of commission. I guess Boaz ran too close to one of the Highlands and she fetched him one in the chest with a horn tip. The result was a minor, but sidelining, chest wound. Grass, however, does *not* stop growing. So much for horse-drawn haying.

I called my friend Randy, but he didn't know anybody who might bale it. About the time I was ready to give up on getting any hay in, my other friend, Arnold, had David Clark call to see if we still needed our hay baled. Did we ever. We had no sooner negotiated a price than David whisked over here, mowed, and baled. Next thing I knew there were 664 bales of hay lying in the fields, and rain threatening.

A TRUCK'S NOT BIG ENOUGH

Next evening (to beat the heat of the day) we started throwing hay into the Toyota and Ford pickups while Justin hitched up the horses to the Hochstettler wagon, which they had never before pulled. We had already stacked several loads in the barn when Justin finished hitching the horses.

Now to understand what happened next, you must know that the wagon has stamped-steel wheels. That prevents punching holes in your tires, but also sounds like fifty-five gallon drums half full of gravel rolling down the road. Also, the Hochstettler wagon hath no brakes. You stand to drive it, and use gravity to stop it.

ZACH LEARNS TO PRAY

Justin eased the wagon out of the tractor shed. Unbeknownst to Justin, Zachariah had climbed up in the wagon and lain down behind him. We were just walking up from the barn behind the tractor shed. Susan had gone to town in the station wagon. Just about the time Jachin and Boaz cleared the fence posts and turned left onto the road, those stamped steel wheels hit the gravel.

Imagine what would happen if you hit two horses in the rear with a live 220 volt electric line. When they heard the clatter of those wheels hitting gravel, they literally *leapt* ahead, veered toward the driveway fence on the other side of the road. "That's it," I thought, "end of wagon and horses. I hope Justin can jump clear alive."

They missed the corner post and veered back in the road. Justin, a.k.a., Ben Hur, was still pulling back on the reins, trying to stop them. Zach was flat as a fritter on the wagon bed, clinging to the boards with his fingers and skin, praying with an unfeigned and earnest fervor.

About that time Susan turned the corner into our road, about 400 yards away. When she saw Justin bearing down the lane toward her, she first thought, "Now why is Justin running those horses like that?" Her second thought was to pull over—fast.

They never slowed down. Past Susan the road curves away to the right, and your eyes could follow the horses running for over a quarter mile until they finally ran out of gas. We hopped on the vehicles and raced down to Justin.

For the first time, Justin turned around and saw Zach. "Zach, have you been in the wagon the whole time?" he queried.

"Naw," Zach snapped, "I ran up here just now and hopped in to fool *you*."

Once we got the horses off that gravel road and onto grass where the wheels didn't scream, they acted fine. On the way back to the barn with a load of hay, they were too busy and tired to act up.

ONE MORE TRY

On Wednesday we figured that the horses would have settled down to the wagon from the previous day's experience. The wagon was parked in the bay of the barn, pointed out into the fenced paddock. Our neighbor's son, Jordan Uselton, climbed onto the wagon. Zachariah knew that the horses wouldn't run away again today, so he joked with Jordan that if they did, he should just "lay and pray." Justin hitched up the horses, climbed into the wagon, and took up the reins. I went and opened the gate out of the paddock.

A flash of black horseflesh and wood passed before my eyes. It was the wagon, shortly before it broke the speed of sound. I saw poor Jordan lying in the back, beginning his instruction in the Zachariah Sanders's School of Prayer. Justin stood up, pulling on the reins and yelling at the horses.

Now picture the pasture the horses had run into, somewhat bowl shaped. Around the left lip of the bowl are first the barn and then the tractor shed, and the fence at the back of the tractor shed. That runs at a right angle to the shed and along the road. To the right, where the bowl would be, lies a fairly sharp ravine. Instead of heading down toward the ravine, the horses ran around the lip to the corner of the pasture behind the tractor shed, where they stopped at the fence.

We waited, and thought we had the horses calmed down. With Jordan walking and holding Boaz and me holding Jachin, we began to circle them around clockwise, facing the ravine again. After about four steps, they felt the urge, and away they flew, the wagon hitting the ground about every twenty feet. Justin apparently thought better of riding down the ravine. The wagon went left and Justin went right—through the air—as the horses veered back left and headed away from the ravine and toward the corner of the pasture. I thought they'd stop again at the fence.

Think again. Still pulling the wagon, they waded through that barbed wire like it was paper tape and never slowed down. They curved along inside the fence next to the road, and vanished out of sight over the hill, with all of us running after them.

Eventually we got them out of that pasture and led them back up the road to the paddock, where Justin and I left them, still hitched to the wagon.

Remember that. That was *not* a good idea.

YOU STILL HAVE TO HAUL THE HAY

In the truck we headed back to the hay-laden pastures, an hour closer to sunset and tireder than ever. We had no more than half a load when here came our friends, Pam and Arnold, pulling their long trailer. If Arnold had been Santa Claus with a full sleigh and a paid-up American Express card, I couldn't have been happier to see him.

We took our load back to the barn, and about the time we had finished unloading, Arnold backed a full trailer into the barn. Picture now that on one side of the barn there is no loft and we had stacked hay twenty feet high from floor to ceiling. Now we were ready to begin on the other side stacking the hay up in the loft.

With so many people (Justin, Zachariah, Christian, Wright, Jordan, Arnold, Pam, Susan and me) you can move a lot of hay fast. We started stacking the hay at the far end of the loft. About the time we had stacked fifty bales down there, I heard a large tearing, creaking noise, and turned in time to see that end of the loft disappear from view, carrying Justin and Christian down with it.

The horses, still standing in the paddock, heard it, too. Through their minds, insofar as a horse has a mind, one thought sprang: "Time to *git!*" They began circling the paddock at about seventy miles per hour. As they circled back toward the barn, I thought, "Oh, no, they're going to drag that thing through the barn and wreck everything!"

They didn't. Rather, they ran onto the open gate, jammed the wagon tongue into the mower's wheel, and rammed everything together so tight they couldn't move.

By this time I had determined that Justin and Christian had not been crushed to death, even if the barn was somewhat worse for wear. Eventually we got the horses, wagon, gate, and mower disentangled. The rest of the hay we just stacked from the ground up next to the first stack.

Miraculously, the horses were hardly scratched. It was God's own miracle that nobody was killed or seriously hurt. I know it's not funny, but still when I see in my mind Justin standing on that wagon, hair flying behind him and those horses running like their rears were on fire, I still have to stifle a laugh. And in the end, we got all 664 bales of hay tucked safely away in the barn.

I'm telling y'all, this place is *not* Green Acres.

ROOM FOR MORE

We've had another bull calf in the last month, and also Princess (Houdini's girlfriend) gave us nine piglets on my birthday. This is our first experience at pig births and I've never seen anything as pretty as a silver-covered piglet about one hour old.

Our garden is doing well and we are enjoying the produce already. Nothing like organically grown romaine lettuce for that Caesar salad. Also fresh arugula adds just a wonderfully spicy walnut taste. You should try it. I am keeping it from bolting by putting a tarp over it to shade it from the harsh heat of the summer and it seems to be doing just fine. Please announce it: I planned to plant enough to feed three families plus extra, figuring there are always more showing up every day. So if you find yourself over this way, stop by for a fresh salad and lemonade under the shade of two beautiful maple trees.

HORSE-BREAKING OR
HORSE-SHOOTING

The outlook for breaking Jachin and Boaz from bolting was not good. Justin got on his Internet discussion groups and the answer that most often came back was: "Shoot them." Go ahead and kill them now, before they kill you.

Sound advice, but I wasn't buying it. First place, I couldn't shoot them. Second, I just couldn't believe that you couldn't train that runaway out of them, like you can train everything else out of them.

Another less than helpful old hand with mules told us that when he trained young mules, he used a chain bit around their tongue, and if they ran off, pulled back hard on that bit. "They keep going it'll cut that tongue nearly in two." I wasn't buying that, either.

After much inquiry, another old horse-hand told us one thing that *might* work. You hitch the animals up to a hay wagon or mower, then chain the axle of that to the axle of a truck or car following. When they begin to dance—horses always dance right before they run away—the driver in the following vehicle hits the brakes. When the horses hit that collar, not only are they pulling the wagon or mower, they are also pulling a two or three thousand pound vehicle, and they won't pull it far with the brakes locked down. By repeating that several times they will learn that they can't run away, because when they do the load only becomes immoveable.

What did we have to lose? Two two-thousand-pound Percheron geldings, so we tried it.

First we hitched up the boys to a hay wagon. Then we ran a stout logging chain from the wagon's axle to the axle of Uncle Jesse—our old 1981 Ford F150 Pickup. This is a full sized pickup made of real metal, not plastic like the ones they make today.

The field was full of hay bales, lined up in neat rows. Justin started driving the wagon between two rows, with all of us walking along each side throwing bales into the wagon. We hadn't gone far and the horses commenced to dancing. Susan was sitting in Uncle Jesse, and we all yelled at her to "Hit the brakes!"

She did. Jachin and Boaz bolted. Wheels locked up on that heavy pickup, and to give those Percherons' credit, they managed to pull hay wagon and Uncle Jesse, with locked brakes, about 150 feet before they gave out.

I'll give them credit again: they were persistent—one try did not suffice to convince them. They danced again, Susan hit the brakes again. They dragged the wagon and truck a shorter distance than before, and then gave out. After five or six attempts, they gave up for the day and resigned themselves to the task at hand.

Still, I was not convinced they were convinced. The next time we mowed, Justin took the mower seat, but changed the "brake" on the bolting horses. This time the boys used our Terrestrial Titanic—a 1984 Ford LTD station wagon, complete with fake wood paneling (for that added country flair).

I loved that car. Truly. It was the best-riding car in the world, but it was nearly twenty years old and the transmission was going out. As a matter of fact, we couldn't get it out of first gear and, warning us of significant repair costs, our mechanic had convinced us not to rebuild the transmission.

While the horses always seemed more afraid of the hay wagon, I would rank the horse-drawn mower with a higher spook-quotient due to its fundamentally deadly, loud, and cumbersome nature. Imagine a contraption with two giant iron wheels, joined by a sturdy axle, above which is a metal chair, deftly suspended in mid-air by baling wire (well, it *feels* like baling wire). While you perch in said oddly-contoured metal chair, not three feet in front of your fragile face are the four deadly rear hooves of two enormous, and terribly nervous, horses. To your right is something akin to *forty* giant pairs of scissors on a bar, constantly rattling loudly and *cutting*. Now, twenty feet back there is a lead-footed teenager driving an enormous hunk of metal to which you are all chained.

With two horses you need a "double tree" or "evener." A "single tree" is a stamped-metal or wooden shaft about thirty inches wide and the thickness of your forearm if it's wood. At each end it has hooks to attach the trace chains from the horse's harness, and in the middle an eyelet to attach to the equipment. You hook up both horses' single trees to the double tree, and then hook the double tree to the equipment. When one horse lurches ahead of the other, the double tree moves to even out the equipment's weight between both horses. Nothing else attaches the horses to the equipment except the double tree.

Needless to say, Jachin and Boaz danced, and Wright hit the brakes. This time, however, all inanimate equipment stopped, but the horses rolled forward at top speed. Apparently the stamped-metal double tree, which attaches the horses to the mower, was a little more affected by rust than we thought. When the horses lunged, it snapped in two. I have since been told it is a surprising thing to be yanked forward by the reins in your hand when the seat under you abruptly halts.

Once Justin stood up and cleaned the rocks out of his mouth, he and Wright searched the farm and found our industrial-strength double tree. Once Jachin and Boaz were hooked to that, there was nothing left to do but dance *while* they cut grass. By the end of that day's mowing, those two horses wouldn't even venture a slow waltz. It's amazing how tame a dog-tired horse can be.

They had learned the lesson. They've never run away again. On top of that, the most mysterious thing happened. That old station wagon's transmission? Those horses healed it. Hasn't given another minute's trouble, and shifts smoothly into all five of its ancient gears!

FARMING

JULY 2000

It has been a year since we said good-bye to urban Shelby County and Memphis.

The last week in June Justin, Wright, and Mercy drove with me to Beersheba Springs, Tennessee, for a weeklong League of the South seminar on the Southern Agrarian Tradition. On beautiful Ben Lomond mountain, in an inn built before the War of Northern Aggression, my other name for the War for Southern Independence, listening to lectures from the finest and best-read minds, anybody would be tempted to wax romantic and sentimental about the country life.

Then you remember the *sweat*.

Listening to the professorial eloquence at Beersheba [locally pronounced *BURshubba*] Springs it occurred to me that we four seemed to be the only ones there *practicing* this agrarian lifestyle.

Why? Beyond the questions of moving out to the country and making a living (you just about have to have an outside source of revenue to be able to farm these days), there is the question of *work*. Lots of it. Hard. Unrelenting. Unforgiving if ignored. Face it: we are a society accustomed to easy living. For most people, "work" consists of sitting and typing or shuffling papers for a nominal eight but actual six (or fewer) hours a day, and then "leisure" (TV) for another six. *Light years* separate that life from the demands of the earth (and we *by no means* come close to answering

207

them all). In the end, however, working on the earth pays far greater rewards. To go to bed exhausted from that sort of labor is as satisfying a pleasure as I have ever experienced.

It occurred to me the other day that this is what I have *wanted* to do all my life, but somebody or something was always keeping me from it. Now it is here, and the only thing that gets in my way is my duty to write and take care of my other business so that I can indulge my weakness for working outside.

Which reminds me of Thomas Malthus:

> If those stimulants to exertion, which arise from the wants of the body, were removed from the mass of mankind, we have much more reason to think that they would be sunk to the level of brutes, from a deficiency of excitements, than that they would be raised to the level of philosophers by the possession of leisure.

> — Thomas Malthus,
> *An Essay on the Principle of Population*, chapter 18

It seems self-evident that since "exertion" has been removed from the American scene, leisure has indeed produced more brutes than philosophers.

The old proverb rings true which warns that "an idle mind is the devil's workshop." God created man for *work*. Remembering the goodness of God, the difficulty of the labor after man's disobedience set all creation against him, the "sweat" of the curse should be understood as *redeeming us* more than it punishes. A cursory survey today of the results of scant work and abundant leisure in America solidly supports that conclusion.

Whoa, slow down—I'm waxing too philosophical myself. I was supposed to be telling y'all what it was like to escape the city and live in the country.

WORK APLENTY

The chief reason people don't live on farms any more has little to do with the amount of money you can't make. It's the *work*. I know that's the reason my grandfather left the farm in 1912. Every day brings some new job—fences down, beans in, corn up, blackberries out. Failure to catch it at the right time means that you miss it altogether, or, worse, bring a lot *more* work on yourself.

Whoever said (and lots of philosophers have) that farming forms an independent and responsible character knows what he was talking about. *Responsible* because there is no one else to answer for things. You care for them, you foresee the needs, or it doesn't get done. *Independent* because you are in charge and no one else.

TIME SLOWS DOWN

Although it seems like you never have enough time to do all the jobs shouting at you, the *rural dilation of time* compensates for that. Yes, that's right, as Einstein theorized, time does actually slow down—*in the country*. More accurately, country people move according to their own internal clock. They won't and can't be rushed, so you might as well settle down and enjoy yourself. When you pass them on the back roads, everybody waves. If your vehicle is stopped, they stop to ask if you need help. The idea of "instant" everything—food, service, gratification—dies pretty fast. Besides, you enjoy not only the *end* of the trip, but the *trip* as well.

As a great by-product of this move to the country, the frenzy of modern life falls away the same way a healthy snake sheds his dead skin. You know what I mean by *frenzy*—that frantic but pointless urgency that infects you when driving in traffic or shopping in a mall. A genuine and patient calm wants to assert its rule over your soul.

Focusing on all the work skews the true picture, however. Farm life is not just grinding drudgery all the time until you collapse on your face in the dirt. Some of the work—like picking blackberries—becomes more social occasion than labor. We can't seem to find the time to watch much TV, but have lots more time for conversations with each other.

CEREMONY AND SACRAMENT

Days have become much more ceremonial and sacramental. We have become more aware of our part in each day. Perhaps because we are more likely to be outside, we notice how glorious the sunsets are.

Jim Kibler warned me before I moved that you couldn't get to know a place in anything less than a year. Jim was right. Every day some changing face of the land changes your appreciation of it. In the winter you can see for miles and miles. You learn to appreciate its austerity and solemnity. Then the spring comes and you can't wait to wake up and see what has happened overnight. First redbuds and crocuses warn you that spring is coming, then dogwoods come floating among the trees, then overnight, *whoosh*, the leaves are out. Then you can forget about the florist, because (as Susan says) you can pick your dinner bouquet off the roadside.

MONEY IS NOT THE CURE

I know that Ecclesiastes 10:19 says that "money answereth all things," but you have to construe that in the whole context of a farm. Money will *not* cure everything, but a farm will eat all your money. We would have been a lot better off if we had followed Charlie Ritch's advice more closely—*start small, go slow, learn the land and your animals.* Make haste slowly—*festina lente*—has to rule when you undertake any new project, and nowhere is that more true than on a farm. I've fed enough chickens and ducks to dogs, coyotes, weasels, skunks, foxes, and owls to stock two farms with poultry. Given the learning curve with cattle, swine, and chickens, *thank God* we didn't buy any sheep or chinchillas—yet. Learn before you spend.

NOT MUCH TO MISS

When we visit the city, we don't find much to miss. The traffic is terrible, and it takes a day or two afterward to shed that infectious frenzy.

The ever-present urban racial tension is absent in the country. It's true, we don't have air-conditioning (Justin and Ellen and Lib and Johnny do, those *slackers*), but even the hottest day brings a cool evening and night. We have to drive twenty-five minutes to the nearest Walmart Super Center, but we lived the same distance away in Shelby County. There are friends we miss. We wish they lived out here with us. Other than them, we didn't leave anything behind.

We have no plans to move back.

The best part of living in the country is that daily the mighty works of God are played out before your eyes. I know living in the city doesn't *prevent* you from seeing the works of God, but when they are played out so dramatically and majestically and personally before my eyes day after day, it's easier for me to hold on to the presence of God. This in itself would be reason enough to live out here.

> *The heavens declare the glory of God; and the firmament showeth his handy-work. One day telleth another, and one night certifieth another. There is neither speech nor language; but their voices are heard among them. Their sound is gone out into all lands; and their words into the ends of the world.*

> — Psalm 19:1-4
> (Reformed Episcopal Church, Book of Common Prayer)

PORK ON THE HOOF

After last month's letter, Georgia subscriber T.C. wrote, "I love to read about your family. I see you are getting a new education. I was raised on a farm and most everything will—bite you—kick you—run over you—or make you itch. It is the best place to raise a family."

Maybe I've been out here too long, 'cause that makes *sense* to me.

THE PONDEROSA

My daughter Liberty, her husband Johnny, and their sons Tucker and Bedford decided to join us. Last year they sold their house and were renting while they waited to buy another. They had already bought a trailer and moved it out here in case of Y2K catastrophe. Actually, this is Susan's story to tell:

> Liberty and Johnny had bought a trailer for Y2K and put it out behind our farmhouse. When Y2K didn't happen, they went back to Memphis. But they had sold their property there and couldn't find anything now to buy. They moved into the trailer, to save money in the meantime.
>
> Johnny was traveling a lot, Lib was working in the garden here, and the three boys (our three grandsons) played together from May to September. I was steadily

praying that they wouldn't leave, but they're city people, they love what the city has to offer, and this is not the city.

Then on 11 September, right before Liberty and Johnny's joint birthday on September 15, time was running out. I got an email from Johnny saying that they had weighed all their options, pros and cons, and realized that the cons of moving back to Memphis outweighed the pros. If they build a house out here, all the cousins can grow up together. And because living out here is cheaper, they could get more house for their money.

I framed that email and hung it on my wall.

We've named every place out here. The refurbished log house where Susan and I live is called "The Shoe." The farm where Justin and Ellen live is "The Top." Surrounded by pastures, the whole place lies atop a broad ridge. The wind misapprehends that this is Kansas, and so blows most of the time.

Liberty has named her trailer "The Ponderosa." When I asked her why, she said, "I just can't imagine telling anybody I'm going to 'The Trailer.' 'The Ponderosa' has more class."

First thing we did once Liberty moved in was to pick blackberries. Around here this has been a perfect year for them. First time we went out four of us picked about five gallons in about one hour. They became pies, cobblers, and, of course, cordial. It's amazing. None of us got even one chigger bite!

SWINE TIME

Princess had ten piglets on my birthday, May 24. One was born dead, and a dog got another. That dog's days at the Top are numbered. We still have eight piglets. Trouble is: what do you do with them?

Raising pigs is only slightly less trouble than raising children. They can escape any pen; hence our boar's name, Houdini. Once they get out, they can run 1,400 miles per hour, and make right-angle turns like a flying saucer.

This is what Susan wanted to capture and train to an electric fence.

After several phone conversations, reading a book, and more phone conversations, Susan and I decided we would have to drive down to our friend Charlie Ritch's in Hartselle, Alabama. Let's see some electric fencing before we spend any money. Two hot hours in the car there on Tuesday, a hot hour-and-a-half touring Charlie's establishment and quizzing him about electric fencing, and another two hot hours back.

Charlie, who patiently answered all our dumb questions, always has a *method*. He pasture-raises his pigs in fields fenced by electric wire, but *first* he trains them to the wire. Out of four welded wire panels, he builds a sixteen-foot square pen. Just on the inside at piglet nose height he installs a two strand electric fence. Then he puts the piglets in for a few days to teach them the virtues of an electric fence. Put a little feed under the wire and sooner or later they will hit it with their nose. Once zapped, they are forever wary, and then he can turn them out in a larger fenced area. (If you don't keep pigs in some way, they will destroy your whole place. What they don't root up or turn over they befoul. Repeatedly.)

Armed with our new knowledge, Susan goes to town and buys everything needed. While I am otherwise detained writing a newsletter, she labors in the hot sun Wednesday afternoon. By the time I break to see what she has done, it is raining briskly. The piglets are running all over everywhere, and catching them is out of the question, even with Susan's six assistants. After a few tries I finally convince her that the catching will have to wait till the next day, when they will be hungry and easily lured with food. *Lure, don't chase*, is my motto.

That wasn't good enough for Susan. She has built her pen, and she wants to see something swinish in it. I didn't witness this, but it was later reported to me that she herded Houie the 300-pound boar into the pen.

Now the pen had not (as someone had recommended) been reinforced with two more T-posts behind each panel. Instead, at each corner there was one T-post. The wire panels were attached with *plastic* zip-ties.

For about twenty nanoseconds Houie was okay. Then his rear hit that electric fence. *Grunt!* Again, it zapped him. *Grunt, grunt!* Now he was *mad.* He charged the corner of the fence, scattering electric fence and wire panels everywhere.

The next morning Susan repaired the fence. Then she drafted all the children on the place and a few strangers and went out chasing pigs. By the time I saw her about noon, her face had that dazed, bright red lobster look of sunbaked tourists at the beach. The boys ran down every piglet but one with a fishing net. Susan ran after boys and piglets both.

Once inside the pen, the piglets imitated balls in a pinball machine. They gaggled together, and grouped in a corner. One would hit the wire, sending the shock through the whole touching gaggle. Squeals, grunts, and scramble for the opposite corner, where again the same shock-squeal-scramble was repeated.

By the time I took a break and wandered over there, they were plenty stirred up. The biggest piglet lay in the shade under the tarp, glassy-eyed and panting.

"What happened to her?" I asked Susan. The story came back that she got in the corner *across* the electric wire, then grabbed the wire panel with her teeth, thus forming a perfect pathway for electricity from the fence to the wire and on back to the ground. Pigs make good bacon but terrible electrical engineers.

I grabbed the pig (that I could grab her at all was proof of her dazed condition), threw her in the water trough, and started splashing water over her. Zachariah brought some cool well water and by the time we had poured several buckets over her, she was perking back up.

None of this was for sentimental reasons. Come November, that piglet will be 250+ pounds of pork on the hoof.

It's two days later now and those piglets won't get *near* that wire.

Susan is still determined to train Houie to the benefits of electric fencing. In another three days, she's going to reinforce the panels with more T-posts and use metal fasteners and three strands of fencing. That should fix Houie's wagon. Then it'll be Princess's turn. That whole lot is learning who is boss and to stay out of Susan's garden.

PIG VERSUS MAN

AUGUST 2000

All at once Susan said to me, "We can't leave. The weather's too bad." There was a storm blowing up. Susan and I were just getting ready to drive to the post office mid-afternoon, somewhere about 3:45 pm. The truck was parked facing east in the lee of Justin's house (From above it's an "L" with the upright on the north pointing east and the tongue pointing south). Our weather comes from the west, so the inside of the "L" stands in the lee of the building. We were already in the truck.

I looked to my right, where The Ponderosa (Lib's trailer) sits about 300 yards away. There was a terrific wind blowing, but not like a tornado. It was a perfect wall of wind (we later found out it was blowing sixty miles per hour!)

Johnny had a chain-link dog pen outside with a tarp on top. This was twelve feet square and eight feet high. As I watched, the wind picked it straight up, and carried it high enough to clear the barbed wire fence, then on another hundred to a hundred-and-fifty feet.

About that time tufts of pink began flying through the air. The wind had peeled back the Ponderosa's tin roof and was blowing away the insulation.

(A somewhat frantic Susan wanted us to get up there while it was still raining! I do have a point where I say *no*. That was it. No.)

That storm marked the first time the wind ever blew the glasses clean off my face. The wind was unbelievably powerful, forcing the rain at a ninety degree angle. It passed fairly quickly.

Once the storm passed, I became willing to climb up on that trailer. Justin and I hurried to get a ladder and some tarps to cover the hole in the Ponderosa's roof.

A roofer I am not, but little by little we hoisted up everything we needed—tarps and boards to weigh them down. Justin and I had been up there twenty or thirty minutes when I noticed lightning in the distance. Fairly rapidly, my mind made the connection between the lightning and my position on the roof, about twenty-five feet higher than the next highest object. Next lightning flash hit closer, and we began to smell smoke in the near distance. About this time Justin and I were fairly *flying* through our work. The wind was enough. I wasn't about to test the lightning, too.

The storm also peeled back several metal sections off the barn roof that then slammed into the Shoe, flooding the summer kitchen with four inches of water. Susan is still trying to get the mud out of everything.

PIG POLICE

The Amish man who was fixing our horse-drawn mower finally wrote that it was ready. Justin and I drove over there and picked it up, and Eli had done a *great* job. He installed all new cutting teeth, timed the mower, shortened the Pittman stick (the stick that transfers force from the geared wheel to the cutting blade), put on a new sickle and guide, and I don't know what all else. Justin and I couldn't wait to try it out the next morning, so we made arrangements to get up and out early. I left the Shoe (our house) before seven. It was one of those glorious, close days where fog hugs all the world, but you can tell that any minute the sun will appear to burn it off. The light doesn't come from any particular direction, but seems to glow out of the air itself.

I got over to the Top as Justin was coming out the door. I couldn't see Boaz and Jachin anywhere. Their pasture rolls quite a bit, so sometimes the ground hides them. We started whistling and pretty soon they came up. They're suckers for corn, and so deduced that was the only reason we could be standing there. Jachin came at a run.

Surprise, surprise, no corn. Great thing horses don't hold our dirty tricks against us. They are gentle enough that we could lead them across the road and to the barn just holding them under the chin with our hands. I left Jachin in the bay of the barn and went back to my truck for a bucket of scraps for the pigs. That previous night we had a birthday supper and party for my son Worth, so I had a *full* pig bucket.

Here you have to "think" like a pig for a moment. What Bach, Shakespeare, good friends, Schlitz, the Mona Lisa, MTV, social climbing *and* crack cocaine represent to humans is, for pigs, all wrapped up in one word: *food.*

So you can understand that Princess, our sow, got a little *excited* when she saw me holding the magic white bucket. Her mind and taste buds were running wild at the thought of molded bread heels, egg shells, salad trimmings, plate leavings, sour milk, bacon grease, and leftover rice and gumbo, all sauced with coffee grounds. She just couldn't think about anything else.

That's why she stepped over the electric fence.

It surprised her as much as me. See, an electric fence *pulses.* It also requires that the *shockee* make good contact with the ground. When the weather and ground are very dry, and when the shockee times it perfectly, the fence may not deliver an *immediate* shock.

And since pigs aren't notable jumpers, the top wire of the electric fence hangs only about fifteen inches off the ground. Our boar Houdini and Princess previously having shown no inclination to get *near* the electric fence, much less make a break, we had constructed it mainly for the lower-to-the-ground piglets, but, seduced by the pig bucket, Princess just *stepped over* the fence.

Now, to my great disgust and rising anger, the day is passing and I am already sidetracked chasing a *pig.* Not just a pig, but a practiced peripatetic

219

pig. Molly, Johnny Bain's Golden Retriever, was there, and usually she's a competent pig herder. That day she wasn't even sure she was a dog. Justin was stuck in the barn with the horses. No help there.

Princess had a good time running me around the trailer at first. To divert the swinish mob behind me, I poured the scraps in the trough. Then I opened the gate in the electric fence. No good. She wouldn't get *near* it, not even with all those slobbering hogs behind me devouring her share of the scraps. Pig psychology failed.

About that time she remembered her "salad days" munching dry dog food in the farmhouse carport across the road. Thither she trotted a beeline, with me in hot pursuit, shovel in hand. The shovel I had acquired as a Pig Persuader. If I had gotten close enough to apply it, I would have had to use it as a Pig *Planter*.

All right, we ran three times around the house, once clockwise, twice counter-clockwise, before she grunted "Uncle!" and ran back across the road. No sooner did she get near the pen than Jachin emerged from the barn. Cannily sizing up the situation, he appointed himself Pig Policeman, and started chasing Princess. That drew off Justin, who had to get Jachin back into the barn. Princess withdrew to the hill across the pond where she could graze in peace. I cast her one disgusted look and returned to the barn and the horses. If I couldn't *lure* her, I sure wasn't going to waste any more time *chasing* her.

We hitched up the horses and then—in memory of their escapade when they ran away with Justin and the Hochstettler wagon in the summer of last year—we sweated them in the fenced paddock. "Sweating" is working them as a team but without any load. Object is to get them hot enough to work the smart aleck out of them. Then we hitched them to the mower. For the first time since we bought the mower, we successfully completed a job without a breakdown.

However, it took us till 10:30 am, and by then the sun was hot. Don't bother telling me that we were only *riding* on the mower while the horses were *pulling* it. I know that, but I was soaked with sweat and worn slap out.

The rest of the day in the office was still staring Justin and me in the face. We survived, but by 6:00 pm I was ready to go home, tired and angry and irritable. Then as I was pulling out of the driveway, my eyes happened to light on the pigpen, and it dawned on me that no one had taken the pigs their evening libation. I was the only candidate for that job.

The old timers used to "slop" hogs with swill made from "shorts," broken scraps of wheat thrown out in milling. They filled a barrel with a hundred pounds of shorts and water. Every day when they took out a bucket for the pigs, they added back another bucket of water, until the mixture got too thin. Then you had to add another hundred pounds of shorts.

Several weeks ago, as I was pondering these piglets, it had occurred to me that I had a cheap and plentiful source of grain nearby that we had *already paid for*, namely, the two *tons* of rice we bought for Y2K. Sitting there, tying up money, doing nobody any good. At first Susan and I thought about boiling them a couple of gallons of rice every day, but then we tried soaking some rice for twenty-four hours, leaving the barrels in the sun to head and ferment the rice. We fed rice, water, and all to the pigs.

Our experiment was an unqualified success. In fact, the pigs gave us the swinish equivalent of applause, i.e., blowing contented bubbles through their snouts while they scrounge the bottom of the trough for kernels of rice. Our Y2K preparations were not for naught after all.

So I drove the truck over into the pasture next to the barn, where the pigs are penned, with a load of said rice swill. When you're carrying five gallons of rice and water in your bucket, it's easy to be the most popular man in Pigland. A burst of porcine excitement broke out. In every heart and eye, I was a hero. Never despise life's small victories. Admiration, even from pigs, is still admiration.

Amazement! There in the pen, staring at me expectantly as if nothing had ever happened, stood Princess. Now since memory runneth not to the contrary, no pig has ever broken back into a pigpen.

I'm telling you, we're not just raising pigs, we're making history.

AMBITION

've been pondering daisies. The roads here are a wild riot of daisies, stretching in solid five foot walls for half a mile and more on both sides—short daisies, tall many-branched daisies, and tiny white daisies bunched like puffs of smoke. All among them are tall purple-tufted flowers, stalky yellow and blue flowers, and little furry cornflowers, or bachelor's buttons. All this springs from the dead, dry dust of summer.

I kept remembering something G.K. Chesterton wrote in *Orthodoxy*, and Reverend Steve Wilkins helped me find it:

> The sun rises every morning. I do not rise every morning; but the variation is due not to my activity, but to my inaction. Now, to put the matter in a popular phrase, it might be true that the sun rises regularly because he never gets tired of rising. His routine might be due, not to a lifelessness, but to a rush of life.
>
> The thing I mean can be seen, for instance, in children, when they find some game or joke that they specially enjoy. A child kicks his legs rhythmically through excess, not absence, of life. Because children have abounding vitality, because they are in spirit fierce and free, therefore they want things repeated

222

and unchanged. They always say, 'Do it again'; and the grown-up person does it again until he is nearly dead. For grown-up people are not strong enough to exult in monotony. But perhaps God is strong enough to exult in monotony. It is possible that God says every morning, 'Do it again' to the sun; and every evening, 'Do it again' to the moon. It may not be automatic necessity that makes all daisies alike; it may be that God makes every daisy separately, but has never got tired of making them. It may be that He has the eternal appetite of infancy; for we have sinned and grown old, and our Father is younger than we. The repetition in nature may not be a mere recurrence; it may be a theatrical encore.

Some modern writers view life as a ghastly repetition of the pointless—another child is born, only to rear more like him and die. The labors of our life can seem pointless and burdensome.

What they fail to see is that the repeated journey, universally alike but perpetually unique, delights the heart of God, who never tires of making daisies—and men. In our frenzied striving, we long for the Great Hit, the Excitement, the Stimulation. We miss, all along, the tireless mystery shown us in the sacramental procession of our days. *Ahh*, kiss the ones you love, and sing in your heart for the work given you this day, and bless your Creator!

OUTSMARTED AGAIN

Zachie walked into the office dressed only in his drawers. "What's wrong?" I asked.

"I've been feeding the pigs," was his disgusted remark. I failed to follow up. I should have.

Once again I had outsmarted myself.

A few days later I put up another barrel of rice to soak for the pigs. I forgot about it and got on with my work. A couple of days passed and it fell my lot to feed the pigs. About thirty yards from their pasture I noticed an indescribable smell. "Whew!" I thought, "we've gotta enlarge the pig pasture."

Then I opened the rice barrel.

You've heard the phrase, "The smell took off the top of your head," but that really doesn't do it justice. This was a stench so bad, so fetid, that merely living in the same county with it was pure pain.

Duty overrode distaste. I scooped out a bucket of rice and juice. The pigs had tuned up into an oinking mob. I poured this disgusting froth into their trough, and pandemonium—panswinery?—broke out. They *loved* it.

Observing that some of the liquid had gotten on my hand, I beat a hasty retreat to the house and scrubbed my hands—*twice*. One sniff proved my efforts bootless. I hastened back home to the Shoe, stripped off my clothes, and jumped in the shower. I took a fingernail brush and scrubbed my hands foamy—*twice*. Foolishly assuming the job done, I climbed out of the shower and sniffed my hands.

Might as well have not washed them. The *dead* don't smell that bad. Mercy! It took twelve *hours* for the stench to vanish. And I had another, oh, say, thirty-five *gallons* of that stuff to feed the pigs.

OCTOBER 2000

GRAND AMBITIONS

Maybe I'm not sorry as gully dirt after all. I'm always flagellating myself for lacking ambition, but maybe I just misunderstood my own ambitions. Maybe the ambition I've been taught to admire isn't the right kind at all.

A couple of days ago I had worn myself out all day in front of the computer, so before supper I took a break to feed the pigs. That involves a lot of fussing around. First you have to dip out soaked rice, carry it to the pigs, pour a little in one trough first to decoy them off so you can fill the other feeding troughs without getting pig snot all over your jeans. Then you have to go back to the barn and set up their food for the next day, feed Hillbilly and her calf (recuperating in the paddock), and throw some scratch feed to the chickens.

By the time I finished, dusk was lowering. Where I was standing in front of the barn is just enough lower than the corner of the pasture across the road that I could see our draft horses, Jachin and Boaz, silhouetted against the sky. That reminded me they were expecting an evening snack.

I scooped a quart of sweet feed out of the barn and crossed the road. Standing in front of the gate, I talked to Jachin, trying to teach him some manners. No good, he was in an uppity mood and Boaz was unapproachable. I opened the gate and poured their feed into the rubber basin. A few days before, we had moved our Highland Cattle into that bigger pasture because they had eaten down the smaller pasture. The horses are very picky about what they eat, and had left big patches of tall grass. I wanted to see how much of that the cattle had eaten down.

Ahead of my left shoulder the three-quarter moon was waxing, and over my right shoulder the evening star was just peeking through the blue-black sky. A sunset like that one only shows in the fall—the horizon glows red-orange, pale blue above abruptly shifting to midnight blue. The air was as crisp as a Granny Smith apple.

I hadn't walked more than a hundred yards when a burst of drumming wings startled me. In the dusk my nearsighted eyes couldn't tell whether they were dove or quail, but I think they were quail. I went another twenty feet and *another* covey drummed the air, curved away, then drifted into invisibility back in to the earth. All in all I must have flushed seventy-five to a hundred of them.

The cows' progress in eating down the pasture astonished me. Cutting back across the pasture I walked over the pond dam and past our Highland called Tartan. After shaking her horns at me, she graciously allowed me to approach and be sniffed. (Cows are *very* formal.)

Crunching on across the pasture, I could just make out Jachin and Boaz ambling toward me. His stomach full, Jachin had waxed friendly, and approached for me to scratch his jaw. He and Boaz both like for you to whisper to them. They followed me back to the gate, probably motivated more by hunger than affection, but with horses the two are hard to distinguish. Who cares anyway?

I stopped at the gate. The sun was nearly gone, but the horizon still burned red. The moon was bright enough to cast a shadow. The gentle hills had blackened into silhouettes against the evening sky.

Now who could think about *mutual funds*, or *gold and silver*, or *IRAs*, or *geopolitics* with all that going on?

Maybe I had the right ambition after all.

PIG PANTRY

This is the last pig story; I promise, but I'm so proud of myself I have to tell it.

In addition to the two tons of rice we bought for Y2K, Susan and I bought a year's supply of dehydrated survival food. We've hung onto it all these years, but some things, like dried eggs or milk, must be used and rotated every five years or so. Since it's out of date and we can't eat it, I decided to feed it to the pigs.

I've been having a great time every evening concocting new "casseroles" for the pigs, guessing what will please their palates. The base of the mix is beef, vegetable, or ham-flavored (*whoops!*) TVP (texturized vegetable protein). To this we add dehydrated potato granules or slices, carrot slices, cabbage dices, bell pepper, or soup mix. Now they *like* that TVP, but a little dehydrated fruit *really* tickles the porcine palate. Cabbage dices they only tolerate, and beans of any kind guarantees they will flip the trough out on the ground, dried apricots notwithstanding.

Every evening I fill two six-gallon plastic buckets with water and head for the "Pig Pantry." This is a stall we cleaned out in the barn where we installed a big shelf for the dehydrated food. There I open up the No. 10 cans and pour it into the buckets to soak overnight.

Not long ago I struck a big hit with *Beef Piganoff*—dehydrated sour cream, elbow macaroni, onion slices, beef TVP, and just a *hint* of dried dates. It was, I discovered from the pig's reaction next morning, *to die for.*

But here's the really great thing about raising pigs. No matter how long you have them, no matter how close you get to them, you will *never* mind loading them onto the trailer for that last ride to the butcher. In the end, a pig remains a pig.

TENNESSEE HOMECOMING

This weekend the whole Sanders clan (with all three married branches) headed out to Tennessee Homecoming at the Museum of Appalachia in Norris. It's billed as "one of the nation's largest and most authentic old-time mountain, craft, and music festivals." If you live within three hundred miles of Knoxville, next time it happens you ought to climb in your car and head that way. Not only did we get to see all sorts of mountain crafts, but there was also more old-time and Bluegrass music than anybody could possibly take in.

NOVEMBER 2000

PRINCESS

A few nights ago I got my comeuppance for my anti-pig remarks.

I hate the sudden shift from Daylight Savings Time. One day you're feeding your pigs at sunset, next day midnight.

Have mercy, it's *hard* to love pigs.

Princess, our sow, is curiously colored. She is mostly white like a Yorkshire, but just on her eyes she has black spots—just the size of her eyes. So help me, it looks like she's wearing too much badly-applied mascara and false eyelashes.

It was hard dark, except for the light from our barn streetlight. A pig is an appetite with four cloven hooves. Pigs are a pain to feed because they won't step back from the trough long enough for you to pour it full. That engenders all sorts of dodging back and forth to fool them. As time passes and the pig snot accumulates on your jeans, it also engenders a certain irritability on the part of the feeder toward the feedees. Said irritability has been known, in certain irascible individuals, to seize the lower leg and foot with a vigorous kicking motion. Patience dies.

So fumbling around in the dark I am dodging pigs and trying to fool them. I pour a little fermented rice juice in one trough to pull them off, then race over to another to fill it before they follow. As I am leaning across the electric fence, Princess hustles over to the trough. Although it's dark, I can see her white form. I halt as I am about to pour.

Her whole face is turned up, those ridiculous mascaraed eyes staring at me through the false eyelashes. Her aspect is so hopeful, so pathetic that it fills me with compassion. Yes, for a *pig*. I'm almost sure I heard her say. "I'm doing what I'm supposed to do. Why aren't *you*?"

If you still think this is a story about a pig, read it again.

LEARNING CURVE

NO HIDING FROM GOD

As I write here in my office the soft, regular snores of Cleo, our Great Pyrenees, thrum in the background.

Why, you ask, should she take up residence in my office?

Simple. On the night of November 6, during a cold rainstorm and outside the warm doghouse Ellen had built for her, Cleo gave birth to six pups. One was born dead; one died the next day. The mewling of another led Zachariah to him in the dark, wet pasture, so him they have named "Lucky."

The next day Ellen, Justin's wife and Chief Canine Midwife, decided Cleo looked "depressed." She bundled up Cleo and the remaining four pups and took them to the vet. He diagnosed a slight infection (not mastitis), and recommended we feed the pups every two hours (for two days) on a special formula.

Never underestimate the sympathy of women for their kind—I mean, *one female for another*. If they are mothers and offspring are involved, the hormones pull them in like a junk-yard magnet. That's probably why Ellen, Susan, and Liberty all ganged up to feed the pups, leaving Cleo free to snore her way through the day. Actually, Cleo is a fine mother, nursing the pups and doing all the other things that mothers do for pups. To tell the truth, I just love the wet dog smell that Cleo brings back from her frequent trips outside, the smell that has taken over my workspace. Only Susan gags.

Oddly enough, this fall the trees have had glorious colors. As dry as it has been, I expected all the leaves to just turn brown and rattle to the ground. Not so! Everywhere we drove there was a riot of color.

DECEMBER 2000

DEATH AGAIN

Y'all may remember that on one terrible September Saturday a year ago a string of accidents took off our Great Pyrenees puppy, Kaiser, and Justin's horse, General, in a few short hours.

Life and death persistently humble us with their unpredictability. Today I am hurrying to the office because an ice-storm is predicted and I am finishing a newsletter before Susan and I have to drive two-and-a-half hours down to New Albany to have it printed. It's bitter cold. I pull into the driveway and look out into the pasture. One of the cows is down, and our black Percheron Jachin is pawing at it. I still have to feed pigs across the road, and while I'm there I see Justin and Susan looking over the cow, which has to be our oldest, Lassie. Actually, things can be worse than just finding a dead cow, i.e., finding her not *quite* dead yet.

There ensues a long back and forth to dispatch Lassie, the details of which I will spare you, but it involves a pistol. In the midst of this we discover that Susan's sole surviving home-grown chick who was attacked by a stray dog yesterday is also dying.

O Lord, how hateful death is! What a terrible fate Adam inflicted on us all! When I think on this, how much more precious Christ appears. The thought of Christmas manages to send a frantic joy through my heart.

RUSSELL'S DRAFT HORSE SCHOOL

After Justin attended last February, it took me seven months to drag Susan down to Kenny and Renee Russell's draft horse driving school in Poplarville, Mississippi (about an hour from the Gulf Coast). She exercised all her ingenuity to escape. I exercised all my stubbornness to persevere. I won, and as I expected, Susan was very glad I did.

Kenny and Renee are hospitable as only Mississippians can be hospitable. After two minutes, you're convinced you've known them all your life. I was amazed to learn that *most* of the folks who attend the school don't own draft horses. What's more, many of them are professional people—doctors or lawyers. I guess a lot of people just *wish* they owned draft horses, and want to learn how to drive.

Before we left, Justin told me that we would really enjoy the people we met at the school. For some reason that didn't sink in until after we got to the school, but he sure hit the nail on the head. One of our greatest delights was meeting and socializing with the other folks there. (Also the food was good—and hot. All meals are included.)

Unfortunately, for the first time in four years, it rained all week, which severely curtailed our opportunity to drive any of Kenny's splendid horses. In spite of that, we learned enough (and had enough fun) to make the

week worthwhile, although I think the rain and the cold embarrassed Kenny. If he had known how good a time we were having, he wouldn't have thought twice about it.

Kenny owns mostly Belgian draft horses, from 1,500 lbs. and up. Harnessing horses obviously precedes driving, and Susan got her turn at that. Kenny and Renee host three schools a year, in February, April, and November. The $450 tuition includes room, board, *and* training (add $150 for a spouse). I don't know how they can do it for that price, but they do. If you're interested you can contact **Russell's Farm**, 12055 Highway 11 North, Poplarville, MS 39470; (601) 795-4200.

KIDNAPPING ELLEN

No, that's not the name of a new Meg Ryan/Bruce Willis movie, it's the plot my elder daughter Liberty and Susan hatched to celebrate my daughter-in-law's birthday. Susan was taking Mercy to Atlanta and Liberty's best friend Judith lives there. Judith's birthday is the 11th; Ellen's the 19th, so they decided to celebrate both the weekend of December 9th. On Friday Susan and Liberty conned Ellen with a story about Mercy twisting her ankle at school. When they got to school, they sprang the trap and all headed to Atlanta.

Yes, you're probably asking yourself who took care of Justin and Ellen's eighteen-month-old son, Elijah, not to mention Liberty's two-year-old, Tucker, and twelve-month-old, Bedford? *Good question.* Justin and Johnny Bain did, but they stayed at my house both nights. We made a nutritional discovery, viz., small children, even infants, thrive on frozen pizza and hamburgers. We also fed them plenty of Vitamin C (candy). *No problem.* I needed a fire hose to clean up my kitchen on Sunday, but other than that, *no problem.*

Wishing you all a wonderful Christmas making memories with your loved ones!

JANUARY 2001

I believe I am sentimentally unfit for raising animals. It's not that I mind taking care of them—feeding, watering, doctoring—or that I mind terminating those raised for the table. It's the in-between casualties that lay me low.

A few days ago Zach and I were feeding the animals. I had pulled the pick-up into the barn, fed the horses, fed the cows, fed the chickens and ducks, and was pulling out to go feed the cows across the road. Three of Cleo's ten-week old Great Pyrenees pups remain with us. They hang around vehicles like ticks around a blood bank. One was over at the barn, so I carefully checked where he was before I backed out. There he was, a couple of points off my bow and fully twelve feet in front of me. I started backing and about the time I began to turn, I heard that awful *yelp!*

Zach ran around to the driver's side wheel and there was the pup. I had to back off of him. Zach and I rushed him to the vet's. I writhed as I drove, inwardly tormented by the accident but sure I had taken all possible precautions.

The vet kept him overnight, and this time I was delighted to hear that he was all right, except for the fractured pubis of his pelvis.

I have now switched from feeding animals in a pickup truck to a four-wheeler and trailer.

A CHRISTMAS TO REMEMBER

A friend of mine tells me that the soil is a discipline on your soul.

Living next to the soil truly disciplined us last month. In fact, it like to froze us to death. It showed up every detail we had neglected.

Like insulating the well house at Justin's. And the water pipes under The Ponderosa.

Everything froze up, and neither Justin nor Liberty had water. For reasons that will probably never become clear to me, Susan *loves* plumbing. Well, she got her bate of it at Christmastime.

Oh, yes, and at our house we found that the plumber had unaccountably run the upstairs cold water pipe *outside* the house for about ten inches—easily enough to freeze the line solid in ten-degree weather. (Funny how bad work always makes itself known.) So we had burst pipes at the Shoe, too. They burst right after Ellen had soaped herself up in the shower, but they didn't stay burst for long. Plumber Susan came to our rescue.

THE HOLIDAYS

Pigs, by the way, do not like cold weather. It turns them pink. We had an old dog pen in the pasture, and Susan sided it up with some old tin to make a pigararium. On the outside she actually painted, "Heavenly Ham Hotel." in big bold, white letters that you could see from the road. Plainly.

We were late getting a Christmas tree up, and when we did it fell over *twice*, taking a multitude of ornaments to their graves. Susan didn't get up her porch lights until Christmas Day at dusk. Now she has decided she likes them so much, she's going to leave them permanently.

That same night twenty-three people slept at our house. The Klingers came from Georgia with their five children, we were there with four children; Erica Augustin, Mercy's friend from school was spending the night; Jordan Uselton, Christian's friend who might as well be named "Sanders" since we feed him most of the time; and sundry other friends. They just all seemed to come together at the same time. Maybe it was a conspiracy to figure out how many people the Shoe could sleep, four bedrooms, upstairs hall, sleeping porch, floors—it was entirely maxed out. I made sure I got a bed, even though it wasn't my own.

That was when it started snowing—with the Shoe filled to maximum holding capacity.

Usually it doesn't snow much here, but it kept on and kept on. We built a big fire in our limestone fireplace, which, like the bumblebee that shouldn't fly, shouldn't heat because its flue runs straight up without a bend, but since nobody told the fireplace it can't heat, it happily heats anyway. The stone gets hot and acts as a heat sink, giving back heat all night as the fire dies down. We popped popcorn and played charades and drank some wine and laughed and then hunted for pillows and blankets and comforters and quilts.

Then came the thaw. The gravel roads are almost as much fun as hot melted rubber, and not nearly as neat. The pigs have churned, pugged, and stewed the pasture into a mud pit. Thanks. Doesn't matter, I got an oilskin slicker for Christmas, one long enough to keep the mud off my jeans.

Never mind all the bother. Even with all the work, dead plumbing, duties of hospitality, and mud pits, it was one of the best Christmases I can remember.

HARROWING

He went back and forth a long time in the decision, but Justin recently acquired two registered Percheron fillies about seven months old. They arrived today. Do not let the glowing eye of the front horse confuse you—she is *not* the Horse From Hell, but actually "gentle as a dog," as the man who sold them to us says. The other one, now, comes close to HFH rank. She's wild as a March hare in bankruptcy. We'll keep them penned up about two weeks, talking to them as we feed and handle them. That should help. Until they arrived I hadn't realize how *huge* our Percheron geldings, Jachin and Boaz, really were—and they haven't finished growing *yet*.

BRAGGING

Last fall Justin started back to college to finish his degree. He pulled a four point! And Wright, who attends Mississippi State, made an A in *Milton*. Any veteran of Milton will testify that it is an exceptional occurrence just to stay awake in Milton class. I never could.

SPRING IS IN THE AIR

Even though the weather has been severe and seems like it will never change, spring eventually will come. Liberty and Susan remarked that since we've already had such a bad cold spell, they are fully ready for spring. Just this past week we had forty-degree weather and they were looking for the tree buds. They better not hold their breath. I heard another cold, hard freeze is on the way.

FEBRUARY 2001

On a farm you can't just do things whenever you get around to them. If you miss some things– like planting clover—you miss them for a whole year. So we sat down to organize and work out an agenda for the spring. Of course, before you can do *any*thing, you must first do something *else*. Take planting clover. If you want to raise cows or horses, you have to have grass. If you want to have any kind of pasture at all without using colossal and expensive truckloads of nitrogen fertilizer, you have to plant clover. You can't plant clover until you harrow. And it's no good harrowing if there's still long grass standing, so you have to mow before you can harrow. And you can't harrow until you hitch up the horses. Besides all this, if you never put down lime to lower the soil acidity before you did anything else, the clover won't come up anyway.

We sat down and discussed everything we wanted to do and Susan then spent a long time breaking everything down into tasks and setting up a schedule.

Two weeks ago Monday I said to Justin, "We need to do some harrowin' tomorrow."

He flashed me the funniest look, and said, "*You* want to do some *heroin*?"

"Sure," said I, thoroughly puzzled, "we *have* to do some harrowin.'"

"Heroin?"

"Harrowin.'"

We fell into a loop of feedback disbelief there that we nearly couldn't escape from. I'd look at him and say, "Harrowin'!" and he'd look back at me quizzing, "Heroin??"

Sometimes you just have to spell things out to people.

PEREGRINATING PIGS

At our meeting Zachariah came up with a brilliant idea. We wouldn't have to spend so much time turning up the garden if we just put a few pigs over there to root it up. That was a *great* idea, so one afternoon Susan put up an electric fence around the garden plot. When it came time to transport the pigs from their home across the road to the garden, though, we were stumped. No loading dock, no trailer. Susan had a flash of inspiration: take a sixteen-foot welded wire pig panel, bend it into a bobby pin shape, then set that down inside the rails of our little six-foot trailer. It made a perfect portable pigpen.

Next problem: entice pig into portable pen. Pigs have only one word in their vocabulary: *no*. And swinish suspicion rises exponentially with your urgency to capture them.

Remember our rule: *lure*, never chase. The initial luring naively positioned the trailer in the open field. That failed, so we *lured* four of our eight pigs into an old dog pen in their pasture. (Luring works best with *aged* table scraps.) Now cast your eye upon the assembled entourage. There stands our four wheeler, pulling the trailer with the pig panel on it. There is Justin's wife, Ellen, with Elijah (1½), and Liberty, with Tucker (3) and Bedford (1), and Susan, and Zachariah, and Justin, and Franklin.

And eight 150-200 pound pigs, and our sow, Princess, vastly pregnant, and Houdini, our boar, but he's so lazy he doesn't count. Biggest threat from him is that you'll trip over him. By now, *all* the pigs are stirred up and barking, and Princess is grunting threateningly.

So we lured four pigs into the sixteen foot-square dog pen and backed up the trailer to the gate. (Don't miss that: *backed* the trailer, a skill some of us still have not perfected.) Justin and Zach, inside the pen, would *drive* the pigs into the trailer. The driving created an immediate pig panic, sending pigs in every direction, like flies in a bottle. One found a loose place in the wire and actually escaped under the fence. That dictated guards outside the fence to keep them away. The only place the pigs would *not* run was into the trailer. They would practically climb an eight-foot fence, but not that trailer. Finally the boys drove two into the trailer, but the slacker (who will remain unnamed) manning the back of the trailer failed to close the ends of the pig panel together quickly enough so one escaped. We delivered the one captive swine to the garden, and returned.

The second came not so hard. We returned for the third, and most diabolically clever, of all the pigs. This one was a *thinker.* Justin chased him round and round the dog pen, but he refused to run up into the trailer. Finally Justin cornered him at the mouth of the trailer, and to our astonishment, he just sat smack down, *plump!* Then (I promise you) he flashed a look of smug satisfaction, and I thought I heard him chuckle, "Checkmate." Completely taken off guard, none of us moved. That gave the pig time to notice that one side of the pig panel was loose. He reached over with his snout, flipped it back, and *walked* out of our trap into the pasture.

Now it was pig round-up time again, and they were in no mood to be lured. Pigs were disappearing, and they knew it. At last we got four more pigs in the dog pen, and Justin and Zach, by now wielding large truncheons, forced two pigs into the trap.

By the time we had driven them over to the garden, the runt was literally climbing the pig panel out of the trailer. In the end, we did get four of them into the garden, but once we did, I noticed the funniest thing. We had eight pigs—two black and white spotted, two red and white spotted, and four white. By the time we finished luring, chasing, and transporting, there were *two* black-spotted and *two* red-spotted pigs in the garden, and *four* white pigs across the road. So much for random selection.

STRANGLES

Before the pig peregrination occurred, two other panics broke out. About a week after they arrived one of our new Percheron fillies—the wildest one, naturally—came down with *strangles* (shipping fever). That's a horse upper-respiratory infection, something like the flu, and it's no fun. The horse feels ratty, hangs her head down between her knees, drips green snot out of her nose and coughs up great ropes of brown phlegm. The lymph nodes under the jaw swell to the size of baseballs, and often burst and abscess. The treatment for strangles is 20 cc (about an eighth of a cup) injections of penicillin daily and plenty of water. But it doesn't stop there, because there are *other* horses. I knew better, but had failed to quarantine the fillies from Jachin and Boaz for two weeks, and strangles is *highly* contagious. Our local vet came out to begin treatment.

A friend we met last November at the draft horse school is a vet in Oklahoma specializing in horses, so I called him, too. To avoid the disease or lessen its severity, he recommended vaccinating all the other horses and giving them prophylactic doses of penicillin for a week. Our vet came back out and administered the vaccine nasally, but we were left with giving all those shots. It takes about one or two rounds of penicillin to make a horse shot-shy. Now with a child when he sees the needle and starts screaming and squirming, you can hold him down for the shot.

What do you do with a shot-shy eight hundred pound horse?

You *twitch* her. That is, you take a stick with a loop of rope in the end, put the horse's upper lip in the loop, and twist. (I know it makes no sense, but the horse *will* hold still for you to grab him by the lip. I sure wouldn't.) You tighten down the loop until the horse becomes reasonable, then you can give her the shot. (Do not try this at home with your kids except under a veterinarian's direction.)

The blessing in this strangles was that it forced us to handle the fillies quite a bit every day. The wild one started to calm down considerably, and is no longer wall-eyed and scary. The drawback is that her frightened temperament has now lodged in her formerly mild sister. But by now everybody is just about well.

Last Sunday, though, we had to give the girls one last dose of antibiotic. By that time we had shifted to *oral* antibiotic. Oral administration is *easy*. First you dissolve eight big pills in a 35 cc syringe full of water, then pinch off the plastic nipple with a pair of vise grips, channel locks, or a neutron bomb. Next somebody grabs the horse, while the administrator stands at the horse's head with the horse to his left. With his left hand he reaches up and forces his thumb into the gap between the horse's front and back teeth. Then he gently crams the syringe over his thumb into the horse's mouth on top of his tongue. Now he begins to press down the plunger, and discovers that, kept too long, i.e., more than three nanoseconds, antibiotic pills set like concrete. The solution: go get more water and re-dissolve. Repeat process until syringe is empty. Then hold horse's head up with left hand while horse drools and slobbers spit and antibiotic juice all down your left sleeve.

After we had finished this with *both* fillies, it occurred to me that a year and a half ago there was no earthly way I would have stood still for horse drool to run down all over my arm, let alone allow pigs to wipe their noses on my jeans.

Living in the country, I think, changes you.

POPULATION EXPLOSION

When our long-suffering vet came out that first time, I asked him about Princess as he was climbing in the truck. "I've been having a difference of opinion with my wife. That sow looks pregnant to me. What do you think?"

He glanced at her and said, "Well, it looks like her sacks are filling out."

"What does *that* mean?" I shot back, wearing my ignorance like a crown.

"Well, her *milk* sacks are filling. She ought to farrow in a week or two."

"WHAT! WHAT! WHAT!" I huffed, panicking on the spot. It was freezing cold and we had made no preparations at all to separate Princess or provide her and her new piglets with protection from the extreme cold we had been having. Justin and Susan found a picture of a farrowing crate and Justin got busy on that at once. A farrowing crate looks like two Ls standing back to back. The little spaces on either side of the main passage (Great Hall?) offer the piglets a refuge where the sow can't roll over on them.

Unfortunately he built the farrowing crate *outside* the old dog pen where we had to separate her. Now I have one son who uses three times as many nails as any project needs, and one who uses twice as much wood, but neither of them builds *light*. By the time Justin finished, he had a 300-pound farrowing crate that had to climb *over* a five-foot fence. I absented myself for that episode.

THE DEMON COW

In the midst of all this frolic, we learned that our friends who had been milking the cows in our "milk co-op" were moving. We would have to take in another cow (and calf). Not only that. *If* we want to keep on having fresh milk, we have to learn to milk.

Okay, no problem, we'll just go learn how to milk a couple of evenings. We can set up our milking parlor in one of the barn stalls. We'll let the calf have the overnight milk, and we'll separate them in the day. That way we can milk her every evening. Simple. Neat. Clean.

I reckoned not with *The Demon Cow*.

Arnold assured me that even though they had not been milking Molly for the last three weeks, she would be no problem. Susan and I first, and then all of us, went for milking lessons. It was a breeze—choke, pull, squeeze—presto!

Fresh milk! Easy.

Last Friday Molly and calf, Ginny, arrived. Before this could happen, however, the barn had to be redecorated. Simple? Not so. We had to build a paddock out one door to keep them up. (Remember my lapsed quarantine with the horses? I wasn't going to make the same mistake twice, this time with the cows.) Then we had to build a gate at the door of the barn. All of this sounds simple, but remember that before you can do *anything* you have to do something *else* first. In our case, that usually means running down the tools first. Then nails. Then bolts. Then wood, and so on.

Let us forego recounting all that pain, and just report that by Saturday morning early cow and calf had already escaped and run down the road. Let us forbear to repeat the name of the child that drove by without reporting said escape, or recapturing said escapees. Let us fast forward to Sunday evening, when Susan and I went to milk for the first time. Let us rejoice in the ease with which Susan milked out that first pint into the stainless steel pan. Let us forget when Zachariah walked through the stall with a bucket for the horses and incited The Demon Cow to overturn the bucket. Let us only remember the nearly two big cups of milk we did salvage.

Nor should we dwell too long on Somebody's failure to separate cow and calf Monday morning, but pass ahead to yesterday's happy milking. Yesterday, long after dark, I realized that the cow must be milked. I finally assembled all the necessary personnel and equipment and marched to the barn.

The Demon Cow's udder was filling out nicely. She didn't seem to need the shackles to keep her still, but we put them on anyway. It was scary, it went so smoothly. First I milked, then Justin, then Zach. We were up to nearly a quart when the trouble started. Not able to leave well enough alone, I took off the shackles and got into a discussion with Justin about the right way to put them on. The cow promptly walked off.

Now don't forget what a cow does all day, every day. The very *air* was full of it.

So the chase began, Justin and I trying first to push a seven-hundred-pound cow into place, then entice her with feed. In and out of the stall, in and out of the paddock. Oh, did I forget to mention that it was raining fire hydrants? There was one point there when I actually had a vision. I saw red neon letters appear on the cow's side, spelling out "H-A-M-B-U-R-G-E-R." I was so mad I was ready to flip her over on her back and milk her like a fountain with a plumber's friend. The quart or two of milk we did get was thoroughly contaminated with manure, which was flying everywhere, so in the end the *dogs* got the milk, and we got the shaft.

Tonight, I have to go down to New Albany to get this newsletter printed. Tonight, I don't have to milk. Tonight The Demon Cow will just have to torture somebody else.

I'm getting to where I don't even like milk anyway.

JUST A LITTLE BURN

Some of the fields were still covered with tall broom sage. The choice was either 1) mow (a lengthy process involving people, schedules, horses, and refractory machinery) or 2) burn (a quick process involving two people, a little diesel fuel, and a couple of matches). I'll admit it: I was the one who opted for burning.

It was a *beautiful* day, warm for February, but sometimes windy. The Top is seated on a high ridge full of open spaces. There are very few trees to break the wind, so it can really blow at times.

The day we picked to burn off the Sunrise pasture was one of those. One minute Justin and Zach were nursing a tiny fire, the next minute Susan was calling 911. By the time I got there smoke was boiling through the woods (*not* on our property) and I could see flames leaping five feet high and ten feet wide. I rejected my first response, which was to lay down in the ditch and die right then, grabbed a big rake, and headed into it. Thank God, the trees weren't burning, just the leaves. But the wind was out of the west at our backs, whipping the fire in a long line (a quarter mile at least) eastward down the holler and up the next hill.

There's nothing like a little forest fire to add hot fervency to your prayers and urgency to your efforts. I can really understand now how people get killed in forest fires. The smoke can quickly confuse and smother you, not to mention its bewildering speed. I was fighting buckthorn and raking like an electric gardener, trying to pull leaves out of the path of the fire. I walked all the way around to the far horn of the fire, in the woods, and fought my way all the way down the line, extinguishing the fire as I went. I thought I had been successful until, after about thirty yards, I looked back to see that it had rekindled itself in the very crescent I had just put out.

Faster than I could rake, I was praying that the wind would change as the fire crested the hill. Off where I couldn't see them, but could occasionally hear then hollering to each other through the smoke, were Justin, Susan, and Zach. When the smoke finally parted and Susan emerged, only half the teeth remained on her rake.

At some point the West End Volunteer Fire Department arrived, sometime after we discovered that we don't have 911 out here. They had a truck with a tank that went behind us spraying out the fire—and the wind *did* change, blowing the fire back on itself. Finally somebody came out from the forestry department with a bulldozer to cut a fire lane through the woods.

When all was said and done, the only thing that *actually* burned (other than most of the teeth off Susan's rake, some of our pasture, and my eyebrows) was the leaves in the woods. The forestry fellow, however, was aggrieved because we didn't have a "burn permit." Turns out, though, that getting a burn permit involves nothing more than *calling* some office and telling them you're going to burn.

What good *that* does I confess I can't divine, but I'm not planning on doing much burning in the near future anyhow.

MARCH 2001

Can you believe this? A subscriber from Ohio bought something from us that cost five bucks. When it came time to pay us, he sent five dollars all right—*in genuine Confederate money!* Shoot, if I'd known he was going to do that, I'd have sent him *two* of whatever he wanted.

A FAR CRY FROM KROGER

I have been steadily learning that *experiencing* agrarian life differs utterly from *thinking about* it. For a long time I was just thinking about it. Not so now.

The pigs from Princess' first litter, born May of last year, just keep on getting bigger. Since *no*body keeps pigs as pets, at least not for long and not in great numbers, sooner or later *some*body had to kill them.

Herding us all down the road to reality, Susan appointed Monday, February 26, as E-day for two pigs (and the "E" didn't stand for E-mail). We selected two of the four in the garden behind the Top. The week before, Susan read up on butchering (as if reading anything *ever* prepared you for the reality), negotiated with the butcher, and made an appointment for us to take them in. *The Catch*: transported pigs are excited pigs, and the adrenaline in excited pigs toughens the meat. Solution? Kill them where they stand, and transport the *carcass* to the butcher.

So before 7:00 a.m. on Monday morning, when the sun had just finished winking over the horizon but was still too stingy to warm anybody up, we foregathered by the garden. From somewhere in all our disorganized stuff Susan had fished out a game hoist for butchering. Justin produced a suitably sharp knife and a .22 rifle. The process is in two steps: 1) shoot pig, 2) slit throat. In silence I will pass over who got elected executioner.

The pigs were on one side of the light electric fence, and we were ranged on the other: Johnny Ray Bain in his impossibly clean white duster; Justin in army green and his knit cap with earflaps (looking like a conscripted

Laplander longing for his reindeer), Liberty holding Bedford and wearing pink plastic shoes, Zachariah in camo, and Susan and I. It looked like a lunatic asylum had burst open, spilling inmates all along the side of our garden.

Susan had kept the pigs fasting the day before, and we scattered some corn next to the fence, which they greedily attacked. The executioner did his work, and then exploded a flurry of throat cutting and bleeding and wrestling and hanging up. The essential puzzle piece we didn't know was that when you shoot a pig, he quivers, rigors, flops, spasms, and shakes from side to side most unpredictably. Believe me, a 250 lb. pig in that state *ain't* manageable. A man in a clean white duster with a very sharp, long knife trying to cut the thrashing pig's throat with five other people clustered closely around is not the best idea either, we found out, highly likely to result in cutting the people rather than the pig. What seemed like a lifetime later we had two pig carcasses in the back of the truck ready to drive to the butcher. Once we got to the butcher his Amish hands took over and they were adept.

We saw some other hogs while we were there, and I felt proud of my yard-raised hogs. We had never fed them anything but grain, table scraps, and leftover dehydrated Y2K food, and had never used any chemicals or antibiotics on them. Certain local acquaintances had sniffed at them, remarking that it was taking an awful long time to feed them up to killing size. Well, I saw a couple of other hogs there, and I was not impressed with the product of feeding them fast in confinement. Instead of a pale pasty color, our hogs had a healthy glow. There was only half as much fat on them as the others, and the carcasses still weighed 190 and 226 lb.

About a week later we went and picked up the meat. The butcher had asked Susan what size pork chops she wanted, and without reflecting she said, "two inches." For our first home-raised pork feast she pulled out a package of pork chops wrapped in butcher paper. When she unwrapped them, they stood up about the size of your spare tire. Huge. But she patiently grilled them, and I modestly must say, it *was* some of the best pork I've ever eaten.

Let us not wax *too* philosophical, but also let us not pass this point without remarking on the difference between *buying* pork chops out of Kroger's meat cooler and *raising* your own—the difference between looking in the eye the butcher who sells the meat and the pig who *is* the meat. Once you have lived through all that, raised the pigs from newborns, fed them twice daily for months, and killed and slaughtered them yourself, you will never look at another pork chop or slice of bacon quite the same way.

On the other hand, let us not wax too vegetarian or vegan, either. If you need convincing that animals have no souls, just hang around at killing time. Our surviving pigs never blinked when the others were removed, they just stepped over to their brother's corn.

WORKING COWS

Once or twice a year, cow working time rolls around. Cows have to be vaccinated and pregnancy checked. When our cows calved last year, they gave us five little bulls out of five. Those little bulls now have to be converted to steers.

We called our longsuffering veterinarian, Dr. Bell, and made an appointment for what promised to be several hours' work. Now, remember, you can't *work* cows until you *herd up* cows.

At which we are *not* very good.

Admit it. We are almost as good at herding cows as we are at building and launching intercontinental ballistic missiles.

Not that we didn't put a lot of thought and work into it. Rather, there's always some *little* thing that trips you up, like cows noticing an escape hatch you *didn't* notice.

Because the cows are trained to electric fence, they won't even walk between two white plastic electric fence posts *without* wire. Nor will they test an electric fence wire. If it's there, that's threat enough for them, so you don't *really* have to electrify it. We plugged up the wrong turn on the road with a couple of fence posts, and actually put in posts and strung wire in the driveway and through the barn. The plan stipulated that with a bucket of feed we *lure* them *out* of the pasture across the road, turn left out of the drive way, then immediately back right into the drive leading to the barn, through the barn, and into the paddock behind the barn where we could shut them up. From the paddock they could be led a few at a time into the holding pen for the chute, and then through the chute.

Simple. Clean. But *not* cowproof.

With Dr. Bell scheduled to arrive at 11:30 a.m., Susan and Zach got busy early in the morning putting out fence posts while I strung wire. Unfortunately, some unnamed person left the gate to the cow pasture *open*. And he left the bucket of feed just outside the gate. Not surprisingly, we discovered this about the time we got ready to move the cows. Pilgrim, our 1,800 lb. bull had already found the feed, pushed aside the gate, and begun munching contentedly out of the bucket. Behind him worked a moil of anxious cows, all fretting that they were about to miss breakfast. When we spied this situation, we tried to mend it by grabbing the bucket and leading them out of the drive.

About that time things started going wrong. Across from the gate was an unfinished wooden fence, mostly uprights but with a few slats. Rather than follow the bucket, the cows all walked across the drive, under the fence, and into the front yard. Remember, now, that cows are not individualists. There is a *lead* cow, and everybody follows her. Belle, our lead cow, came right behind Pilgrim. Rather than try to explain what happened next, I have just drawn a diagram. The diagram depicts the *planned* cow trajectory versus the *realized* cow trajectory. One glance at that will show you what went wrong.

In addition, in the field behind the tractor shed we had a cow and a young bull, Hero. When Pilgrim got across from the tractor shed, Hero spied both him *and* six cows and four calves. This sent him into a fit of bellowing and running up and down the fence on his side of the road. Pilgrim, two cows, and a calf got out in the road and headed for California, in a hurry, with Hero hot on his heels on the other side of the fence, bellowing his head off. Susan and Zach hopped into a car and headed down the road after Pilgrim and his posse while I rode the four-wheeler into the pasture to pull off Hero.

Again, you probably won't want to hear the details of this excursion. It's enough to say that I got to apologize to *everybody* after we finally got all the cows safely into the paddock. Dr. Bell arrived and little by little we pushed the cows down the chute to him. (I will pass over in silence as too embarrassing for a fifty-four-year-old to recount the episode where one of the cow herders got *in front of* one of the cows in the chute and had to be rescued by Dr. Bell pounding on the cow's snout. I really did appreciate his help, though.)

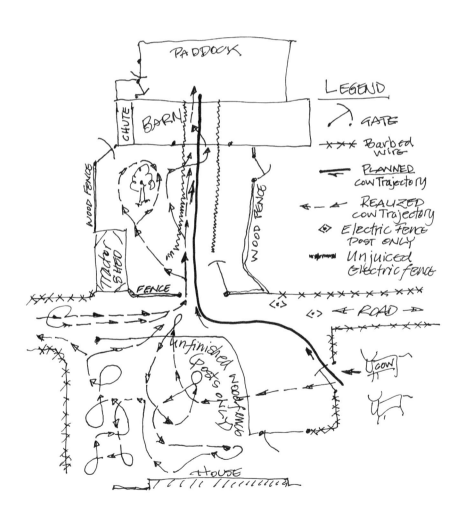

The results were great. Out of our seven Highland cows, five are pregnant. Two, Dr. Bell said, were within thirty days of delivering. I had him check the Demon Milch Cow, Mollie, too. Even *she* is pregnant! In addition, he successfully fixed five out of our four calves, and doctored on the horses.

I may have discovered a reason why not many vets do farm work any more. To preg check a cow—no delicate way to explain this—the vet pulls on a rubber glove that nearly reaches the shoulder, inserts his arm into the cow's anus, and feels the cow's uterus to determine how far along the calf is. For this Dr. Bell charged us $1.85, which seems to me would hardly buy the rubber glove. More than that, a vet does *strenuous* work.

HORSES

Don't even mention horses. That filly with the star is a little too smart for her own good. Sunday a week ago we came to feed everything and she knocked out the top boards in her stall and jumped into the next stall. Then she started pounding on the gate and knocked the latch off the gate. We've been working with the fillies every morning and evening for just a little while, and their abilities and dispositions are improving, but we're not done yet.

DOGS AND COWS

Molly the Demon Milch Cow has settled down quite a bit. She has some sort of antenna that can tell when she's making you mad, so you have to *really* keep the lid on your patience and watch her every second.

The milking team consists of Fast Finger Eddie (a.k.a. Johnny Ray Bain), Zachariah, Justin, and Christian. These are the best milkers and the rest of us just get drafted into it when they are absent. It takes at least two, and better, three, to milk her. One to milk, one to stroke along her neck, and one to wrestle her back into place when she bolts.

So Johnny Ray and Justin and Zach were milking a few mornings ago, and made several big mistakes. Do you recall that we have *lots* of dogs around here? And they follow us to the barn. So Johnny Ray finished milking, and set the pail down outside the milking stall—*Mistake Number One*. While he went back into the stall, one of the pups stuck his head into the pail and helped himself. Johnny stepped back out just in time to witness his work going down the drain.

He went back in to clean up the stall. Justin was working on the panel that closes off the back of the stall, and Mollie was outside in the paddock. *Mistake Number Two*: for one brief moment there was a straight line of open apertures—gate to the paddock, panel at back of stall, door to stall. That was all she needed. *Whoosh!* She blew by Johnny Ray, down the drive to the road, and took a left, murmuring something about a hair appointment in Lawrenceburg. Happily, Justin and Wright had witnessed the escape attempt and could angle across the field to head her off.

I tell you, I'm losing my taste for milk.

A HEIFER CALF

On Tuesday after Dr. Bell had worked the cows I went to feed them and found a new Scotch Highland calf, still wet, and this one was a *heifer!* She looks like an Ewok.

The next morning Justin was out harrowing (*har-row-ing*, not *he-ro-in*) the pasture and my grandson Tucker remarked that there were *two* calves in the pasture. Justin looked closer and saw that, sure enough, there was another little calf that had just been born, this one a bull.

AGRARIAN WORRIES

I certainly don't need to live in the city to tie myself all in a knot about work. Last year we spent a lot of money planting red clover and almost none of it sprouted. If you don't plant clover in late August to September, there's only a short time window to plant it—from February 10 to March 10. Before you plant clover you have to lime the fields, because it won't germinate on too acid soil. (*Check!* Did that last fall.) Then you need to mow and harrow so that the seed doesn't fall on grass but gets good ground contact. *No check.* It has rained and rained and since January one thing and another has kept us from getting into the fields with the horses.

Days kept passing without any progress and the Clover *Führer* got more and more anxious.

Naturally, getting anxious has done me no good whatever. I cannot stop the rain. I cannot make the ground dry any faster than it will. I cannot spread seed any faster than I can spread it. Once seed gets on the ground, I cannot make it sprout.

John Calvin once wrote: "Ignorance of the providence of God is the cause of all impatience." Planting clover or doing any other work, we depend *utterly* on the providence of God. You might plant eight pounds of clover seed to the acre, at exactly the right time, and it might come up that year, and it might not. It might never come up. Under the sky with your feet on the ground, it is harder to avoid that dependence than it is sitting in the air conditioning in front of a computer. Oh, this is true both places, but in front of a computer you can hide from it for a while.

I had been watching the dogwoods because our spring has been so late and they always know to bloom before Easter. When I was seven we lived in the mountains of southwest Virginia, where I first learned about dogwoods. The four-petaled blossom is shaped like the cross. The red tips on the blossoms stand for the wounds in Christ's hands and feet, and the red center for the spear wound in his side. Later I heard the legend that the cross had been made from dogwood, and the tree had been so ashamed that it had begged God that it would never again grow big enough to be used for such terrible work. That's why now dogwoods all grow crooked and small.

Every spring now I watch for the dogwoods to bloom. You can always spy them in the woods, their blossoms floating like clouds among the naked trees. Last week we had friends from Kansas visiting. They had hoped to see the dogwoods blooming, but *alas!* By the time they left on Friday, no blooms. Now mind you, we have dogwoods all around our house. I have been scrutinizing them for weeks, searching for buds and signs of blooming, but nothing.

I promise, the day after our friends left, I looked out my kitchen window and leaves were greening out everywhere. They had *exploded* overnight. The next day, Sunday, the blossoms too had begun to open, and by Monday they had popped out everywhere.

This morning I looked out my bedroom window—three stories high right there because the hill falls away from the back of the house—and there our most glorious dogwood, more than thirty feet tall, was heavy with blooms. Now I've waited all this time for the dogwoods to bloom, searched their limbs diligently for buds without encouragement, and all at once, blossoms everywhere. If I rummage around in here long enough, I'm pretty sure I'll find some hidden meaning. It just feels that way, doesn't it?

CELEBRATE SENIOR CITIZENS

Tomorrow is Susan's birthday and she probably thinks I've forgotten. Most likely, she is so sure she won't even notice this when she lays out this letter, but I got the jump on her this year. Thanks to timely reminders from my children, I have already done my birthday shopping. I decided to stick with Sentimental Stuff—a new cover for her steering wheel first, the kind made out of that shiny pink synthetic fur with a matching set of furry sponge rubber dice to hang from her rear-view mirror. That'll look great in her Volvo. She also needed a good .22 rifle, and a new asbestos oven mitt, and a good square-tipped shovel.

I never stint on presents or good tools. Walmart was glad to see me coming.

ON THE FARM

The clover *is* coming up—not everywhere, but strong where it is. Best of all, it came up gangbusters where I planted *last* year and had thought my effort vain. After I had given up all hope, it sprouted.

My friend Charlie Ritch made a good point the other day. People like us—trained in chemistry and math and living in an urban industrial world—expect things to work "scientifically." You put X inputs in, and get Y outputs out, world without end.

If you're farming or gardening or raising animals or doing anything at all with *real* life, forget all that. Life is not science, it is mystery. Mystery overtakes science and leaves it in the dust. One year you throw out five times the recommended dose of clover per acre, and only Johnson grass comes up. The next year you spill gasoline on the ground and the clover pushes your feet out from under you.

> *The mind of man plans his way,*
> *But the Lord directs his steps.*

> — Proverbs 16:9 (New American Standard Bible)

AN INVITATION TO FARMING

Justin walked in a couple of months ago and threw down a magazine on the table. "What's the matter?" I asked.

"Nothing," he answered, "I've just been reading an interview with this man about agrarianism, and I feel sorry for people who never get to experience an agrarian lifestyle. Doing it changes the way you think." That precipitated a discussion about how we could share our experience, a discussion that drew in Susan and Liberty and Ellen and eventually all of us.

Thus was hatched "Agrarian Challenge."

From Thursday evening, June 21, when we will make plans for the weekend over homemade dessert through Sunday dinner after church, June 23, we will open our lives to seven people, age fifteen to fifty. They will eat what we eat and work where we work, whether we're hauling hay or picking blackberries, and we'll share all our experience with them, including church on Sunday morning. One hundred bucks covers room and board. Nashville is the nearest airport, so we'll run a car up there on Thursday afternoon to pick up anybody who needs it. Reservations are on a first come, first served basis.

NO LONGER STUMPED

The contest for naming our new Percheron fillies is over, the committee has sat and judged, and a winner has been chosen. There were some *great names*, but only one pair could be chosen. The winner, from Front Royal, Virginia, chose names from Isaiah 62, *Beulah* ("Married") and *Hephzibah* ("My delight is in her").

261

AN OLFACTORY EXCURSION

MAY 2001

I have a cousin who nearly failed organic chemistry one summer because the lab professor caught him sniffing unknowns. His nose was so accurate that he could sniff the unknown chemicals other students were supposed to identify as their lab assignment, and then go to the shelf of reagents and sniff through them one by one until he identified the same one as the unknown. I ranked it as a *virtuoso* performance of the smelling art, but the professor was neither amused nor inspired. (*Nasal Philistine!*)

My cousin's skilful nose runs in the family. I am nearsighted and somewhat selective of hearing (as my children delight to point out: "*Soap?!*" "No, *peanut butter!*"). Nevertheless, I am a *world class* smeller. But that has its drawbacks. Like the other senses, you can't just *turn off* your nose. The odors of this world assault your nose and insist on extorting their share of attention.

So it happens every spring that no matter how tightly I wind up my self-control, my nose seduces me from duty's straight and narrow path to the shirking dreaminess of spring. And just about the time *one* tree or flower plays out, *another* more sweetly beguiling takes its place.

About three weeks ago Susan and I were driving home to the Shoe along the ridge. A smell so sweetly piquant, so new to me, forced me to stop the car and investigate. It *looked* like an apple, but was growing in the fencerow, a leggy tree. The flowers resembled apple blossoms, but I had never seen any apple quite like these. Before they fully bloomed they were closed up like little round bells. The petals were white, and faded to pink along the tips. We cut several branches and put them in the dining room, whence they perfumed the whole house for days.

A few days later Justin and I were walking the electric fence down Pig Hollow, looking for breaks. Another sweet odor lifted me into the air by my nose. There in the understory was a tree with a leaf somewhat like a dogwood's, but clinging tightly to the flat branches like a bell was a white, round blossom with a spike of a yellow tongue. I have no idea what its name is, but I could identify that smell again anywhere.

All of this was just the beginning. The wild roses (some people call them "rambling roses") began to bloom two or three weeks ago, just after the blackberries. Now blackberries just barely smell, but rambling roses fill the air with sharp sweetness. The wild rose's sweetness keeps an edge on it that always saves it from going overboard. It never palls.

Then comes the honeysuckle. It's great, but it's like a friend with a very powerful personality. You love him, but you can only take a little of his voltage at a time. Otherwise he overamps your system.

Last night I worked late on the newsletter. I could hear the hammers still pounding outside where Justin and Wright and Johnny were working in the solar house. When we moved out here, at both the Top and the Shoe we put in solar power installations. They needed their own little houses with roof for solar panels, and a dry home for the charge controller/inverter and batteries. Now Johnny Bain is making himself an office in the Top's solar house. Unbeknownst to me, Susan had abandoned her newsletter layout post to race around the ridges spreading mulch on the newly planted trees. We have planted an orchard with cherry bushes (not trees), peaches, pears, and plums. I gave up on locating her and headed to the Shoe.

It was after 8:00 p.m. but the western sky still showed a band of blue and yellow and red, and after the day's heat the air pinched with a light but pleasant chill. Once I got past the fence posts that mark the boundary of the Top, the smells hit me. The honeysuckle was so sweet it smelled almost like grape juice, but the way grape juice would smell if it weren't too sweet and too *grapey*. Then I'd pass a band of roses, and they would tug at me. The roses and honeysuckle worked me over until I reached the pastures before the ridge drops off into Suck Stem Hollow, where the spicy cow-smell reached out to greet me. I made the sharp turn off the ridge onto Suck Stem Branch Road, full of the secret mystery of the damp leaves beside the branch. A little further down, the spring called from the dark. All this time the radio was playing one of those almost melancholy and very thoughtful late-Baroque chamber pieces. By the time I reached the last turn toward home onto Little Fishtrap Road, I was in a deep and dreamy rhapsody.

About which time I saw headlights in my rear view mirror.

Closing fast.

Now at Roy Haggard Road there is a little triangle where the roads converge. You can take the first very sharp turn and fight the too-deep ditch and turn left, or you can go to the intersection proper and turn left. Since I was driving Susan's new and as yet unmarred 1990 Volvo station wagon, Sven, I avoided the ditch. (I also avoid driving the Volvo in the daytime, for fear somebody will see me in it and assume I am a liberal.)

The headlights were Susan and Zachariah in our 1984 Ford pickup. While I made the turn the long way, they took the short cut and got onto Roy Haggard ahead of me—laying down a trail of stinking oil-soaked exhaust all the way to the Shoe.

It didn't matter. About a quarter-mile down the road the *pines* kicked in.

TEACHING PIGS TO JUMP ROPE

When somebody told me you could drive off flies by hanging up a plastic bag full of water, I laughed. Then the flies got so bad we tried it. Folks theorize that the flies stay away because the plastic baggie full of water looks like a hornet nest. Frankly, I don't care what the flies see, as long as it keeps them away from the door. I laugh no more.

Bearing in mind that some researchers hypothesize that Mad Cow disease might be caused by organophosphate insecticides, *and* that strong chemical insecticides can have unexpected and untoward side effects, *and* that we ourselves eat the animals we raise here, we decided never again to use chemical fly sprays.

But when you see the swarms of flies plaguing the poor horses and cows, you have to do something. Here's a natural (non-chemical) fly spray we used first last summer, until Susan waxed too cheap to spring for the crucial ingredient, eucalyptus oil. This year our renewed determination to avoid chemical fly sprays sent her flying to the Internet to find eucalyptus oil in bulk and cheap. Last summer she paid eight dollars for four ounces at retail, but this year she bought three *gallons* for $145.51 with shipping from **New Directions Aromatics**, 705 Jadecrest Court, San Ramon, CA; (800) 246-7817; newdirectionsaromatics.com. They also carry sizes smaller than three gallons.

The recipe for fly spray comes from the *Rural Heritage* website.

Natural Fly Spray, one gallon:
– 4 sixteen ounce bottles Avon *Skin So Soft*
– 5 tablespoons pure eucalyptus oil
– Enough white vinegar to make up one gallon

I highly recommend you subscribe to *Rural Heritage*. It's full of great information every month. **Rural Heritage**, 281 Dean Ridge Lane, Gainsboro, TN 38562-5039; (931) 268-0655; ruralheritage.com.

Do not put the eucalyptus oil into the mixture first, as it melts your plastic bottle. Start with the *Skin So Soft*, then add the eucalyptus oil, then fill up to one gallon with white vinegar. From that gallon of finished spray fill up smaller spray bottles. Best for large animals is a two-gallon sprayer.

The spray lasts from several days to a week. Before the animals get used to it they probably won't like it or stand still for a full application, so apply every day until you see it working. It will literally kill flies and certainly keep them off, including cattle horn flies. As far as I can tell, it will keep off ticks as well, but you have to be careful to thoroughly spray the animal's underside and behind the legs.

We have used this spray on horses, cows, and pigs, but not yet dogs. That, however, is coming shortly.

TWENTY YEARS STRONG

Last month's issue marked the first issue of *The Moneychanger*'s twentieth year. *Twenty years!* There were several times during those two decades that I thought I wouldn't survive another twenty *minutes*, let alone twenty *years*. We even published one issue from jail back in December 1996. That June we had just put an issue in the mail the day before I was arrested for my *first* vacation in the Penal Farm.

God gave us grace to stand and to continue publishing month by month for twenty years.

Looking forward to another twenty, I pray God will give me the grace to recall Psalm 77's cure for fear:

I will remember the years of the right hand of the Most
Highest. I will remember the works of the Lord, and call to
mind thy wonders of old times.

— Psalm 77:10-11
(Reformed Episcopal Church, Book of Common Prayer)

TEACHING PIGS TO JUMP ROPE

The old proverb says: "Never try to teach a pig to sing. It wastes your time, and it annoys the pig." I understand the meaning of this, but in defense of pigs I must point out Revelation 5:13:

And every creature which is in heaven, and on the earth,
and under the earth, and such as are in the sea, and all
that are in them, heard I saying, 'Blessing, and honour,
and glory, and power, be unto him that sitteth upon the
throne, and unto the Lamb forever and ever.' (Authorized
Version)

In that glorious setting of universal worship, who can doubt that even *pigs* will sing most harmoniously?

Most people don't know it, but pigs can dance. Quite well, as a matter of fact. Young piglets do it all the time, and larger pigs as their joy overcomes them. I have seen them before a coming storm, pirouetting on their back legs, throwing their heads up and down for excitement, ears flouncing.

But I had never seen a pig *jump rope*, at least, not until last Friday.

AN ESCAPEE

Exactly one week before, on the previous Friday night, our neighbor from down the ridge toward Still House Bottom (one of the locals says it's called that because the *government* used to have a still down there; you can believe that if you want) came up to report that one of our pigs had stopped by his house. Justin and the neighbor chased the pig through the dark, ruining the fence around the garden, and finally gave up. This was one of those pigs from Princess's first litter, now weighing about 280 pounds. One of his sisters just gave birth to nine new piglets, but that's a scandal we don't mention.

I gave up on him. If he was lost, he was lost. If he came back, he came back.

I'd been getting up extra early to drive Mercy and Christian to school. One morning I was about a mile from the Top on the Ridge Road when what to my wondering eyes should appear but *our pig*. He stood thoughtfully at the side of the road, noble snout held high, sniffed the air, then ran across the road and promptly entangled himself in a pine deadfall. Covered with mud, he showed no signs of remorse or repentance.

I was in Susan's famous Volvo station wagon. There was no way I could get that pig to ride with me. Then I hit upon a stratagem. Perhaps the pig would remember grand feasting days of yore and respond to my call. I rolled down the Volvo's window, and began to call softly:

"*Soooooo*-ee. Pig. Pig. Pig." He jerked up his head in recognition. Gently I nudged the Volvo down the road, calling all the time.

For the next mile I nursed and teased him down the road. From time to time he would stop. If you've ever ridden in one of those Swedish coffins, you know you can't see anything right behind you, so I could only watch the pig's shadow in my rearview mirror. I led him triumphantly through every intersection and past every distraction nearly to the driveway at the Top, at which point I remembered: *dogs*.

We currently are enjoying a bumper crop of dogs, *fifteen* in fact. We still have three *huge* (eighty-pound) Great Pyrenees puppies left from Cleo's last litter, and she just had eight more. (By the way, could any of y'all use a dog? Cheap?) Then there is Cleo's mate, Orion. And Liberty and Johnny's Golden Retriever, Molly. And Shawn and Worth's yellow Lab who moved in with us when they moved to Nashville. Every dog that can open his eyes and walk will chase a pig, given the chance, in the direction just opposite to where you want him to go.

Susan had just pulled up at the Top when the pig and I arrived and was soon joined by Justin, Ellen, Wright, and Zachariah. From somewhere Princess, our sow, suddenly materialized, to make matters worse. At least she was on the correct side of the fence.

Let us not now drag this out. It was 8:00 a.m. By 9:30 a.m. things had not gone well, and all were sweating profusely, except the pig. We had finally coaxed the pig into the right pasture, the one next to Pig Hollow, and chased him over every inch of four and a half acres. We had thirty times herded him *near* the gate to Pig Hollow, without once successfully driving him *through*. He had bathed and swum and cavorted in the pond. He had proven Justin knew absolutely nothing about lassoing. He was impervious to singing and tempting with food.

What a pig.

About that time Justin came up with a bright idea. He handed Wright (20) the end of a fifty-foot black nylon rope. They spread out on either side of the pig, and began swinging the rope up and down to herd him along. At the touch of the rope, the pig jumped.

Susan fell out laughing. "They're teaching that pig to jump rope!" I have to admit, it *did* look like that.

By 10:00 a.m. the pig still couldn't jump rope, and every attempt to hang him had failed. I gave up again. I had work to do.

A week later, the pig is still in the pasture. Every morning he lies by his fence with his relatives on the other side, all waiting for somebody to feed them. A couple of days ago, I hit on the solution that will take him *down*. In the pasture under the trees are two pens where we used to keep pigs. Every day, I put down a handful of corn in the pen, just enough to whet Pig's appetite. I checked after the first day. All the corn was gone. Every day, I will put down a few more kernels of corn, and by and by Pig will get used to his morning handout. One day, while he's munching on breakfast, I will sneak up and shut the gate behind his wandering carcass. It will be easy.

Pigs, you see, have a welfare mentality.

HOEDOWN

In our family we always celebrate July ninth as a high holiday. This was the day that God delivered Susan and me and fourteen other friends with an acquittal in federal court. This year marks the tenth anniversary of that Great Deliverance. This year we are going to celebrate with a *bodacious big party*, the Balm of Gilead Hoedown on July 14, 2001. We have convinced the 12th Louisiana Band to come up and play War Between the States period music. The dance will begin in the early evening, but other events will last most of the day. We will kill the fatted hogs, our own homegrown hogs, and serve barbecue dinner with all the trimmings and blackberry cobbler. Somehow we've got to pay for all this, so we'll ask an entrance donation of twenty dollars per individual or fifty dollars per family (limited to relatives of the first degree, please—no eighth cousins twice removed). Come join us for a leg-slapping, toe-tapping good time, one you won't forget for a long time! Guaranteed!

JUNE 2001

You won't believe this, but I have discovered a new kind of whippoorwill.

Every morning about 3:00 a.m. the bird flies to our windowsill, perches, and commences a loud and *unending* repetition of his call. He kept on waking Susan and me up, but there was something strange about his call. You know, when you're half-asleep-half awake, you don't perceive sounds precisely at first.

A couple of nights ago the bird cranked up as usual, and I started listening. We have both *chuck-will's-widows* and *whippoorwills*, and they sound alike. I wanted to determine which bird it was before I got my shotgun.

To my surprise, it dawned on me that this was *neither* species, but a new one altogether. Over and over he was crying:

> *"Krugerrands-krugerrands-krugerrands-krugerrands-krugerrands-krugerrands."*

DISCOURAGED

The week after Memorial Day was, I believe, the most discouraging I've had since we moved to the country.

It shouldn't have been. We had just come back from Monroe, where I spoke at the 11th Annual Southern Heritage Conference. We had a great time, and my two speeches were well received. When we got home, the rain that had already soaked us through May cranked up again. We had missed putting out a garden early in the month when for a short time it was dry enough, and now we are lagging. Liberty and Ellen, however, have gotten out quite a few plants in spite of the mud. Seeing Lib's mud-caked boots on the back porch testifies unequivocally that moving to the country has made an epochal character change in her. She used to be allergic to the *word* "garden."

Monday it rained buckets, enough to make you think—uneasily—of Noah and the Flood. It has rained so long that even my *soul* is damp and dripping. Worse, the only raincoat I have is a lined oilcloth job suitable for outdoor work in Antarctica, so my soul was also *sweating*—profusely, as they say. The ongoing rain foreclosed our cutting hay. The bright side was that perhaps, just perhaps, the rain would fill out the skinny hay crop.

That morning early we discovered that our silky white Highland cow Bonnie, *Queen of Cows*, had delivered her calf, and it was a heifer. Somebody named her "Bonnie Blue." The next afternoon our last pregnant sow—unnamed, because you don't get attached to pigs as you do to cows, nor do you desire their intimacy—farrowed, a disappointing five piglets.

The rain continued.

Wednesday morning I went out to feed the pigs and found that the sow had killed one by lying down on it. She probably would have killed *me* if she'd lain down on me. Just before that I had discovered that an un-named Sanders child brought a big can of eggs cleaned out of the incubator, supposed to be eggs too long incubated without hatching. When the pigs began to eat them, however, I noticed a live duckling in one. Obviously, the Unnamed had not properly checked the dates written on the eggs.

On Wednesday for no good reason the well pump at Justin's house expired. This entails 1) finding somebody to fix it, and 2) a long trip to Florence, Alabama, to buy a new pump.

On Thursday Susan and Lib left early, i.e. only an hour later than they intended, to buy the pump. Lowe's in Florence was out of stock, so they had to drive to Muscle Shoals to get the pump. (Beginning to get the picture?) That was the morning all my kids, *sua sponte*, all on their own authority, decided to sleep in, so when time came to feed animals and milk, nobody appeared but Johnny Ray Bain and I.

Now replacing a well pump is a huge job. To pull the pump, you also have to pull the pipe that reaches to the bottom of the well. How do you get out 150 feet of pipe when the roof of the well house is six feet above the well mouth? You take off the roof. *Whoops*—don't forget the rain. Wednesday the sun began to shine, but Wednesday night the storms cranked up again. Thank heaven Susan had remembered to put a tarp over the well house. I hadn't.

By Thursday evening the pump had been replaced and the workman left. The well ran for about three minutes before it threw the breaker. I went home to the Shoe.

Friday morning dawned wet and crisp—dripping, in fact. The truck was out of gas. The four-wheeler that pulls the trailer for feeding the animals every morning was out of gas. The one-thousand-gallon gas tank, we had just discovered the day before, was out of gas. Either somebody had been driving back into the pasture stealing it or my children had been filling out of it without telling anybody. *Hot ziggety*, we'll get to buy the refill gas not at $1.20 a gallon, but at $1.60. I probably shouldn't complain. I haven't lost money filling up that gas tank since we moved out here. Price of gas keeps climbing, so a month from now even $1.60 gas will look cheap. Isn't inflation wonderful?

I located a gas can brimming with almost two quarts of gas. Enough for the four-wheeler, and enough to get Susan, with crippled back, down to Country Bob's Store where she could buy enough gas to reach her chiropractor.

But first, before I can feed the animals, I have to drive out to the Ponderosa to get water, because remember there is no water at the Top. Later, when I finally drew near Pig Hollow, I remembered that Susan had told me to check on the *second* duck setting on a clutch of eggs.

Lame Duck was already setting on eight eggs. Lame Duck is a Rouen duck we got last summer. She turned up with a broken leg and we thought she'd die or something would get her (slower speed, readier prey) but not only did she survive, she became the leaderess of our other three surviving ducks. Lame Duck had been setting for about two weeks. Her nest was in one of the pig pens under the trees, the pens we had used for Princess and Houie before we fenced off Pig Hollow. The second duck had a nest next to the fence outside the pens.

Lame Duck was gone. There was something yellow on the bottom of the nest. Only one egg remained. Second duck's nest was empty, but had seven eggs left. Ne'er a duck was in sight, so I reasoned thus: "Varmint enters pen. Varmint eats Lame Duck. Varmint eats eggs. Varmint leaves. On his way out, varmint eats Second Duck."

It started to drizzle again lightly, just enough to dampen what was left of my spirits. The pigs were clotted around the gate, waiting to wipe pig snot on my jeans—their morning duty. They were grumpy and picking at each other. I poured the bucket with their food into another, to make sure it was thoroughly mixed, and spilled about a quart. Once I had the big pigs fed, I went over to the pens where we keep the two sows with piglets.

First thing that met my eye was that dead piglet I still had to pull out of the pen and bury, but then I turned and spied the four *ducks*, playing in a mud puddle. I know it wasn't much, but the sight of those four ducks, *alive*, was at least something to feed my hope.

Ahhh, humanity! Is thy spirit so weak, so fragile, that even a duck (and a lame one at that) can cheer thy soul? How low canst thou sink?

THINGS GET WORSE

I was pondering all these things when the sun finally came out on Wednesday. I got an e-mail from a friend that contained this line from a turn-of-the-century Kansas farmer: "I know farming is hard, ruthlessly hard, but what you might call *hard*, God called *good* when He made it. I have to stay a farmer."

Now that cheered me up a good bit.

Until things started falling apart again. After shifting it once already, I had my telephone interview with Walker Todd, a lawyer and economist who worked for the Cleveland Federal Reserve for twenty years, scheduled for 10:30 a.m. on June 6. The day before, one of our horse-drawn mowers had thrown bolts essential to its operation. The other was already *hors de combat*. Mandatory trip to town, gigantic time-eater.

Wednesday promised to be a late day to begin with, thanks to the trip to town, but my boys were also late getting out of bed, somebody having fed them a powerful sleeping potion. I dodged the aggravation by *leaving* them behind. Driving from the Shoe to the Top, I feel giddy and wildly free, having no one to nag. Arrive at the Top at 7:40 a.m., no Justin outside getting ready to leave for town. Find Justin and Wright inside, one of them actually awake.

Skip the rest. About 8:35 a.m. Zachariah comes into the office to inform us that Molly the Milch Cow is acting strange and can hardly keep her feet.

Molly has bloat.

Bad bloat.

Molly will die, quickly, if we can't do something.

Molly walks as far as the barn and then goes down (i.e., lies on her side), preparatory to expiring.

Run to the office.

I call the large-animal vet where we had taken her the day before for scours and mastitis. The lady there tells me to get a six-foot piece of garden hose and run it down her throat to relieve the gas in her stomach.

Run back to the barn.

We—Franklin, Susan, Christian, and Zachariah—convince Molly to sit up. Molly weighs 600-700 pounds.

I begin my unsuccessful attempt at intubation. Garden hose collapses. I run out of barn across the road searching through the grass for stiffer hose to cut a piece out of. I find, cut, and run back to barn.

Susan must leave, vowing she cannot stand there and watch the cow die. I look at Molly's big suffering frog eyes, and sharply repent our earlier differences of opinion.

Christian (not I) manages to get garden hose down Molly's throat, and it *does* let off some gas.

Our regular vet, Dr. Bell, whom Susan had called, finally arrives. If he had been General Patton riding a Sherman tank at the head of the Third Army and I had been the leader of the French Resistance, I couldn't have been gladder. I resist hugging him and kissing both cheeks. Dr. Bell is too grave for such outbursts.

Dr. Bell has a twelve-foot tube.

No wonder our six-foot model wouldn't work.

We spend another hour helping Dr. Bell work over Molly and drain out her stomach (he's puffing and blowing and sucking on the tube). We run dishwashing detergent down her, just in case it's *frothy* bloat from eating too much clover. The detergent breaks up the tiny bubbles. Administer massive doses of calcium intravenously and *per os* (i.e. by mouth) in case she has milk fever, a condition induced by calcium deficiency immediately after calving.

Molly releases large quantities of gas, exceeding yearly US limits for CO_2 emission under the Kyoto Accords.

Finally, Molly regains her feet. I felt like Shirley Temple's daddy in one of those cheesy Grade B movies from the 1930s, where Walter Brennan dies and everybody watching it cries whether you want to or not.

It is now 11:30 a.m., and I have definitely and irredeemably stood up Walker Todd, waiting in Cincinnati.

"But God called it good when He made it."

I believe. Help my unbelief.

THE SWINISH SEQUEL

That was the same day I quit waiting for those piglets to die on their own. Consulting with Dr. Bell, I concluded that the sow had suffered a postpartum uterine infection that had also given her mastitis. Mastitis equals no milk, a death sentence for piglets that are little more than appetites with legs and a snout.

We took them away from the sow. Where to put them? My office, naturally—it doubles as a veterinary surgery, animal obstetrics clinic, and compost heap. Susan sets to work bottle-feeding piglets. She quickly discerns that one of the pigs has a lot longer row to hoe back to health. Susan separates that one out.

These piglets had been so rain-soaked and malnourished that two of them have rotting tails. Not a single one is an accomplished bottle feeder. Nonetheless Susan perseveres. Friends loan her a heat lamp and she buys a milk substitute. She adds Citricidal grapefruit seed extract for whatever infections they might have. If it works for us, maybe it'll work for piglets, too. (Citricidal is an extract from grapefruit seeds. It was developed as a wormer, but found also to kill systemic infections. Great to take when you feel a cold or stomach flu coming on, but some kind of bitter. You can find it in health food stores as "Grapefruit Seed Extract.")

By Sunday it becomes apparent that the sickest piglet would not make it. To me falls the lot of disposing it. Now before you say, "Well, there's nothing to that," let me ask you why *you* wouldn't volunteer for that job. After all, what's one piglet more or less? The world is full of them.

Pig or human, I'll tell you why nobody volunteers. It's because you have to admit that Death has won, and Death is our enemy, the hateful enemy with whom we can never make peace.

In the last three days the three remaining pigs have begun to thrive. Susan always puts on her yellow rain pants to feed them. She put the piglets in a little enclosure in the yard, and hung the pants over the fence. The little piglets all curl up to sleep right next to those yellow pants. Apparently, they think they're Mama.

I believe. O LORD, help my unbelief!

Help it when the dogs eat Susan's last chick.

Help it when the pig only has five piglets.

Help it when one of the piglets dies.

Help it when the cow bloats.

Help it when it rains for two weeks and the hay can't be cut.

Help it when the army worms eat the grass before it can become hay.

Help it every morning, and every evening, and every moment, because that's how much I need it.

I do believe; help my unbelief!

— Mark 9:24 (New American Standard Bible)

A WAITER AT THE ZOO

Last Monday dawned the appointed day for three more hogs to visit the butcher. You remember Peripatetic Pig from last month, the escapee that cost us so much trouble to recapture? Recapture him we did, but on Monday morning, the very morning he was destined to Make the Big Trip, he broke out.

That pig knows something.

We had borrowed a stock trailer and parked it in Pig Hollow. I threw a couple handfuls of corn into the trailer every day, to accustom the pigs to the trailer. I knew it would work. I told y'all about the welfare mentality.

Come Monday morning, I threw corn into that trailer and those pigs rushed in. That trailer started shaking and rumbling and squealing like there was a bar fight inside. Our problem was to get pigs *out*, not in.

When Susan pulled away, the trailer held Red Pig, Pink Pig, and our original boar (now not a boar) Houdini. What's one pig more or less? I know it sounds silly and sentimental, however, but I hated to see them go. Pig Hollow looked empty without them.

On the other hand, Houdini weighed 475 pounds, and will become *famous* whole hog sausage. Every creature, I suppose, must fulfill its own destiny.

I LOVE CATS

I am just about plumb sick of dogs and pigs. I pulled up at the Top a few days ago and got out of the truck. The carport sounded like the waiting room at a bus station right before suppertime. Susan's three little pigs—Bertha, Penelope, and Mabel, the world's hairiest, hungriest, and ugliest piglets—were snorting and oinking. Eight—*yes*, eight—Great Pyrenees pups were moiling around them whimpering and complaining for breakfast.

I'm no more than a waiter at the zoo.

My wife made me take the bumper sticker off my car: "I love cats—dead ones." She said it was mean-spirited. Anyway, Ellen got a new kitten, Stella, to replace another kitten that tragically passed away before his time. Stella weighs about three-quarters of an ounce and is white with black spots. Like every other cat I have ever known, she is very loving until she gets tired of you and tries to convert your hand to sausage—without warning.

Stella is very respectful. She waits patiently and quietly until I am fully concentrated, then begins a long, silent run across the room. Halfway through the room she leaves the floor, flying through the air to land open-clawed on the back of my office chair, producing a sensation not unlike being attacked by a runaway fire hose or an enraged dust bunny with claws.

I am only the waiter at the zoo.

While I am working Stella climbs up on the back of my chair to sharpen her claws and chase her tail behind my neck. When she's awake, that is, which isn't often in the daytime. Usually she sneaks in to nap in my chair when I leave the room, so that when I go to sit down everybody can scream, "Don't sit on the cat!"

Why not? I wonder.

She and the grown cat, Emeril, play chase around the office. They are certainly no more destructive or messy than, say, the Great Khan's Golden Horde on a liverish day.

Man, I *love* cats. Let's get some more.

AGRARIAN CHALLENGE

On Midsummer's Day began our *Agrarian Challenge*. We originally planned to give seven people a chance to experience our agrarian lifestyle. By the time everybody got here we had eleven.

Since the emphasis was on *experience*, we didn't spend any time lecturing. Everybody arrived by Thursday evening, with, of course, the predictable snafu at the airport. That evening we had enough time at least to talk briefly about our theme: Psalm 106:14-15. Speaking of the children of Israel in the wilderness, the psalmist says:

> *But lust came upon them in the wilderness, and they*
> *tempted God in the desert. And he gave them their desire,*
> *and sent leanness withal into their soul.*

> — Reformed Episcopal Church, Book of Common Prayer

That's the modern world. It satisfies every desire, but leaves us with "leanness in our souls." What good is it to have everything you want at the tip of your fingers when none of it satisfies?

Friday morning we fed animals just in time to dodge the rain. It actually proved a kindness, because the rain forced us back to the Shoe and we got to visit a while. After noon the sun came out and most of the men began work replacing our barbed wire fence. Here I made just a minor mistake in judgment. Well, *two* mistakes. First, don't take down a fence when you have cows in the pasture. Second, not even six men can put in six hundred yards of four-strand barbed wire fence between 1:00 p.m. and

6:00 p.m. I can still see Philip Elder running from fence pole to fence pole in the headlights, stapling in the last few staples.

By the time we got finished at 9:00 p.m. we were ready to eat. And eat we did. Liberty had been planning menus and gathering recipes for two months, and every meal was a treat. Of course, Ellen was right by her side helping, along with Susan.

Saturday morning we got up early. The ladies picked blackberries, and made chicken hoops to hold setting hens, and worked in the garden. Susan taught them how to work with step-in posts and electric fencing—and how to chase calves.

Justin and I had left some hay standing in our Sunrise pasture, because we knew how much one of our guests likes to ride a mower. Justin showed everyone how to harness up horses, and then we hitched Jachin and Boaz up to the mower. We decided just to set a post and make a haystack. I don't know what all sort of grass was in that hay, but it was the sweetest smell-

ing stuff I have ever had the good fortune to fall into. Once it was mowed Justin pulled out the forecart and hooked the dump rake to it. Philip Elder drove the forecart and I sat on the dump rake, with my right hand resting on the lever that lifts up those curved tines to dump the hay.

After raking the field into windrows, the hay raker would bring loads up to the haystack. Johnny Ray's job was tromping down the hay on the haystack to settle it. That's Sam Elder and me leaning on our pitchforks, the only time that day we allowed ourselves that respite. Philip Elder is driving Jachin and Boaz, and that's Justin behind him on the hay rake.

We finished before sundown, so we got to gather at the swing and watch the sky redden. We had launched full career into refreshments and conversation when something went "*Boom!*" I turned toward the Ponderosa, Liberty and Johnny's trailer, in time to see a perfect volcano of flame sheeting a hundred feet into the air. It appeared to be the trailer burning.

We all ran out there as fast as we could, to find to our relief that the fire was *far* on the other side of the trailer. We had piled a lot of old wood our there for a bonfire, and unknown to anyone else, Susan had instructed Christian to go out and light it, which he did. With the help of some gasoline. After that, the rest of the night had to look pretty uneventful, except for the absolutely stellar blackberry tarts Lib made for supper.

Sunday morning early a few had to leave. Our bishop, Dan Morse, came over Sunday morning all the way from Memphis, so we had communion at church. After dinner that afternoon everybody else headed home.

MOST BODACIOUS HOEDOWN

We hadn't even cleaned up good from Agrarian Challenge when we had to start getting ready for the Most Bodacious Hoedown. We rented a forty-by-sixty tent for the dance, and just kept mowing for four weeks until we had a perfect *carpet* of clover. Susan and Justin were pretty clever about a stage. They pushed the big Hochstettler wagon under the tent. The wagon is sixteen feet long and over six feet wide. It made a perfect stage.

People came from Virginia and North Carolina and south Georgia and Mississippi and Tennessee and even Indiana. Justin had Jachin and Boaz giving wagon rides, so I spelled him. Across the road they were cranking up a greased pig race. This I didn't see, but Jordan Uselton, Christian, and Nicholas Augustin got busy greasing a pig. Actually, they were using oil, so I guess they were *oiling* the pig. Unfortunately, the pen was too small and the people were too fast. Besides, the pigs had been sitting out there so long they got sunburned. Hence there were four winners, and ne'er a pig among them.

Somehow Susan had conceived the notion that a pig kissing contest would be fun. We caught poor Penelope and gave her a quick bath. Now you have to understand that *no* pig *ever* suffers anything in silence. That's not a pig's way. They hit a note and hold it at maximum volume like they're dying. This continues until they lapse to the side like they've passed out. Pig possum? I don't know, but Penelope weighs a hefty twenty pounds at least. I grabbed as many trotters as I could reach and carried her over to the tent. She vacillated between her *faux* fainting spell and squealing.

Susan managed to convince the crowd that they needed to join in the kissing contest, and divided them up into classes. In the adult class Paul Paskey won, and his daughter Suzy won in hers. Three pigs and a number of Charlie Ritch's range-fed chickens gave their all for supper that evening. Besides barbecue pork and chicken there was homemade coleslaw, Susan's squash pie, sliced tomatoes and Vidalia onions, corn on the cob, baked beans, ice-cold watermelon, and blackberry cobbler. I'm telling you, you could *hurt* yourself eating.

Then the band cranked up and the fun really started. About half the folks had never attended a Southern ball, so they had no idea how much fun they were facing. We danced reels and waltzes and round dances and we danced some more. Big kids danced with little kids, and adults with toddlers. We danced barefoot in the grass, and my heart broke and my eyes filled with tears to remember that it was the tenth anniversary of the day God with almighty power delivered us from our enemies. They tried to put Susan and me and others in jail for *twenty years*. We'd have still been in jail today. Instead God had set us free and we were dancing *barefoot in the grass*.

And all our enemies have vanished, like smoke in a bad dream.

Bishop Dan Morse had been one of the defendants in that trial, and he and Marianne came over for the party. On Sunday we had one *bodacious* worship service under the tent. By Sunday evening we were already planning next year's Hoedown.

PROS AND CONS OF
A WET SUMMER

AUGUST 2001

The rest of the country is panting for breath, but we've been soaked. Normally it hardly rains here in July and August. This year it hasn't stopped. From Friday to Friday last week it rained nearly four inches. During this rain I have made a discovery about the purpose of air conditioning. It is *not* to keep the air in your house *cool*, but *dry*. We have no air conditioning in the Shoe, having cleverly constructed it with skylights in every upstairs room and clerestory windows to let the hot air rise and escape. Wet air, however, just *sits*, circulating with about the same speed and fluidity as wet cardboard in a blender. The delightful result has been a light dusting of mold on everything below the top story. Even my books look like they've been dipped in flour. Just about the time I was out in the garage, rummaging around for a can of gasoline to burn the place down and start all over, the sun came out. I couldn't have burnt it down anyway, even with gasoline.

The matches were too wet to strike.

ONLY A FEW BUGS

One benefit of the rain has been a much smaller crop of Japanese hornets, wasps, ticks and chiggers. Alas, there have also been fewer lighting bugs. To make up for this want, however, Nature has smiled on us with another denizen previously unknown. We have named this the Blister Bug, for reasons that will shortly become clear.

We had already hired a fellow to come cut hay once, with his tractor and mechanical hay baler. We had almost thirty acres to cut, and just couldn't get it all done with horses—at least, not with it raining all the time.

We had already put up seven hundred bales of hay, but still had hay standing in one field. That we decided to cut and rake with Jachin and Boaz, and pile in a haystack in the field. Oddly enough, our neighbor has a fifty-acre hayfield next to us, and that was the same day he was moving hundreds of round bales of hay out of the field, at about a ton each. Justin drove the horses, Zach stood behind him working the dump rake, and Wright pitched hay by the pole.

Justin rigged up a Rube Goldberg apparatus. He hitched the horses to the forecart, which looks like a chariot. Justin stands to drive, and with his "Neck Heat Shield" looks like a Tennessee version of Lawrence of Arabia. He hitched the dump rake to the forecart so there would be one person to drive and one person to operate the rake. Otherwise one person would be right busy, trying to do everything at once. A dump rake has a long bank of curved teeth. As you drive over mown hay, it piles up in the curve of the rake. Once you drag the hay to where you want it, you push down a lever (requiring only about four hundred foot-pounds of force) and the tines rise up and dump the hay. Ideally, you dump the hay right next to the haystack, so the stackers don't have far to pitch.

All this sounds fatiguing, but actually it's easy-paced and pleasant work, no matter what your job. Now I got in on this after noontime, so it was pretty hot. At one point we were waiting for Justin to come back around with hay, so I lay back on the haystack and took a little snooze.

This, as it turned out, was a mistake. This wet year we don't have many ticks or chiggers, but we have something else abundantly: blister bugs. The next day I counted thirty-six on my lower body. They itch like fire and make a tiny blister. These are not chiggers, as a load of thirty-six chiggers would have outright killed even a strong man. These just made you *wish* you were dead.

I got to take the blister bugs to Abbeville, South Carolina with me, where I could enjoy them all week at the League of the South Summer Institute. Justin and Wright went with me. The theme this year was "Total War and Reconstruction" and the speakers were superb: Tom DiLorenzo, Clyde Wilson, Michael Hill, James Kibler, Joseph Stromberg, John Chodes, and Don Livingston—great historians, great thinkers. This was the third Institute I've attended, and every one has richly repaid my effort, both time and money.

A few days after we got back from Abbeville Susan somehow got into the blister bugs, or, more accurately, they got into *her*. Several years ago Shirley Hull introduced us to Balm of Gilead. We bought all she had when the company that makes it went out of business, because it is bar-none the best anti-itch/healing salve we've ever found. Susan asked me to help her apply Balm of Gilead, and I counted seventy-eight (78!) blister bugs. I don't know how she kept from losing her mind.

BEFORE YOU KNOW IT

On a farm things can go bad before you know it. Our old John Deere No. 4 Big Mower weighs heavily on the tongue. That and all the other work gave Boaz a big sore on his neck where the collar rests. One day he was fine, the next he was a mess. Didn't matter that we had called ourselves checking him out daily, and had really meant to, he still got sored.

Same thing with pigs. Remember we had a sow that got mastitis, so we had to take away her new piglets. I noticed that she was only picking at her food, and knew something was wrong. A pig that shows no enthusiasm over food is a *sick* pig. She disappeared and a couple of days later the atmosphere changed. When we finally found her remains back in the woods, it was a big clean up job. The boys *really* enjoyed that.

Her piglets were the ones Susan had been bottle feeding. She was keeping them in a pen in the backyard, and finally moved them to a pen in Pig Hollow where we could train them to electric fence. They were bad to climb the fence when dinner time drew near. I think that's how Mable, the smallest, injured herself, falling off the fence. Anyway, she didn't make it. That left only Bertha and Penelope.

Meanwhile the litter of pigs older than Bertha and Penelope, now at forty to sixty pounds and *really* destructive, decided the price of a slight electric shock running under the fence was not too great to pay for freedom. Every morning they infest the barn. The chickens haven't had an undisturbed meal in days. The upside is that the pigs, disgusting creatures that they are, clean up after the cows. We finally let Bertha and Mable out, but they couldn't make too much social headway with the other pigs. They gave up on the barn side of the road and transmigrated to the house side, which they liked better anyway. A thirty pound pig, however, is *not* a pet. It's a *pest*. You'll be standing outside, minding your own business, when out of nowhere you feel a cold, attention-demanding snout on your ankle.

I'd been meaning all summer to go buy another little boar to replace Houdini, who was transmogrified into whole hog sausage. The man I buy pigs from had only one little pig that had escaped fixing. Frankly, he looked pretty sorry, all skinny and scared, but he was my only choice. Mercy decided his name was Bernard-Alphonse. It should have been Houdini, Jr., because he didn't stay in the pen even twenty-four hours. After three other escapes, I believe we have at last got him. I put Bertha and Mable in with him, just to keep them out from underfoot. First mealtime Bertha promptly commenced to biting on Bernard every time he tried to get his snout in the trough.

If that pig escapes being hen-pecked, it'll be a miracle.

WATER WITCHING

S ome things just have to remain a mystery. You see them, but there's no explaining them.

High in that mysterious category ranks *water witching*.

Yes, I know that the ignorant scoff and deride water witching as a worthless medieval relic. That's because they've never seen anybody witch for water. Last night, Justin and I did.

I knew my neighbor, Mr. L., witched for water, and I had a friend that needed a well. For a month I've been trying to get by Mr. L.'s, but one thing and another kept me from it. Finally I recognized in my own mind a haunting reluctance that resembled fear, so I faced up to it and made myself drive over there. Twice. The second time Justin was with me. Mr. L.'s truck was parked in his driveway, but I couldn't get anybody to answer the door. I went back to my truck and was writing him a note when his wife came to the door and hollered. I told her I was looking for Mr. L. and she said he had just stepped into the bathtub and would be out shortly.

In a few minutes he came out of the front door, putting on his shirt. He must be in his early sixties, craggy-faced, wiry, pure country and extremely pleasant. He's tanned like all of us in the country—red and brown around the head, neck, and forearms, milk white everywhere else. I hemmed and hawed about what I wanted and he finally said, "Oh, you want me to witch for a well? Well, when do you want to do it?" I sputtered that any time

290

would be all right, and he nailed me with, "How about right now?" Fine by me. He knew where the place was; he would meet us there.

We waited for him up on the road, and very shortly he drew up in his truck. We drove out to the point of the ridge where we wanted to put the well. Mr. L. got out of the truck with a forked twig in his hand. Now the length of the fork wasn't more than thirty-six inches, and at the tips it was just a tiny switch, hardly more than a twig. He cut off one wild shoot, stuck that in his back pocket, and then picked off all the leaves with his knife. "They'll catch my stick on the grass," he explained. The stick, he explained, was cherry, but any fruit tree would do.

The weeds were shoulder high where I pointed out that we wanted the well. He held the forked ends of the stick in his hands, one hand high in the middle of his chest, the other about the navel. The joined end of the fork stood out in front of him. The stick's ends, which he held, were too thin for him to control the rest of the fork with them. He started to walk, and suddenly the joined end of the fork swung around to his right. "Well, there's one stream." He took the fifteen-inch twig out of his back pocket, and knelt down over the spot where the stick had turned. He held his hand up against his stomach, and started the free end of the stick bobbing. He didn't say anything for a long time while it bobbed and bobbed and then fell still. "It's sixty-two feet down," he said.

"How do you know that?" I asked.

"I counted," he laughed. He had been counting the number of times the stick bobbed. "Now," he continued, "we want to find another stream, and then they can put the well where the two cross." He stood off about twenty feet from where he had found the first stream, turned and began to walk back toward that stream at a right angle to it. In about six feet the fork turned to his left, pulled back toward me, and then back around his shoulder. "There's a whirlpool here or something," he said. "See how the stick's going around toward my back? Don't want to dig there. Might be a cave or something and you'd never get your water."

He stepped on and shortly the stick pulled again to his left. He knelt down with the bobbing twig in his hand, and I silently watched and counted it bob forty times. "Forty feet," he said. He stepped over where that stream would be, and came back the other way, searching again for the first stream. In a few steps the fork turned again. He had it, the place where the two streams crossed.

By this time it was nearly dark, but Justin and I were full of questions. Water witching, Mr. L. says, is a gift, not a learned skill. His daddy had it, he has it, his son has it, and one of his grandsons. He let Justin hold his hands while he walked across one of the underground streams, so Justin could feel that he wasn't manipulating the stick himself. Then Justin tried it by himself, and it turned again—maybe Justin has the gift, too. We kept on firing questions about water witching to Mr. L., and he seemed delighted to answer them. I reached around and pulled out my wallet and started digging for money. "How much do I owe you?"

"Oh, no!" he said, "Water witching is a gift. If you charge for it, you lose the gift," he said. Short pause, then, "But I *can* take a donation."

Just to show me how it worked, he asked if I had any change. I handed him a penny out of my pocket. He split the end of the fork and stuck the penny in the split. Then he stood off ten feet or so, and started walking past me. As the stick passed me, it pulled to the left, just toward me.

"It's looking for the change in your pocket," Mr. L. explained. "I can do the same thing with paper money and a dollar bill." He went on to tell some hilarious stories about people trying to fool him, swapping rolls of money around among themselves, but the stick always found the one with the biggest wad. His son had even found a lost wallet under three feet of silage in a silage pit!

We called the drilling company.

When the well driller came out, he pooh-poohed Mr. L.'s water witching. "Works half the time, half the time it don't," he said. That may be, but when they dug where Mr. L. marked the spot, they hit water at about fifty feet. I reckon we got in on the half of his time that it worked.

A SPIRITUAL CURE
FOR DEPRESSION

For a recent newsletter I wrote an article called "Studying God," with this paragraph:

> Susan once told me that the best cure for being
> downcast or depressed or alienated from God was to
> praise him. By the time you have gone through even a
> short list of God's mercies, the color of the world begins
> to change. No coincidence, then, that we find psalm
> after psalm where the psalmist practices exactly this
> cure.

In July, one day when I was out of the office, the phone rang. Susan answered and heard this story from a subscriber in California:

> I've been battling depression for years. I tried drugs,
> but they just wouldn't work with my body. Then I got
> on Sam-E for about two years, and it was helping
> my depression. When I read your article in *The
> Moneychanger*, I thought, 'Well, it's worth a try. It can't
> hurt.'

So I started praying the psalms and praising God. After ten to twelve days it seems that the Sam-E just wasn't doing its job. Later that night it came to me that my body didn't need Sam-E. The prayer had taken over, and I just went on my way.

Of course at times I get slack in my prayer, and then I have to get right back to it.

I had *heard* I was supposed to "glorify" God, but I wasn't sure what that meant. I went and looked it up and it said "glorify" meant "praise and worship." I thought to myself, "I can do that!" And I can. Now I'm not sure yet, but it seems I'm also getting a *physical* benefit.

You write a newsletter for twenty years waiting to hear a story like that just once.

I called him back toward the end of August and asked how he was doing. Was he still praising God and praying the psalms? Was it still working for his depression? *You bet!* I asked him if he minded our printing his story but without using his name, and he said, "You can not only print my story, but you can print my name and address and phone number!" Just for privacy's sake, if you want to ask him any questions, call our office and we'll give you his number.

All this set me to thinking. I'm sure there are *physical* illnesses or disorders that may cause depression, but surely most of it is *spiritual*. Isn't depression after all despairing in God? I'm trying to avoid putting this in a way that sounds like I'm pointing the finger at people who suffer from depression, but I can't because in the end I *am* pointing the finger at them. Some people have a constitutional bias toward depression. I know. I'm one of them, and I've made a lot of progress—by the grace of God—and I'm surely no Giant of Faith. There's a moral failing here, a refusal to trust God and trust his good will toward us. *But what curse is there that God cannot remove?* And if something physical isn't causing the depression, then am I not *obliged* to work at a *spiritual* solution?

If there is some answer other than this, I don't know what it might be. If you're depressed, why not just try praying the psalms and praising God? What can it hurt?

> *Why art thou cast down, O my soul? and why art thou*
> *disquieted within me? hope in God: for I shall yet praise*
> *him, who is the health of my countenance, and my God.*

> — Psalm 43:5 (Authorized Version)

PIG PERSUADER

If you're like me (pray you're not), you probably wait until December 22 or 23 to start thinking about Christmas shopping. This year, don't do it. Here are a couple of suggestions.

For children, grandchildren, godchildren, nieces, and nephews, instead of giving them cash (that is, green paper money), why not give them *silver*? A gift of silver thrills and fascinates everybody. It's also a great way to *save*, because the silver can't be prised out of a piggy bank and spent at the 7/11. The shiniest, showiest way to give silver is simple, one troy ounce 99.9% pure silver rounds. More expensive, but still always a hit, are the silver American Eagles. You might also give US silver dollars minted before 1936, Peace or Morgan type.

For those folks you want to honor and remember at Christmastime, here's another suggestion: *Harper's Country Hams*. They sell hickory-smoked country hams, bacon, jams, syrups, sorghum, and gift baskets full of all sorts of Southern favorites. The Sanders family has laboriously taste-tested almost everything the Harpers sell, and granted it our Seal of Delight. (If you order any of their "Smokin' Hog Ham Jerky," I recommend you keep it under lock and key. If your children get to it first, you'll never even get a sniff at it.) Liberty especially loves their country ham, which she ranks equal to imported Italian prosciutto. Around our house we often quote our friend Michael Hill's wisdom: "If nectar is the drink of the gods, and ambrosia is the food of the gods, then red-eye gravy is *the gravy of the gods*." I don't know what they eat for gravy on Mount Olympus, but from the ham juice left in the skillet after frying ham here, Liberty always makes "the gravy of the gods." Harper Country Hams is a family-run business, and here's their address: **Harper Country Hams**, P.O. Box 122, 2955 US Highway 51 North, Clinton, KY 42031; (888)-HARPERS; hamtastic.com.

NOT A GOOD DAY

I thought I had everything under control on October third. I got up especially early to make my appointment with Eurice (pronounced *Your-iss*) to buy a boar. I had been trying to get this off my list for months. I climbed into the truck ready to roll.

Remember that our first boar, Houdini, was also a graduate of Eurice's establishment. By default, Houdini wound up as whole hog sausage, but without a boar you are shortly *out* of the pig business. A couple of months ago I went and bought a young piglet to replace him. However, what looked like the right equipment on Bernard-Alfonse was in fact a hydrocele hernia, and he was never going to prosper or sire progeny. So I borrowed a friend's horse trailer and that morning set out for Eurice's to return the piglet and buy a full-grown boar.

Climbing into the truck was the last time that day that anything went just exactly right.

Now Eurice is a jovial man with about four hundred pigs (all sizes, shapes, and colors), a hundred goats, sheep, hundreds of chickens, geese, guineas, and turkeys, not to mention pigeons without number, all crowded onto a small place that resembles a nuclear test site. However, he is one of those folks that have an intimidating presence. Not gruff, just the sort of person whose time you know not to waste—not a person to trifle with, as we say in the South. Add to that his recent back trouble, which will soon require surgery. In getting this boar I didn't want to waste his time or take him farther out of his way than I had to.

First, I forgot where to turn off after I got east of Lawrenceburg. I drove all the way to the Giles County line before I could find a place to turn around. I got to Eurice's by guess, and just on my 8:30 a.m. appointment. He was gracious, but obviously in pain from his back. Then he saw my trailer, with its flop-down ramp as a back gate.

"That won't work. You can't back it up to the hog ramp."

Impasse. He soon broke that by offering to take his pickup back to the hog lot, load the boar, and then transfer him to my trailer. He took off in the truck, then stopped and leaned out the window. "Why don't you just bring that pig on back?"

I nodded, and picked up Bernard-Alfonse in his cage. I had brought him back for a refund. I then *walked* the quarter mile back to the hog lot. Eurice looked at me astonished. "Why'n't you bring him in the truck?" Huffing, I set him down. Yes, why *didn't* I bring him in the truck? After a brief inward examination of the circumstances and my action, cosmic stupidity was the only plausible reason I could name.

Now it was time to catch and load the boar, and I had not a *clue* how we would do this. Pause to ponder, dear Readers, that no pig can be captured without increasing your proximity to a *number* of pigs. Eurice's feed pig lot was *full* of pigs in all sizes, some easily tipping the scales above 400 pounds. And pigs are *not* cuddly. In large crowds they can be downright intimidating. There was, however, nothing for it but to jump over the fence (if the verb "jump" can ever be performed by the noun "Franklin Sanders").

Eurice's plan was simplicity itself. He had a maze of pens leading from one to the other, cobbled together out of every material that an active ingenuity and inscrutable Providence could bring together: barbed wire, hog wire, old pallets, wire panels of every size and manufacture, you name it. He would spread out food on the ground, enticing the boar (and about a hundred other pigs) into that pen, then separate him out into another pen, and finally into the chute leading inexorably into the ramp. At the mouth of the ramp was parked his pickup truck, with a tubular steel cage on the back, ready to receive the two hundred and fifty pound boar.

In Eurice's hand was a Pig Persuader, a.k.a. an electric cattle prod. The pig has not yet been born who will not yield to a Pig Persuader. Mercy, *I* would yield to a Pig Persuader.

My job was to manipulate the gates from pen to pen as we separated the pigs. Nervously keeping an eye on a hideous—truly hideous—four hundred pound sow in the next pen, I waded through pigs to shut the first gate. "Good!" complimented Eurice.

I beamed with pride in a job well-done, but had no time to rest on my laurels. Wielding his Persuader, Eurice somehow herded the boar and three other pigs into the pen leading into the chute. In that pen was an oak about two feet through at hip height, with roots all tangled on top of the ground. Eurice started playing merry-go-round with the pigs. I winced every time he moved, thinking about his back, but he never even groaned. He shouted at me to man the gate, and "Don't let that boar out!"

Right. No need to worry about me choking up at this point, *no, sir!* I might be trampled to death by frantic pigs, but when the dust cleared they will find my gnarled knuckles still clinging to that wire panel.

Whoops! Out ran the first pig, then the second, then the third. *Slam!* The boar was successfully isolated into the chute, then charged out and tried to leap the three-foot fence beside me. *Whang!* He mashed his face up against the hog panel strategically leaning inward from the fence, only to turn and face Eurice closing in with his Persuader. Evidently the boar had already met the Persuader. Eurice urged him into the mouth of the chute, where he immediately lost his enthusiasm, turned three or four circles, and tried to make it out past Eurice—far too slow for the Persuader. *Flip, OINK! whirr*, then up the ramp into the pickup, and quicker than you can look Eurice has hopped the fence and *Clang!* slammed shut the sliding door on the cage.

Step one successfully accomplished. Step two, transferring boar from pickup to horse trailer, lay ahead.

Eurice backed his pickup slam up to the horse trailer, straddling the ramp. Now we had to convince the boar to jump down about three feet into the trailer and not wriggle out through any gap between the truck and the trailer. *Hmmmm* . . . How to keep him from wriggling out? Eurice cast his eye around 180 degrees, and lighted on a pile of old pallets. "We're gonna see how strong you are. Go get one of them pallets." I hefted the pallet, about as handy as a mainsail in a whirlwind, but not nearly as nimble. I managed to lift it up to bulging-eye level and drop it into the trailer through a slot window, taking care not to shear off my hands at the wrists. Then I had to worm my way into the trailer around the pickup, and stand in the trailer behind the pallet, covering the corner next to the pickup. Eurice, using the Persuader, would encourage the boar to jump down. Once he was in the trailer past me, I would block his way out of the trailer with the pallet. Then Eurice would lift up the ramp and I would back out of the trailer.

The boar was not hard to convince, and the rest of the plan went off without a hitch. However, once the ramp was up, Eurice wanted his unique pallet returned to his world-famous pallet collection, so I had to reach down and deadlift it out by the tips of my fingers. I had—just *barely*—quit myself like a man.

Alas, the day was not yet over. Back at the Top I drove through the pasture and into Pig Holler. Susan and Zach were there to strategize. You have to picture that where we were intending to put the pen for the boar stands to the far right side of a sort of shoulder of land. The farther out you drive straight from the gate in the fence, the more the ground drops off. Twenty yards back from the fence the pigs have rooted out everything to the dirt. Beyond that stand briars and brush and little persimmon trees half the size of your wrist.

Zach and Susan recommended that we pull the truck and trailer into Pig Holler past the gate, then back it up past the existing pen to where we intended to build the new one. Justin and I, on the other hand, insisted that this was too conservative and we could just pull the truck and trailer around through the brush, back up the hill, and thus miss the painful exercise of backing a trailer in a tight spot and do everything faster to boot.

Justin and I prevailed. Justin drove the truck. Justin almost got there. Then the trailer wheels both—no, all *four*—hung up on little persimmon trees. The truck's rear wheels whirred and smoked. The birds chirped, the crickets sang, the boar slept in the trailer, and Franklin's blood pressure shot to the tree tops. Alas, I could only blame myself. Susan and Zach, wise as always, never said I told you so—probably in foresightful self-defense.

Justin, Zach, and I laid to with machetes, saws, and hatchets and soon had the trailer tires freed. We loosed the trailer from the truck. With Susan behind the steering wheel, spraying us with sod and dirt, we slipped and slid and pushed the truck on up the hill and out. Then we borrowed Liberty's four-wheel drive Explorer, backed it down to the trailer, and pulled the trailer back up the hill. Now we were ready to kneel in the mud and manure for a couple of hours building a pen out of welded wire panels. Around the inside perimeter we strung two strands of electric fencing. We completed everything except the last panel, where the trailer was parked with the sleeping boar.

Meanwhile Susan was busy elsewhere. She had gone to fetch us another hog panel from the pen under the trees. In the process she put down the electric fence and opened the wire panel gate to Pig Holler. Quicker than you can say, "Sod-annihilating renegade swine task force" out walked our younger sow with *eight* half-grown pigs—bee-lining, no doubt, for my long-suffering neighbor's pristine pastures to root them up as energetically as possible in the little time left before sundown.

Finally we got the boar out into the pen. Susan energized the fence, and the uproar began. He closed in on the fence to sniff at one of our sows on the other side. Little by little his ear edged closer to the wire—closer, closer, *ZAP! OINK!* He bounced from one side of the pen to another. His first solution was to back into a corner so he could see whatever it was coming from either direction. This worked until his backside connected with the wire. *ZAP!* To the other side of the pen. Then he lined up alongside the fence. This worked until his ears touched the wire. *ZAP!* Back and forth and crosswise he bounced around the pen. Finally he just lay down dead center of the pen with a look of defeated disgust on his face.

The weekend before, Justin had built a prototype Swine Chalet, a winter shelter for pigs. Since we already had the truck there, we chained the Swine Chalet up to the truck and dragged it through the gate into Pig Holler. Then we moved Penelope and Bertha, Susan's two bottle-fed pigs, into Pig Holler, *sans* their co-operation.

The pigs all attended to (such as hadn't made good their escape), we turned our attention to the long-neglected chickens. We had to move their electric net-fence ("varmint fence") to give them new turf to tear up. *But first*—all life is tortured by those two words—we had to weed-eat the three-foot-high *wire-weed*. I don't know its real name. I just know that you can't pull it or cut it with anything less than an acetylene cutting torch or wire pliers. I put the saw-toothed blade on the weed-eater. This worked well on everything except the electric varmint fence.

By the time we got the varmint fence back up and the hole mended, the sun was pretty plainly making known his intention to shut down. Those children responsible for feeding animals at evening had disappeared into their accustomed hiding places. They shall remain unnamed. When they were finally rousted to their duty, I began trying to call up the missing pigs.

Never before had they failed to come home for supper. I called and I called until I was nearly hoarse. No pigs. I went to the top of the pasture and called. I called down the hollers where the echo might reach them. I called across the high pasture to the pine woods. I called to the east, and to the north, to the south and west. No pigs.

By now the sun was just glowering above the horizon. I couldn't leave those pigs out all night to wreck my neighbor's pastures. I was tired and thirsty and hungry and—let us admit it—*far* from nicey-nice. I spied the four-wheeler parked in the barn, another source of infuriation. It was useless as fangs on a canary. The battery cables had been broken for weeks.

I asked Susan to pull the Toyota pickup into the barn. Looking for the jumper cables—*de rigueur* equipment in any Sanders' family vehicle—I could find ne'er a one in the Toyota. To my delight, I realized that once again my children had failed to put them away. I told Justin where he might find some over at the house, and before too long he returned with them. By now I could barely make out his form in the dark. He squatted down on the left side of the four-wheeler to attach the cables, while I stood on the right where I could attach them to the truck's batteries. Justin handed me the cables in the dark.

AT HOME IN DOGWOOD MUDHOLE, VOLUME ONE

While I struggled to distinguish red from black clamp so we wouldn't blow up the truck battery, I felt something squishy on the black clamp.

"What is this, Justin. Did you find those things lying in oil or something?"

In the dark I could see his head turn from side to side, then down to the ground. "Oh, no," he whispered in hushed tones. "There was turkey poop on the ground."

Cause and effect quickly met in my mind—one turkey, sixty-five acres, one hand—defying the whole science of probability. Now lest you count me less than a good sport, I want you to understand that nothing on earth has quite the same viscosity as turkey poop. It combines all the unique properties of motor oil, molasses, and Super Glue. It cannot be washed off. The smell must be surgically removed.

I had a whole handful of it.

At this point I was not quite able to laugh, and too weak to cry. Miles from the nearest rag, I stooped down, scooped up a handful of hay, and futilely began trying to scrape it off. Much to the credit of the onlookers' self-control and instinct of self-preservation, *no one* said a word. A hushed silence, as they say, fell over the crowd. Cloaking myself with the shreds of my dignity, I climbed onto the choking four-wheeler. As I attempted to put it in reverse, it died. I dismounted. Quiet, anxious hands pushed it out of the barn, filled the flat tires with air, and reapplied the jumper cables to re-start it. It coughed to life.

I mounted the four-wheeler and roared off into the night, searching for my lost sense of humor, too angry to laugh now, hoping I would be able to laugh later, if I could only get away from the scene without losing my temper. The turkey poop was just the last flashing neon message of a day that said, "You live in a fallen world, where your job is to make things work that never want to work. Get used to it, and smile."

TERRORISTS IN WAYNE COUNTY

Y'all ought to know that when I recommend anything, I've usually tried it myself. That applies to both Mild Silver Protein (MSP, a form of colloidal silver married to a protein molecule) and grapefruit seed extract.

Back in the summer our milch cow Molly broke out in another case of mastitis. She already has one dead udder quarter from mastitis, and this was the second or third time this year it had flared up. I talked to Bill McFarland, who makes MSP, and he recommended we treat her with a spray made of MSP, a little MSM (methonyl sulfyl methane, bioavailable sulfur) and DMSO, a deeply penetrating solvent, to take the mixture deep into her udder. We sprayed it on twice a day for a week, and without any antibiotics her mastitis disappeared. MSP also worked for our Percheron draft horse, Boaz, when he developed a boil on his neck from a collar sore.

Not long ago I went out to feed the pigs and noticed that Bertha, a pig Susan had bottle raised, was acting all wrong. First of all, she had no appetite, a distinctly unpigly manner. Second, she could hardly stand up, and when she did, she walked around in circles. Susan mixed up a stout dose of grapefruit seed extract in water and fed it to Bertha. Next day she was the same old pig. *Well*, you know what I mean, she felt fine. Later our vet opined that she probably had an ear infection. Grapefruit seed extract also worked for our Great Pyrenees, Orion. He had some terrible skin ailment on his rear and had lost a patch of hair six inches in diameter in front of his tail. Susan mixed up thirty drops of grapefruit seed extract in a quart of water and poured it on twice a day. Orion *loved* it—*not*. In a few days the bare spot scabbed over and hair started growing back.

THE TROUBLE WITH TREES

One night a few weeks ago we had guests from the great Commonwealth of Virginia when a terrible windstorm suddenly blew up around the Shoe. It passed as suddenly as it appeared. When Lib and Johnny Ray went out to go home, they found one of our tulip poplars blown down on their car! Thankfully, it didn't damage anything. We pulled it off and they left, only to call a few minutes later and report that their way home by Suck Stem Branch Road was blocked by two huge downed trees (thank heaven for cell phones!). They took another long circle around to avoid that stretch of road. That way they got across the low-water bridge fine, but when they started up the ridge on the last leg of their drive, two downed trees again blocked the road. They gave up and came back. It was a good thing, too, because there was only one other way left to get home, a thirty minute detour. If they had taken it, they would have gotten *within sight* of their place only to find *another tree* blocking the road.

Our guests left the next morning, and Johnny Ray Bain, Justin, Zach, and I hit the road early with chainsaws. Soon after we started to work clearing the first roadblock, a couple of our neighbors began cutting the tree on the other side. I was glad of the chance to make their acquaintance.

We cut everything back to the big trunks and cleared the road, carefully stacking the wood to come back and pick up later. (Some miscreant relieved us of this necessity before we could get back to it, may it clog up his chimney!) Then we drove down Suck Stem and up the ridge to the next roadblock. The tree was better than three feet through at the base, and rested across the road on giant limbs. We started cutting charily and could hear the sound of a chainsaw way off in the distance.

"Durn!" said one of my neighbors. "That sounds like them terrorists, and here we are without a single gun among us."

Through my mind flashed this picture: the puzzled, turbaned terrorist flying over Wayne County looking for a target and wondering why on earth he was there and what on earth he was supposed to conquer. There hasn't been any *loot* here since roughly the end of the eighteenth century. I nearly choked trying to suppress my giggling.

Finally another neighbor arrived who logs for a living. Now he did nothing the way I would have. First of all, he pulled out this mutant chainsaw on steroids. I have a Stihl 029 and a big Husqvarna, no measly saws, but this thing had a bar as long as both of my saws welded together. He stood on the *down*hill side of that tree, cut the trunk first (I would have cut the branches), danced around and in about twelve minutes had it cut into three logs and change. Shows you what I know—*nothing*, in case you need to hear it.

MASSIVE PLANNED
PASTURE ADJUSTMENT

I have already described the pleasure of moving cows. Next to scraping my knuckles on a nutmeg grater, it's one of my favorite jobs, so you can imagine how happy I was to hear Justin suggest it Sunday evening after we had fed all the animals.

Over two Saturdays we had built a new electric pig fence to expand Pig Holler. This was part of a Massive Planned Pasture Adjustment. The MPPA called for removing from our right-hand barn pasture the electric fence keeping our Highland bull, Pilgrim, and his two cows and calves away from Molly the milch cow (and Jeffrey, her calf) and Bonnie the Highland and her calf; moving the horses from their pasture on the left of the barn across the road to the big pasture where the fourteen Highland cow herd was; and the cows there to the horses' former pasture. All summer long Hero, our other bull, has stood in his pasture next to the fence bellowing insults at Pilgrim across the road. Cheap work, since Pilgrim is older and about half again Hero's size, and there were two barbed wire fences and a road between them. Sort of like me making faces at Arnold Schwarzenegger from a locked bank vault through bulletproof glass.

To Justin I had to admit that the Lord's Day sun was about down, and we did have everybody there and some guests besides (moving cows is *very* labor intensive.) But somehow Justin missed my next statement about waiting until I had finished feeding the pigs.

Therefore when from Pig Holler I heard all the commotion across the road, and saw the trucks blocking the road, I was somewhat miffed he hadn't waited. However, by the time I got there he had all the cows and Hero already out of the pasture and across the road where they belonged, except for a couple of steers, a calf, and Hillbilly. Since I had tried to herd her before, my first impulse was just to shoot Hillbilly on the spot, start a fire, and throw a barbecue. I forbore. Justin got mad at me for messing up his plans by driving up in the four-wheeler, I got mad at him for not waiting, and we both got mad at Stella the cat for picking that precise moment to walk in front of the cows and spook them away from the gate.

But we quickly moved the rest of the cows and put the horses in that pasture and apologized and hugged and I thought that would be the end of it.

Until the next morning.

When we rounded the last curve in the road headed to the Top, Zach said, "Look at that hole in the fence!"

What hole in *what* fence? From the gate at the road we have stout wooden fences on both sides of the drive to the barn. Next to the barn at the right and left are gates opening onto the pasture. The fence around Pilgrim's pasture was missing two full sections and a post.

Think about it. One strand of electric wire keeps eighteen-hundred-pound Pilgrim back all summer. Then he decides he wants into the other pasture, and he takes out two sections of wooden fence and a six-inch fence post like pushing aside a shower curtain.

The mystery didn't stop there. Pilgrim, two other cows, and two calves were all in the pasture with Hero's herd, but *the gate was locked behind them.* How? Did he open it with his horns? Nimble tips of his cloven hooves? His lips? Nope. I'm convinced *he climbed the gate.*

Now how the other cows got in I haven't a clue. (By the way, now that they're up close, Hero no longer gives Pilgrim any lip.)

AURORA

"*Wow!* Come look at this!" Zachariah shouted. We all ran out of the Shoe and looked up into the night sky. The moon hadn't yet risen and it was perfectly clear, but there in the sky were huge clear clouds of *red*. Little by little they shifted and changed shape. That was the first time in our lives we had ever seen an *aurora borealis*, but Susan was happiest because we didn't even have to pay $1,500 for an Alaskan cruise to see it.

DECEMBER 2001

TRUE GRITS

Susan, Liberty, Johnny Ray Bain and I drove to Atlanta this weekend to see Judith Morse graduate from the Art Institute of Atlanta. Judith is Dan and Marianne Morse's daughter, and Dan has been our pastor for the past sixteen years. Judith is a few months younger than Liberty, so she grew up like a sister to Lib and a daughter to us.

Both Lib and Judith qualify as true G.R.I.T.S., Girls Raised In The South, but this story concerns the *other* kind of grits, *viz.*, the heavenly manifestation of ground corn that graces Southern tables. On the way to Atlanta we stopped at Walmart in Pulaski. Behind us in the checkout line was a white-haired gentleman who spoke in the soft old accents of middle Tennessee. Liberty, who can strike up a conversation with a goat, noticed that he was buying slices of Harper's Ham, our favorite. Ham led the conversation to red eye gravy, "the gravy of the gods," which may only properly be savored on biscuits or grits. That led to the following story.

Thirty years ago this gentleman moved from Florida to Michigan. Driving back to Florida for one last load, he took along a Michigander friend to help. They stopped in Birmingham, Alabama, for breakfast. The Michigander ordered eggs, sausage, and biscuits. Having spotted his Yankee accent, the waitress looked up dubiously and asked, "You want *grits* with that?"

The Yankee glanced just as dubiously over to his Southern friend for guidance. The friend said, "Sure, go ahead. They're good. You'll like 'em."

"Okay," said the Yankee cautiously, "I'll have one."

SECTION FOUR

———

A REAL FARM

NEW TRADITIONS

Sitting down to write y'all my monthly letter, I asked Susan to remind me what newsworthy events had happened in the last month.

"We've finally contained the pigs!" she shot back. "Think about it: fifteen pig minds [*sic*] working all the time on one point alone—*escape*. And we've *finally* got them corralled." You know why she finds that so newsworthy, don't you? She and Zach are the Keepers of the Fence. They have to walk the mile-and-a-half electric fence line to locate the breaches. That's why it rests on her mind as such a victory.

Our Great Pyrenees Cleo had her pups, but not without disappointment. Ellen built her a really fine large house last year. A few days before pupping time we fenced it off with some pig panels. They're only three feet high, but why worry? Cleo looked like a giant hairy golf ball, so nobody thought she could jump the fence, heavy as she was with pups.

Never underestimate the pull of tradition on a dog. Cleo's tradition is to wait for an icy, stormy night to pup, throw part of the litter in the open pasture, and crawl under the solar house to have the rest. Nor did she depart from custom on November 23. By the time we found her under the solar house one of her nine pups had already died. Even after we moved them four more died. And of course Cleo and her whole litter had to pass through their traditional stay in my office ("the compost heap"). The weather cleared and I shortly reasserted my authority over the compost heap and ejected the lot of them. Now their eyes are open and they're thriving.

A few days ago Zach reported that one of our small calves looked bloated. We put him and his mama up in the paddock and got some pills from our vet, Dr. Bell. I say "pills" but think "hockey pucks." We crushed one and mixed it with sweet feed, but next morning he was bloated even worse. I sighed. I had been looking forward to my first free Saturday in a year. Dr. Bell was scheduled away from the office at 12:30 p.m., leaving me just enough time to drive to my neighbor's, borrow his trailer, drive back, pick up the calf, and drive to Dr. Bell's. When I arrived he pulled out twenty feet or so of clear hose, climbed in the trailer, and started intubating the calf. You can tell he's a professional because every few inches he pauses and sucks on the hose. No sooner did the end of the hose clear the calf's stomach than he deflated like a loose balloon.

I felt so ashamed. I could have done that myself, and not bothered Dr. Bell. It's just that I gag so easily when I suck on a tube full of green cow-stomach-goo.

OUT OF THE MOUTHS OF BABES

Justin's wife Ellen heard Tucker Bain (4) talking to Elijah (2 ½) as they lay in bed supposed to be taking an afternoon nap. Tucker asked Elijah, "Do you know why Jesus died?"

Elijah said, "Why?"

Tucker answered, "So that we could live here. Do you know what they did to Jesus on the cross after they stabbed him? They put nails in his skin."

THE TWELVE DAYS OF CHRISTMAS

Last Christmas a snowstorm hit when our house was filled with guests. For several nights twenty-five or more slept at the Shoe. We had so much fun accidentally that we have decided to try it again this year on purpose, and at the same time revive an ancient Southern custom: the Twelve Days of Christmas, running from Christmas Eve through January 6. When I mentioned this to Johnny Ray Bain he looked troubled. "Take off work from Christmas Eve through Epiphany?"

Sure, I said. Look at the calendar. You won't miss many workdays. Nobody's working on Monday the 24th (Christmas Eve), or on the 26th. So you just miss two days that week. New Year's week will be the same, so you'll only lose two days there. What will we do? First I'll lock up all TVs and video games, and post an armed guard. Everybody is competing to find the best Christmas album and the best Christmas story to read aloud. But we'll also try to have morning and evening family prayer every day, and ponder the ancient church festivals of the Twelve Days of Christmas. That includes *Christmas Eve,* with the odd calm that comes at the end after all the children are in bed, when you get to talk to your wife alone for the first time in weeks, and then *Christmas Day,* a day of worship and explosion and exhaustion, followed by *St. Stephen's Day,* December 26, when we remember the first martyr who prayed for his persecutors even as they stoned him (Acts 7:55). On *The Feast of St. John the Evangelist,* December 27, we can remember Jesus' beloved friend the apostle, who wrote a gospel, three epistles and Revelation. On *Holy Innocents Day,* December 28, we may recall the babes slaughtered by Herod, who glorified God even in their deaths (Matt. 2). *The Circumcision of Christ,* on January 1st, marks the day when Christ became obedient to the law for our sakes (Luke 2), and finally the *Epiphany,* January 6, *The Day of Three Kings,* is when Jesus became known to the Gentiles (Matt. 2). Thus end the Twelve Days of Christmas.

During these ancient festival days we will cut wood or take wagon rides or shoot skeet or hike in the woods, but only enough to work up an appetite for supper. We have invited a lot of people to come stay one night or twelve, so we'll see what happens. Even if nobody else comes, we've got enough people already to have quite a party.

JANUARY 2002

How did our Twelve Days of Christmas work out? Pretty well, for a first try. For me, it was my best Christmas ever. I did banish the TV, except for a very few movies we wanted to watch. On eBay Susan found a copy of Alan Arkin's *A Matter of Principle* and *Improper Channels* (also starring Alan Arkin, both great movies). We also read Christmas stories aloud in the evening (not as often as I wished), and had family morning and evening worship *nearly* every day. I found myself working more than I had intended, and played not nearly enough. And of course, visitors came and came and came—not as many as we expected, but enough to keep us busy.

We didn't get any snow, but we did get a very hard cold snap. Late one afternoon a visiting friend helped Justin and me hitch up the horses. We took the wagon way down Robinson Branch Road, and when we got down in the holler, the sun disappeared. By then we already had fished out an old blanket to stretch across our knees. I kept asking our friend if he was cold. He lacked a really heavy coat and gloves, but he kept shaking his head no. When we pulled up even with the house the sun was almost

down, and I suggested that he go on into the house and warm up rather than help us unhitch. I'll never forget the look he flashed at me when he said, "I'll never forget you for this."

He meant it. It was *cold*.

What do you say about a family that has its picture taken with horses and dogs? Shouldn't they be afraid somebody might not be able to tell the difference? How can I explain all that you see here? The very fence behind us was built by my sons. The horses are working at training us, which is to say rebuilding us from the inside out. Grandchildren are present, and one day may be numerous enough to crowd all the dogs out of the picture. That mower is the latest 1904 technology. Across the road behind us is the pasture we call General, after the horse who lived and died there. Time would fail me to begin recounting the pig chases, sheep hunts, anger, sorrow, frustration, and tragedy that have taken place right there, overshadowed by all the joy.

Maybe all you can say about that family is: they are at home in Dogwood Mudhole.

BOXING THE COMPASS

This week I kept waking up early, so one morning I climbed into our luxurious 1984 Ford F-150 right at dawn. Bear in mind that travelling the five miles (twelve minutes) from our cabin to Justin and Ellen at the Top and Johnny and Lib at the Ponderosa, you literally *box the compass*. You leave our driveway headed *north*. You turn onto Suck Stem Branch headed *east*, and pass down through the hollow. Then you turn *southwest* to climb the ridge, and wind and twist until gradually, you circle back around to the *east*.

When I walked outside it was *barely* dawn. By the time I reached Suck Stem Branch, the sun was still only a yellow and orange glow on the horizon. Before I turned right, I looked straight ahead at the northern sky: it was *pink*, or more precisely, almost magenta. It confused me, because the sun was such a bright orange to my right. Then I drove *down* into Suck

Stem holler headed east and the sun disappeared altogether as I drove lower and lower. In the east only the pink remained. When I made my turn southwest up the ridge, the sky changed color again to *dark baby blue*, while over my left shoulder the glowing orange sun reappeared.

It was as if I had never before seen the sky at dawn. At fifty-four, I'm fairly sure that's not a fact, but that's what I love about living out here. Every day I see something new, or see old things with new eyes.

TUCKER LOVES HOT SAUCE

Johnny and Liberty's son Tucker is four and our oldest grandchild. He habitually makes impossibly precocious pronouncements. A few mornings ago Matt (Ellen's brother) was staying with Justin and Ellen. After everybody had fed the animals, Tucker and Matt sat down to a late breakfast. Before Matt could stop him, Tucker grabbed the Yucatan hot sauce, made from habañero peppers. He thoroughly doused his scrambled eggs with Yucatan, and looked over at Matt. "I love to eat hot sauce on my eggs!" he announced.

Before long the Yucatan began to act. Wordlessly Tucker reached over and grabbed his water glass and drained it dry. He looked over at Matt and never missed a lick. "And I like to drink water real fast after I eat it."

PROVING THE PUDDING

In the last few months I've written a lot about Mild Silver Protein and grapefruit seed extract. We proved them this Christmastime. Before Christmas Susan and I both came down with the family cold—the one the infants pick up from swamp creatures then share back and forth all winter. Both of us hit it quickly with twice daily doses of both Mild Silver Protein and grapefruit seed extract. I also gargled with the Mild Silver Protein and dropped it in my nose. Neither one of us got really sick, and within three days we were fine. The pestilence returned for another shot at Susan about two weeks later and whacked her for several days in spite of MSP and grapefruit seed extract, but I think that was because Christ-

319

mas just exhausted her, with all that waiting on everybody. Meanwhile, we have learned that grapefruit seed extract works for others, too. A subscriber writes:

> Here's a story for the grapefruit seed extract supplement that you introduced to our immune system. [Our] county was experiencing a whooping cough epidemic during December. Germs found their way into our social circles (most of that social circle is under thirty-two inches). I started our entire, unimmunized, Wednesday night fellowship on GSE. I cybershopped and got your quantity suggestion for $90. We all were daily dosing. One family out of seven started to show symptoms. Redoubled efforts and a doctor's visit for the affected ones. After diagnostics, yes, it appears to be whooping cough, but your children just aren't sick enough.
>
> How about that! The rest of the children have had some coughing and congestion, but whether just colds or minimized whooping cough, no one knows.
>
> Like advertising, you never know what is working, but you do know something is happening. And, as usual, Dr. Susan has introduced us to a *good* thing. Thank you and keep up the research.

Another friend in Louisiana was laid low by a terrible cold and flu. He ordered some Mild Silver Protein, and within a few days was singing its praises. It helped where nothing else could. You can pick up grapefruit seed extract at any health food store. Order Mild Silver Protein from (334) 493-0420; mildsilverprotein.com.

MSP works *very* well also on fungus like athlete's foot and yeast. To apply topically, I mix two ounces with ten drops of DMSO to carry it deep into the tissue, but I *never* spray it in my eyes or on mucous membranes. Of course, I'm no doctor and so I can't and don't make treatment recommendations. I'm just telling you what I've experienced. You might use either one of these things and all your hair fall out. But mine hasn't yet.

That reminds me about Shirley Hull's new ointment. She used to sell a cream called "Balm of Gilead," but the manufacturer went out of business. I bought all her stock because I had never found anything like Balm of Gilead to relieve itching and promote healing. Believe me, in the Land of Ticks, Chiggers, and Poison Ivy, anti-itch medication is worth its weight in gold. Shirley has now compounded her own "Special Balm" similar to Balm of Gilead. The label says it "helps with most problems and muscle tension, aches, pains. Promotes healing. May treat fungus and yeast." It contains essential oils, tea tree and grape seed oils, silver, almond, and aloe vera. I have tried it and believe it works *better* than Balm of Gilead. (Being shameless and crazy, I even mix it with Mild Silver Protein.) It's expensive—forty dollars for two ounces—but a little goes a long way. **Shirley Hull**, **Coyote Ridge Ranch**, 11950 SE 67 Pl., Morriston, FL 32668; (352) 486-4395.

LIVING IN A FALLEN WORLD

International Paper Company owns thousands and thousands of acres in our county. In fact, they border our farm on two sides. Although our area naturally grows hardwoods and no pines, they plant pines because they grow fast. A wall of tall pines borders all the south side of our farm.

No longer.

A crew is now working all up and down the Ridge Road harvesting pines. These aren't gigantic trees. I'd guess the biggest are maybe fifteen inches through. They don't cut them with chain saws. They have a machine with a blade at the ground. It snouts up to the tree, grabs it in a claw, and *Whizz!* Shears it off at the ground. Without putting down the first, it scoots over to another tree, grabs it, and shears it off. After its claw is full, it lays those down in a pile, whence another machine with a big arm loads them onto trailers. They start early. Lately they've been working right behind the Top, and when I get here at 7:00 a.m. the woods are already rumbling and growling.

I can't say I like it, or that I won't miss that high wall of pines behind the Shoe sending its perfume over the whole place. I won't like the way it will look as cutover, all stumps and brush and a few scraggly, crooked, worthless trees left standing. Some of that land they may sell cheap (and I do mean cheap) as cutover, but it takes a lot of work and money to put it in shape, working around or removing the stumps and brush piles and fencing. Most they will probably replant in fast growing pines, sending in gangs of uncomplaining Mexicans to set the little trees.

Watching those trees fall is one of those events that are necessary but not very satisfying, no matter how long you look at it. I can't say that I like it, but then, it's their land, so they can do with it what they want. After all, I do use paper, and lumber, so that's got to come from somewhere. That cutover looks so ugly for so long, but then, by the grace of God, it grows back so vigorously that in a few years you could hardly push through it on foot.

It's still a fallen world. Blondie, one of our Highland Cows, has been pregnant forever. We have been anxiously looking forward to her calf, because she had been bred to our young white bull, Hero, and this would be his first calf. A couple of days ago she had her calf, but Justin and Matt and Zach found him dead, and we don't know how he died. Another dark picture you'll never be satisfied with, but it always accompanies that other bright picture: the delight of new calves and grown cows and fresh milk and good beef. Creeping round the pleasure, there's always something to remind you of the fallen world we live in and send your heart longing toward heaven.

MUCK-SPREADING

I started back to work on January 14, but Justin still had some time before his classes begin again. Since Matt was visiting and always offers a ready hand, Justin fled the office to work outside.

He and Matt and Zach shoveled the big manure pile at the barn into our manure spreader. This was our first opportunity to use it since we bought it last year. How does it work? There's a double chain that runs along the floor to feed the manure toward the back, where a series of blades and spiked wheels kick it out behind. What we were not prepared for was the *vigor* with which the manure spreader operates. Blizzard of clods coming out the back. Whoops—they also fly *front*wards, so it is now customary (and a very sound idea) to wear a raincoat and broad-brimmed hat when you drive the spreader.

Once Justin had spread the manure on the garden, he wanted to turn it with the plow. Now I never mind admitting my ignorance. I often stay out of trouble that way. And plowing is something I know *very* little about. It rained that day when I was in draft horse driving school.

Actually, it's very easy. Justin stood off to the side in the plaid coat, driving the horses. That's Tucker sat up on Jachin's back. I held the plow, pursuing a leisurely pace. Imagine first that the plow only cuts on *one* side, so stability is not its virtue. You have to pull *up* to keep the tip in the ground and keep it digging. And if you push to the left, it goes right, and *vice versa*.

Then there is the matter of the horses. Boaz and Jachin weigh about fifteen hundred and thirteen hundred pounds, respectively. That day while I was plowing, Justin forgot the word *whoa*. Imagine waterskiing behind the Titanic at full bore, and you'll get a pretty fair idea what it was like. Fortunately, I had to get back to the office.

HAYSTACKING

You may remember all my fussing about making hay last year. The weather made it hard to get it in on time, and because we don't have a baler, we have to hire someone to come up and bale it, then we haul it out of the field into the barn. And hay is very tricky. If you cut it too soon you won't get much. Cut it too late, and you get nothing but stems without food value.

After we had gone through the agony of loading eight hundred bales into the barn, the grass didn't stop growing. Still, we had a horse-drawn mower, a horse-drawn rake, numerous pitchforks, and a number of off-and-on-willing sons and friends. Back in 1999, one of my neighbors, who raises twenty thousand bales of hay a year, told me you couldn't grow clover around here. I put out a test plot of some stuff called Nutricarb. I think it's no more than ground coal, but I had read two books that its seller, Leonard Ridzon in Ohio, had written about it, so I knew that carbon/organic matter is burned up quickly in our Southern soils. Nutricarb was supposed to replace liming and fertilizer by bringing the microbial life back to the soil. Couldn't tell it was there until the third year, and there

I was suddenly, staring at the impossible-to-grow clover knee-deep in my field. Don't know why or how. I just know it worked. We had clover that literally reached my knees. We couldn't bear to let it go to waste.

The solution was the haystacks. If they've worked for centuries for others, they would work for us. So we stacked. And stacked. And stacked. And stacked some more. And throwing and stacking hay is *not* an innate human skill. Pile it wrong and you'll build a big stack, only to watch half of it slide off on the ground because you failed to weave it right. When the stack gets high, somebody has to climb on top and walk round and round, treading it down. It took some learning, but we ended up with five haystacks ranging from twelve to fourteen feet. The Highlands *love* that stacked hay, and far prefer it to the baled hay. Think about it: we leave the hay where it is instead of baling it and picking it up and loading it in the barn, then in winter pulling it out of the barn, loading it, and carrying it back out into the field. The cows do all the work! Judging by the results, it was a pretty good idea.

So you can imagine my sense of satisfaction at watching the Highland steers feeding on one of our hand-made haystacks.

Clear-cutting paper companies, the risk of getting it all wrong, the steep learning curve, and all the learning by doing—forget how hard it all is and just remember how good it feels when something goes right.

THIS IS MY PLACE

FEBRUARY 2002

It was a perfect crisp, cloudless January day after a week of flooding rains. I'm not sure who spotted it first, but our Highland cow, Hillbilly, finally had her calf. He is tiny (as they all are, barely forty pounds), coated with curly fur, a very light chocolate brown little bull. He hadn't been born long when we found him, because his head and tail were still damp from birth. This is our first calf out of our white bull, Hero. Blondie had one two weeks before, but it was stillborn. This one appears perfect. All the other cows and steers and even Hero were circling around. Poor Blondie kept licking the new calf, missing her own. I think both she *and* Hillbilly are nursing that calf.

SIMPLE VERSUS SOPHISTICATED

I wonder how it is that simple men, against all logical expectation, reach the greatest depth of character.

I have known men—especially country men, and just as many women as men—who seem to know only a very few things, say, two or three. For them, everything starts at those few things and leads back to these few things. They don't worry about the starving natives in far places, they don't set out on Great Schemes to Save the Nation and World, or anything else. Such notions do not trouble them. They are too much absorbed and enchanted with A Few Things. They live altogether under the tutelage of a few simple ideas. They aren't looking for sophistication, and wouldn't know what it was if you told them. Yet these simple men seem to do better than the sophisticates. They seem to understand excellence, for instance, and pursue it relentlessly. It's as if the first and only idea in their heads in the morning is excellence, and then they go out all day and spend themselves wildly on excellence, even if it's only plowing a field or building a shed. And ever afterwards, you can tell where they've been. Their obsession identifies them in their work.

These same simple men seem to understand Love. Children identify it in them most readily, for it betrays itself as merriment, and children have a nose for merriment. Somehow or other, they are always the first ones to play with children, and the last ones that children disobey. Somehow, growing around that Love and decorating it is some not-to-be-gainsaid sternness, too, so that the same merriment that bids children to rejoice at the same time bids them obey. Simple men don't seem to raise their voices. They meet all the crosswise fallen world with calm longsuffering. Calm, not slow. Then again, you'd better hope they *don't* raise their voices, because they understand Wrath, too, and their Wrath won't fade until it reaches Punishment.

For simple men, belief and practice don't ever seem to split. In fact, you aren't even sure if they do believe anything because they probably don't or won't articulate it. They just *act*, because believing and acting are all one thing to them. They're too simple for doubt or duplicity. It wouldn't occur to them. I don't think such people want to be sophisticated. I think that God in creating them wrote on the tablet of their hearts, "Only one thing is needful: choose the good part." *O happy men*, created to steel us against the temptation of distraction!

In the end, the simple men are right. There is, after all, only one thing in the universe worth our notice, and even in its simplicity that one thing is quite complicated enough to busy us for all eternity.

THE TIME OF SINGING BIRDS

Birds make the difference. The weather may warm up, the crocuses may croak, and the daffodils daff, but until you get birds, it's only a quirky warm snap.

"For, lo, the winter is past," sings the lover in The Song of Solomon, "the rain is over and gone; The flowers appear on the earth; the time of the singing of birds is come, and the voice of the turtle[dove] is heard in our land. " Toward the end of January it warmed up here. It was spooky, sixty degrees with the wind kissing your cheek, all out of place in January. It stayed warm and stayed warm, and sure enough the daffodils along the split rail fence in our front yard came up. "Great," I thought, "only to get frozen when winter tires of fooling us."

Winter came back. It froze hard a few nights, then warmed up and in came a wet, slushy snow. My kids are fools for snow. They don't care if it's two flakes on the ground; they'll get out the sleds and pieces of plywood and cardboard and anything else that will slide, and they will play in the snow. I do not fight this. It's an obsession, I'll admit, but it beats hanging out in bars.

I confess, I wanted to get out there, too, but not too bad. *Wet* snow doesn't match my notion of fun, so I waited out the first day. That night it turned cold and snowed again, this time little dusty flakes. The wind blew from the west all night, and in the morning the deck screen outside my bedroom was frosted with snow. The wind had been busy all night, frosting everything in freaky ways. All the broom sage and every blade of grass and weed bent over, dusted with sugar. The sky was grey and the air seemed full, too, with frozen mist. Driving to the Top, I kept wanting to stop and gaze at this plain world transfigured.

That kind of snow never lasts long. It's too fragile, so you have to drink deep when the cup comes your way. I put in my reservation for the four-wheeler early in the day, planning toward dusk to kill two birds with one stone. I wanted to see the snow, and I wanted to see the results of all the tree cutting behind us. I left later than I had intended, and headed down the road behind The Top. Big trucks had been rumbling and wrestling log trailers out of there for weeks, and you could feel the thunder of the tree cutter eating pines all day long. I remembered how the road looked before, a path through deep pine woods muffled by the fallen needles.

Industrial efficiency has changed all that. I have christened their cutting machine "Jaws." Jaws is very hungry. Jaws lays the trees down in little piles, then his pal, "The Wrist," comes and loads them onto trailers. They are parked patiently everywhere, waiting hungrily. The truck drivers have the names of their towns painted on their doors, names close by like Waterloo and Decatur and Savannah, and also far-off names in Missouri and Iowa. Why do they all seem to be such nice fellows? Must be a requirement for driving trucks. All the application blanks have a box to check: "Nice Guy? ☐ Yes ☐ No." No check, no job.

This day Jaws and The Wrist and the truck drivers were all asleep or absent. The snow left everything too slushy to work. I drove along the road in a world new to my eyes. They really don't do such a sloppy job, these harvesters. But it's not what they cut down and take, but what they leave behind that looks so strange, a few twisted, scraggly hardwoods. They leave them standing, like the last few straggling, discouraged holdout hairs on a bald man's scalp. Cutting them would be a mercy.

Before, when all the pines still stood, you couldn't see the land. Now it billows as one broad ridge on either side of the road. At the end of the ridge the cut pines ended and the new ones began. The ridge dropped away into a holler. Hills hung off in the distance, shrouded in mist and mystery. This fork had taken me too far south and west, so I circled back, dreading what lay ahead. Susan and I had ridden this road late one afternoon last summer, and completed the long circle back around to the road to The Top. Where the pines ended at that time brought us to the head of a ridge where a huge clearcut section began. The road down off the ridge had been very badly eroded, so that I doubted the four-wheeler could really make it down without turning over on us at least once.

Down in the holler is a creek and an abandoned house. It was the house I dreaded now. Even with Susan's company, the place had a bad feeling about it, an uneasy foreboding. My friend Jim Kibler talks about the *genius loci*, the spirit of a place. Most spirits must be mute, because most of them don't speak to you at all. But in *some* places that spirit is not mute, and it speaks to you immediately—sometimes a welcome, and sometimes a warning. Something *good* lives at the Top. No other place in the world has ever warmed and filled me with such a feeling of safety and peace. Everything in the world is *right* there. I'm not the only one who has noticed it, either. Numerous people have commented on it.

Likewise, something *bad* lives in that house at the bottom of that dark holler. It *looks* right, but it's not. There flows a perfect, rock-bottomed creek thirty yards from the porch. Once you come down the hill and cross the creek, the road parallels the creek a couple of miles or more until it climbs the ridge again. A long ways up the road from the house, maybe a quarter mile or so, stands a log barn and another odd, high-built shack. Large tulip poplars grow along the creek—big trees, but not friendly. Bad rains during January had washed out roads all over two counties. The road looked sound in the advancing gloom, but when I looked off to my left I noticed that the rain had washed the ditch down to five or more feet. A picture flashed through my mind—the search party, beams of their flashlights piercing through the night, stalking through the woods. On the road, whirling blue and yellow lights of the rescue vehicles and police cars. Finally, a yelp of discovery as the lights converge on my broken body underneath the four-wheeler in that seven-foot ditch.

All the while my rationality was still humming along, reflexes alert and in charge. My fingers never lost their grip on the handlebars, my thumb kept its constant pressure on the gas, my eyes never left the road.

But my mind sure did.

I pressed on, rising out of the holler into darkness that by now had reached full night. The farther I drove out of that holler, the warmer it seemed, although my freezing fingers inside their gloves reminded me

I was only imagining the warmth. I turned right onto our road and leaned back into its familiar curves.

Ahead of me I saw headlights. As I got closer I realized they were *off* the road—my neighbor driving up from feeding his cows. When he stopped on the inside of his gate I sped on by, then remembered I had to tell him about finding one of his steers out on the road, which indicates a broken fence somewhere. The headlights of his truck made it feel like I had walked inside—so warm that I pushed my fur cap back off my head.

Next time I go down in that holler, I'm starting at *dawn*.

My duty done, I mounted the four-wheeler again and sped off into the darkness. As I drove along the ridge it was completely dark until I saw the first sign from the Top: the blue mercury vapor streetlight beside the barn. Next I saw Liberty's trailer, The Ponderosa, off to the right, still boxed by its Christmas lights. Ellen's brother Matt calls it a "little touch of Las Vegas right here in Wayne County."

The lights were on in the barn. Justin was standing in Boaz and Jachin's stall admiring his handiwork. He had spent all day making two stalls out of one. While he and Matt and Zach were working, they had built a fire in the paddock. The fire's warmth reached all the way into the barn. Suddenly, as I arrived, everyone else—Christian and Mercy and Zach and Matt—poured into the barn as they finished feeding. I left the four-wheeler right there. As I crossed the road towards the house, Liberty and Ellen pulled up, so I hitched a ride to the Shoe with them. I climbed into the back seat. Tucker (4) was already asleep in his car seat in the backseat, snug under a blanket.

In the crisp darkness the lights of the Top twinkled through the glass. This is my place—no, not the place I own, but the one place on the earth's face where I belong. Red dirt and chert, broken hills and hollers, maybe everybody in the rest of the world thinks it's poor and sorry as gully dirt, but I know what they don't. It's safe. And if there is a *genius loci* here, I know this much: it loves and protects me and mine.

HEY DIDDLE DIDDLE

Pigs, we are taught, have a gestation period of three months, three weeks, and three days. Back in October our new boar, Nelson, named for the admiral because he rides a sea of pigs, broke out of his pen and immediately entered upon his amorous duty. I counted ahead three months, three weeks, three days and figured Princess ought to farrow on February 8.

Princess, however, counts differently, at three months two weeks, and one day, or January 30. We could tell her time was coming and hustled her into the farrowing pen in time. She had eleven piglets, but one died. Farrowing always claims casualties.

Before we could get the other farrowing crate and pen built, Louise built herself a nest on the south side of Pig Holler and started farrowing. (Yes, sows *do* build nests, actually chewing up grass for the job.) This is her second litter and the second time she has pulled this trick. When I got there on Saturday morning, February 2nd, at about 11:30 a.m., she had five tiny, live piglets and one dead. After wandering to the top of the hill, she came down to resume possession of nest and piglets. As I watched her, she turned around and brought one trotter down square on the head of one piglet, and another square on his rear quarters.

Until you have seen a newborn pig, you have not seen anything beautiful or fragile. The super-fine hair that covers these tiny, trembling creatures shines like lustrous silver. Their eyes are hardly open and their little ribs shiver faintly as they breathe.

Until you have experienced a pig standing on your foot, you cannot appreciate what that piglet suffered. Louise is small, probably tipping the scales at only two hundred and seventy-five pounds, but the business end of that trotter is pointed. With a hoof. It brings a tremendous pressure to bear on a very tiny point. Like your foot. I know, because Princess, who weighs well over two seventy five, once stepped on my foot.

As soon as Louise stepped on that piglet, I counted him a casualty. I jigged around to try to make her move, all to no avail. I gave up. She had killed another one.

Then she suddenly shifted off the piglet. As I watched, the poor little piglet, so recently crushed, stood up, shook himself off, and commenced tottering around like his littermates.

I'm here to tell you, pigs are *tough*.

MARCH 2002

GARDEN PLANNING

You're probably getting ready for gardening. Here's a great source for pepper seeds. Anaheim, ancho, de arbol, elephant's trunk, espanhola, guajillo, chipotle, Mexican negro, serrano, cayennes, japones, pequin, scotch bonnet (habañero), suryamukhi cluster, tabasco, tepin—you name the pepper, Redwood City Seed Company has the seeds. They don't deal in peppers alone—they also have all kinds of vegetable and herb seeds, including hard-to-find items like arugula and radiccio. **Redwood City Seeds**, P.O. Box 361, Redwood City, CA 94064; (650) 325-7333; ecoseeds.com.

MOVING COWS

About two weeks ago it became evident we needed to move the cows. Since we heard Bud Williams at the *Stockman Grass Farmer* grazing conference last October, we concluded moving cows would no longer be torture. We had a protocol. First, we needed to separate the bulls from the cows. More precisely, in our case we had to separate the bulls from the cows and reunite the one big bull, Pilgrim, with the other bulls, since the last move had left him behind in a pasture with our milch cow, Molly, one other Highland cow, Ellie, and a Highland calf.

We did all right until Justin put the curse on us.

Susan fenced the cows into a corner with light electric fence, and set up a corridor into another paddock. We could separate them out one at a time and run them into another paddock. It worked like a *dream*. First we divided out the small bull calf, then Bonnie's bull. Bonnie's first calf was born two years ago and got fly-struck. We nearly lost him. He still has a bald spot on his back, but is otherwise a fine bull, hence his name, "Fly-struck." Then, with a burst of most uncharacteristic cooperativeness on his part, we culled out Hero, our young white bull.

Once the bulls were out, the remaining cows, calves, and steers, fifteen in all, must be led down the driveway, onto the road, and about four hundred more yards further to the pasture we call Sunrise (because it's on the east, of course). With a white bucket (sign of good eats, if you're a cow), I started calling them. They flooded out of the little paddock and down the drive. Unfortunately, they were somewhat distracted by the long grass along the drive, but I kept calling and they kept coming. They headed straight for our new dry-stone wall around the mailbox, skirted or leapt that, and moved on down the road in perfect order.

Maybe they all got to thinking about that new grass waiting for them, but they started *running*. Matt, Ellen's brother, took the bucket and ran ahead and the cows all quickly ran past me. We had blocked the fork in the road with our old Ford pickup on one side and my daughter Mercy on the other. All things considered, it went off pretty smoothly.

Then something happened. On the way back to move the other Highland cow, Ellie, a calf, and Pilgrim, Justin flung the curse. "This is easy," he said, "moving those other cows will be a snap." I could only look at him in horror, knowing what he had done.

Moving Ellie was a nightmare. She had been sharing the pasture with Molly the Milch Cow, who at some point before we acquired her had undergone a complete brainectomy. Her brain has never grown back. Her calf, Jeffrey (Susan calls him "Sir Loin") inherited all her intelligence. We no sooner had opened the gate to let Ellie and the highland calf out, than Jeffrey and Mollie ran through, too—in different directions. And then Ellie and her calf followed suit.

Matt and I already had our hands full with Pilgrim, eighteen hundred pounds of pure bull. We had to walk him out to the road and across into Sunset. Old good-natured Pilgrim was no trouble at all. Just get in front of him with a feed bucket and he's yours.

Sunset is a long, rectangular pasture we had previously divided off for strip grazing. We had four haystacks there, too, at one time, but the cows had long since annihilated them. However, the cross fencing was still there, so when we walked into the first paddock, Hero was still two paddocks away. But he was not inattentive. He started trumpeting and bellowing and pawing the ground. This is an impressive show to a stranger, but I knew the odds. Pilgrim outweighs Hero by about a half. We put down the cross fences and little by little moved Pilgrim into the same paddock with Hero.

Then commenced the fight. It was cool and the sky was clear, the sun just painting the western sky orange. Pilgrim, suave and cool, never let on anything was wrong. He and Hero stood about twelve feet apart, parallel but head to rump and rump to head. In spite of all Hero's bellowing, Pilgrim's expression never changed.

At last they swiveled around and locked horns—slowly, as if they were dancing. Hero scrabbled and strained with all his might. Pilgrim never moved, except to adjust his head and horns a little bit to keep Hero in one place. At last, as if tired of playing around, Pilgrim began to drive him back. Hero would lose his footing and struggle, but it did him no good. He backed off, then made a move to step back toward Pilgrim. Suddenly Pilgrim planted his feet, reared up his head in the air with a spread of horns fully six feet from tip to tip, and glowered at Hero. It was one of the most glorious displays I have ever witnessed.

I will never sell Pilgrim short again. He is all bull.

REASON TO CELEBRATE

First Louise disappointed us with a small litter and lost a piglet, so next it was Dot's turn. This was her first litter, so naturally she waited for the first cold snap to farrow. We had built a farrowing crate for her and filled it with hay. Seen end-on, a farrowing crate has steps on either side, which are really spaces for the piglets to get out from under Mama. Sows have a bad habit of rolling over on piglets.

But that wasn't Dot's problem. Her aim was so bad she couldn't even *hit* the farrowing crate. She had five piglets inside the crate, and six outside—who all died from the cold. Pigs, you see, don't withstand the cold very well, especially not little ones. That's why you always see them in a "pig pile" stacked up on top of each other. They're trying to keep warm. Anyway, Dot's piglets were about *half* the size of Louise's or Princess's. I thought they'd never make it. Now two weeks later they are all little butterballs (*okay*, lardballs), fully twice their birth size.

GRAIN DRILL

Justin put a free ad in the *Farmer's Exchange* looking for horse-drawn equipment. I guess they publish these free booklets all over the country. They take free classified ads but charge for display ads. I can promise you this: everybody in five states reads the thing. We got calls from two fellows in northeastern middle Tennessee, one east and south of Lebanon, and the other north of Carthage. The first one said he had a New Idea hay loader, *built in maybe 1950,* that had been completely rebuilt. The second had a grain drill that he believed was in pretty good working order.

Imagine that this constitutes no short trip for us. Any way you cut it they were nearly three hours away. So early one Saturday, ignoring the drizzle, Justin and I set out in our 1984 Ford pickup pulling a trailer. We took Justin's son Elijah with us. They'll put you in a concentration camp if you don't have him strapped down in a car seat, so we had to mount that unhandy thing in the front seat.

When we finally got to our first stop, the fellow took us out into the field to see the hay loader. True, he *had* rebuilt it. Four years ago. And then left it standing in the weather ever since. Both drive chains were missing. It was a wreck. I offered him a hundred dollars more than I thought it was worth, two hundred less than he thought it was worth, and he said he'd let it rot there for that. We cheerfully bid him *adieu* and headed for our next tryst. North through Carthage the land changes. The hills are straight up, six hundred to nine hundred feet high, and somehow they plant grass on them and graze goats and cows. Branches and rills pouring off the hills everywhere.

Our first sight of our goal was promising, that kind of tight place that says good things about its owner. Nothing fancy, just everything well kept. We met our man and he took us out to the old tobacco barn where he was storing the grain drill. It was an Oliver Superior, made in the mid-1950s. He had greased it and all the parts worked, although it was missing some of the sheet metal tubes. A grain drill is for planting grain or seed; the tubes drop a little dose of seed and fertilizer right by every one of the disk blades. The drill has a wooden box hopper with one side for seed and one side for fertilizer. Since few people wash implements after they use them, the remaining fertilizer usually eats up the sheet metal parts. However, this one still had most of the tubes intact. He wanted two hundred bucks for it.

Justin and I moved off to the side to discuss it. There was a decayed freight wagon out in the field. It was a wreck, but all the metal was there. The man said he'd throw in the wagon with the grain drill. That was enough to save my dickering honor, so we bought it. Our friend loaded the rotten wagon parts onto the pickup, and then we gingerly loaded the grain drill onto the trailer. Then we had to get the eight-hundred-pound drill off the trailer once we got to our destination.

On Monday Justin started digging around for parts and a manual. Lo and behold, he found a fellow in Illinois who had parts for the drill. He also found out that we had one of the *rare* six-foot models rather than the common eight-foot. No matter—we are not collectors. We just want it to plant grass.

LIBERTY LEARNS TO PLOW

It was about sunset, and Justin and I had been plowing a little addition to the garden, one man with the reins and one with the plow. Liberty stood off to one side jibing at Justin about how easy it was. Here's how easy it is: picture waterskiing behind the Queen Mary. About three thousand pounds of horse jumps forward. The plowshare bites into the ground. You have to hold the handles *up* to keep it in the ground, and push them right to go left and left to go right. Understand? Sound easy? Add the three thousand pounds of horsemeat. Add planted stones the size of pumpkins to knock the point of the plowshare up and out of the ground. Now do all this in an area almost big enough to swing a cat in.

So we gave Lib a turn behind the plow, just to see how easy it is. She has not volunteered since.

GREAT NEWS

As we were finishing up this *Moneychanger*, we paused for Saturday breakfast. I was eating in the first shift when Zachariah poked his head in the door: "Belle's had her calf and it's all white!"

We drove out to Blackberry Mecca, the briar-choked pasture where the cows are staying, and sure enough found Belle. Lying on the ground was a pure white calf—and friendly. When it turned around, we could tell it's a *heifer!* Belle is white, Hero our bull is white, and this is our *first* white calf.

We've got a real farm!

Praise God, there's always reason to celebrate.

I LOVE TENNESSEE

5:30 a.m. *Thunk!* Once again, the cardinal hits the window.

Our upstairs guestroom has a corner with a window on the east and a window on the south. Once when we lived in New Orleans on the third floor of an old house we had a similar arrangement and birds were always banging into the big picture windows, thinking they could fly all they way through, but these windows are not that big, so I don't think that's the problem. Susan had foot surgery on the 27th, and she was sleeping in the guest bedroom because it's very quiet. That's when she noticed this cardinal flying into the window.

Thunk! He hits the window with his beak. *Thunk!* Every three to five seconds he keeps hitting the window. Then he flies around the house and starts all over. But he's not trying to fly through the corner of the room. He just flies into the window beak-first, then flits back to the dogwood outside the window. *Thunk,* flit, *thunk,* flit.

Maybe the window acts like a mirror? Maybe he's seeing his own image and fighting that?

Thunk. There he goes again. Why would he keep on flying into the window? His beak-bashing threatens to become symbolic. And why *my* window?

SHEEP

Since our pastures have more than a few weeds and we don't want to douse everything with herbicides, we opted for sheep. Susan and I attended a grazing seminar back in February and ever since we found out that sheep will eat "forbs" that cattle won't eat, we've been looking for sheep. "Forbs" is ag-speak for "weeds."

But we did not opt for shearing. Katahdin (*Kuh-TOD-din*) sheep are "hair sheep," that is, they shed their wool once a year so you don't have to shear them. I am near-sighted, but I can see things the rest of my family, including my beloved wife, cannot see. I can see the future—well, I can see what the future will be if we do certain things, and I can see which way we want to go. I can see where the future will take us. I call that vision; they call it crazy. No prophet gets respect in his own country.

To make a long story short, we bought some sheep, over numerous objections. A neighbor, Tim Stulls, keeps sheep. His herd is mostly Katahdin, crossed with Dorper, another, stockier hair sheep from South Africa. Tim said he would lend us his trailer, so on Saturday we went to pick out some sheep.

First problem: sheep all look alike, I mean, *exactly* alike. "I want that one—no, no, that one. There he is, over there—or is that him?"

Next problem: no sheep were in sight. Not to worry. I was in no hurry. Tim said to his dog, Pat, "Look back!" and Pat raced up the hollow and disappeared over the hill. A few minutes later, heads, wooly heads, started bobbing up over the hill. Tim's dog Pat was a herding machine. Before you could say, "I want a Border Collie," Pat had herded all the sheep up in the barn. Susan picked one ewe with two very young white lambs about two weeks old, a red ewe with two older lambs, and six other young ewes from six to twelve months old.

You ought to know that *dogs*, and not sheep, are Tim's main business. Tim is a world-class trainer of sheep dogs, and sells them all over the country. They are not cheap, these trained sheep dogs. Border Collies. I was only one step removed from heaven.

It doesn't stop there. Tim raises miniature Yorkshire terriers. His front yard is fenced and he turns the Yorkies out in there, but they are not big enough to see over the grass. Looks like a herd of dustbunnies has attacked his front yard.

Tim has all sorts of runs full of dogs. There was this strange looking little black dog with a short, clubby fat tail, not much bigger than a Jack Russell terrier—an ill-favored beast, kept for hunting squirrels or coons or something rendered to me inedible by its possession of hands. We loaded all the sheep into the trailer. While we were on the other side talking to Tim, that blasted little dog reached into the trailer, pulled out one of those white lambs and killed it. Tim gave us our money back and we drove homeward with our now nine sheep. That little dog was still following us a quarter mile down the road. As you may have guessed, I am heavily editing all the comments about that dog, but I will say that there was not a thing wrong with him that a trip to a deep creek chained to a concrete block couldn't cure.

Once we got home we had to set up the electric fence for a sheep paddock. The greatest advantage of electric fencing is that you can string it *quickly*. Liberty reeled out the wire and I came along behind her running it into the holder on the plastic step-in posts. We strung (*straing?*) enough for a forty-five by sixty-five foot paddock in an hour, counting picking up rocks and trash and running six strands instead of the usual three.

And of course, although these sheep were trained to electric fence, ours was a *different kind* of electric fence, black and yellow wire, not white tape. When we unloaded them, first thing they did was run a lap. Then one stuck her head through the widest gap and leapt through. Two more ewes quickly followed, and two lambs. The lambs are so small they could slip through the loop in a key chain anyway. We had to string two more strands of wire.

Today the sheep have been in that paddock for six days. They have eaten down the weeds, but haven't touched the clover or fescue, which the cattle love. So far so good. Maybe we should have bought *twenty* sheep. Besides, if we go back to Tim's, he might be having a Border Collie sale.

PART OF LIFE

In the past two days I have found out that two friends have been diagnosed with cancer, in addition to a third diagnosed in February, Mr. W. I hate death.

I first met Mr. W. in November 2001, I think. He called to talk about silver, and from the moment I talked to him I knew this was going to be fun. When we found out we both knew the famous constitutional troublemaker, Tupper Saussy, Mr. W. said he'd have to come pay me a visit in person. "Come on!" I said.

Mr. W. brought a friend and they both brought their dinner in a paper bag, with a sandwich for me. That didn't do them a bit of good, however, because once we started talking two hours zipped away and we had forgotten all about dinner. When I found out Mr. W. had put three children through college and graduate school raising cows, I knew I'd have to go visit *him*. "Come on!" he said. So one sunny day Susan and I piled into the Swedish coffin (our black Volvo station wagon) and drove an hour and a half to his home. He had invited some other friends and his wife fixed sandwiches and we laughed and swapped jail and court-fight stories.

Part of our conversation centered on Tupper Saussy, who was living up on the mountain in Sewanee, Tennessee, in 1979. He wrote the book *Miracle on Main Street*, in which he explained that we have a constitutional and common law right to use only gold and silver for money. All we had to do was to demand our rights in court. For instance, if you got a traffic ticket, you just say to the judge:

> Your honor, I understand that the Constitution at Article I, Section 10, says that no state shall make anything but gold or silver coin a tender in payment of debt. I would like to pay this fine, but I don't know how

to because there isn't any gold or silver coin circulating. Could you tell me what is the money of account of this state so that I can pay this?

Whereupon a puzzled judge would pull out his constitution, see that you were right, then slap his forehead and say, "Leaping law books! He's right! There isn't any way I can make this man pay a fine with paper money. Bailiff, let that gentleman go and bother him no more."

Legions read Tupper's book. Legions went into court. Legions made the argument. Legions went to jail. A few walked away.

Along the way, legions found out how wily judges can be when backed into a legal corner—and how cruel. Legion others found that municipalities enforce many ordinances that strip us of common law rights and stand on legal footing even shakier than *fiat* money. When ordinary people began to fight those ordinances, they found out that "There's no tyrant like a *local* tyrant." Mr. W. had gone his rounds with the locals, and found out that it didn't matter how much law was on your side; they were always going to rule against you.

After dinner, the ladies went antiquing and Mr. W. and his brother-in-law and I went out to the farm. That day we entered one of those bubbles in time that banish all hurry and care, him showing me his operation and me drinking it in like new wine. I didn't get to see Mr. W. again until last week. He still looked awfully robust and lively for a man of seventy-nine, but the cancer was robbing him of his strength and energy, he said. His wife and daughter were there, and we sat in a comfortable room in the house his father had built in the 1920s. Once again, we entered that bubble in time. His father had been his best friend, he told me. He had sent Mr. W. to Vanderbilt, and Mr. W. had graduated as an engineer during World War II, attending school year-round for three years. We all laughed when he pointed out that the whole three years had cost his father $4,600!

Mr. W. told me about all the things he had worked at in his life, in his own businesses and for other people. He told a lot of what I call "miraculous escape" stories—you know the kind, when you tell them and then wonder, "How in the world did we do *that?*" Like sending three children through college and graduate school. He always had cattle to sell to pay his children's tuition. His daughter laughed at that: "Every time I had to pay tuition at Old Miss., my friends would ask me, 'How many cows did your daddy have to sell this semester?' I trumped them with, 'Well, at least mine's paid for. You've still got to pay back a loan!'"

I was fully engaged in that conversation, but something else kept tugging at my mind. It wasn't anything *said.* The most important things never are said, although they make themselves clear enough. What I saw was how much they loved each other. Some men spend their lives building monuments to themselves in bronze and stone and money. Others build their monuments in the hearts of those they love. Mr. W. had chosen the better part, and had passed it on.

Yesterday I called to find out how Mr. W. was doing, and his daughter told me: not well. I woke up this morning thinking about him. Herodotus tells in the first book of his *History* about how Croesus, proud of his wealth, had asked Solon if he had ever known a man happier than he was. Solon named "Tellus, a fellow-citizen of his own, and told him that this Tellus had been an honest man, had had good children, a competent estate, and died bravely in battle for his country." I suppose many people wouldn't recognize the congruence between "dying bravely in battle for your country" and "raising three children and putting them through college," but believe me, I do. Others, I'm sure, may recognize a patriot who fought the enemies within his *own* country.

You ask me why I love Tennessee so much? Because she raises up men like Mr. W. *God grant that she raises up more!*

NOT A PRODUCTIVE USE OF TIME

This spring, it seems, has been the time for me to face death. In March my elder sister Sandra had surgery for a malignant brain tumor. She recovered well, but last week was forced back into the hospital by further problems. Last Thursday Susan and I drove over to Memphis to visit her and her husband, Adam. She had difficulty talking, but otherwise did not seem badly affected. Last Sunday night she slipped into a coma.

Grief is for the living. My sister is a Christian woman with a hope firm enough to face death calmly, and her husband has the same hope. Their submission to God's will is wonderful to see. It seems her prayer is being answered. After she was told the doctors couldn't do anything else for her, she told Adam that if the Lord was going to take her, she prayed he would take her quickly.

As we left, Sandra got up to take a walk in the hall. We walked on down to the elevator. The elevator alcove was offset from the hall, so I lost sight of them. After a moment I stepped back to catch one more glimpse of them. They stood in that lonely, empty, shiny hall facing each other. Sandra leaned forward and they touched foreheads—a picture of everything terrifying and lovely in life.

I would appreciate your prayers for Sandra and Adam van Drimmelen.

This is the same sister, by the way, who was diagnosed with cancer eleven years ago this summer. After a mastectomy she went to Dr. Nicholas

Gonzalez in New York, who practices a nutritional and cleansing approach to cancer. She improved very much under his regimen, and stayed with him for several years. We maintain an interview with Dr. Gonzalez on our website. You can reach **Dr. Gonzalez** at his office, 36 East 36th Street, Suite 204, New York, NY 10016; (212) 213-3337; dr-gonzalez.com.

GRAVIOLA

When I sent an e-mail to a number of friends asking them to pray for my sister, one wrote back to inform me about *graviola*. The tree grows in the Amazon rainforest, and has shown exceptional anti-cancer activity in some studies, although it has not yet been researched in double-blind studies. You can buy graviola with six other natural ingredients in capsules under the brand name "N-tense" from Rain-Tree Nutrition at www.rain-tree.com/graviola.htm. Judge for yourself.

AGRARIAN CHALLENGE II

On June 26 we will drive up to the Nashville airport to pick up the folks coming in for Agrarian Challenge II. For the next three days they will work with us side by side here on the farm. From the phone calls and questions I've gotten, maybe Susan was right about my first announcement. Maybe I made it sound too harsh—like too much work. We will not, in fact make you dig postholes with only a sharp wooden stick and bent spoon. We will be doing all the things we have to do to keep a farm going—feeding animals, harnessing and working horses, cutting and loading hay, working in the garden, picking blackberries, you name it, and you can watch or work, as it pleases you. Of course, those who do not work shall only eat white bread—*Whoops!* Just kidding. Two hundred dollars per person covers all meals and expenses and we'll give you a pair of work gloves.

BODACIOUS HOEDOWN

Mark your calendars now for Labor Day Weekend. That's when the League of the South and the Balm of Gilead Trust will be sponsoring our next Bodacious Hoedown at the Top of the World Farm, right here just a few miles from the Crossroads of Dixie. There will be draft horse and other exhibitions, Saturday night a period ball (prior dancing knowledge not necessary), and then on Sunday morning a bodacious worship service.

SHEEP HANDLING

I wrote you last month that we had bought some sheep, a.k.a The Stupidest Animals in the World. My opinion has not changed in the last thirty days, and working them didn't improve it.

Bear in mind that a grown sheep, weight about a hundred pounds, can jump five feet flatfooted, straight into the air, hover thirty seconds, and then disappear into the distance faster than your four-wheeler can drive. Electric fence doesn't bother them. At all. Not even five-strand electric fence. Sheep are covered with insulation.

Nonetheless, we had to work them, because they are bad to get foot rot (imagine athlete's foot that takes off your toes.) Also, you have to clip their weird hooves.

In the picture you can see Justin, Susan, the sheep, and me behind our makeshift sheep trap. We bent a pig panel inside our small trailer, tied down another on top, and then spring loaded one for a back door. We held two other pig panels end to end butting up to the sheep trap, and herded them right in—except for Lucille and her two lambs (My grandson Tucker is holding one in the picture). Lucille just jumped the fence, and the lambs went through it, and they all took off. But we still had sheep in the trap.

Trimming sheep hooves isn't a bit more trouble than trimming the toenails on a six hundred pound gorilla, except that sheep don't bite. In the picture you see three of us holding a sheep while Justin trims her hooves. Then you have to treat the hooves with Coppertox. None of this actually hurts the sheep, but that makes no difference to a sheep. Frenzied panic is its middle name.

Once we had treated the five or so sheep from the trap, we had to go run up Lucille and her lambs. This I found to be no more trouble than doing free-hand amputations under heavy artillery and machine gun

fire. The strategy was to run the sheep from one end to the other of a quarter-mile pasture, veering as much as possible from side to side. Most animals can be successfully herded in the same way. Stay back at about a thirty-degree angle behind them, and move up slowly, veering off in the opposite direction from the way you want them to turn. The closer you get, the more pressure you put on them, so you don't want to hurry them (unless you enjoy running after animals). Eventually you run them into a barn, where they will be trapped. Once they are inside the barn, you trap them in a stall and pick them off one by one.

How successful this strategy was you can judge from the picture of four bewildered men trying to corner a single sheep. Success is shown in the next picture, where the three concentration camp victims—*Whoops!* Those are just my skinny sons—hoisting Lucille up onto Christian's shoulders, much the *second* best way to move a sheep.

I've been trying to explain something to the Higher Up. Chasing sheep, herding sheep, catching sheep, and carrying sheep is not a productive use of time. This is why people keep sheep dogs, especially trained Border Collies, and not five miles from here live cages full of 'em. Yet here we are, still wastefully carrying sheep around on our shoulders.

PIGS IN CLOVER

We had nineteen piglets left and Susan had promised them to our friend Charlie Ritch down near Hartselle, Alabama, about two and a half hours away. Because we had to drive to Memphis unexpectedly to see my sister, the only time we could take them down to Charlie was late Wednesday afternoon.

The easiest way to catch small pigs is to feed them, then snatch them up by the back legs one by one as they crowd around the trough. Susan and I asked Zach and our friend Bill, who is staying with us lately, to get the food ready and take it over to Princess's pen and wait for us to come load them up.

Alas, the request was heard, but not acted upon. Rather than waiting for us, Zach and Bill charged the piglets and by the time we got there they were all stirred up and running from section to section of the pen. The only thing that can run faster, and zig-zag more, than a sheep is a pig. With four of us chasing them around their pen, it took only about thirty minutes for Princess and two of the piglets to break out. Seven we managed finally to trap.

Don't forget that these pigs weigh thirty to fifty pounds each. When you capture one, you have to deadlift him over the fence by the hind legs, then swing him up about chin high over the side of the pickup truck and into a wire cage. Since pigs never go easily anywhere, they are screaming all the way. After the last debacle—two pigs breaking straight through a joint in the fence—I just left them running around in the pasture eating clover with Princess, and went on to Louise's and Dot's pens.

By this time I am fairly insistent on following my own prescription for catching piglets: Zach is to fetch a landing net for fish. This goes fine till about the third one of Dot's piglets it lands on. This one rips right through the net like it is wet spaghetti. Re-tie the net. Christian appears, who, whatever his other shortcomings, is faster than a greased pig. Finally, one by one they fall prey to him, Zach, and Bill. I get the best job—deadlifting the pigs over the fence and slinging them up into the pickup, with Susan standing on the pickup to help grab and stuff them into the wire cages.

What a mess. By the time we had finished, our boots were covered in pig manure, which, by the way, is *permanent*. Oh, I suppose you can get the smell off with nitric acid or aqua regia, but we didn't have any of that. We just had a tight schedule and a 1984 Ford pickup full of pigs. Susan and I hopped in and headed down the road, making sure to roll down all the windows first.

By the time we bumped over the gravel roads all the way to St. Joseph, I had to get something cool to drink. Besides, the truck needed gas. Just as I stepped out to gas up, I discovered that no less than three and perhaps as many as six pigs were subject to *car-sickness*. I looked around the gas station to make sure nobody I knew could smell—*make that see*—me.

Pumping gas frantically, I watched through the plate glass windows as Susan entered the gas station. I half expected to see people come screaming out of the station, but both of the brave (and apparently unable to smell) clerks stood by their cash registers. We jumped back into the pick-up as quickly as possible and roared off toward Hartselle. When we arrived, without any ceremony to speak of, Charlie and I dumped the pigs one by one out of the truck and into his pen. No sooner had they hit the ground than they were munching on clover. You can't keep a good pig down. You can't disguise his smell, either.

TAME COWS

We've had weird weather. Before this year I had never noticed just how squarely we sit on the line where the climate changes. On April 11 we left here to drive down to Mississippi to have the newsletter printed. The dogwoods around our house had just *barely* begun to unfold. We hit the Natchez Trace, and by the time we got to the Alabama line (about the length of half a county), the dogwoods were all in full bloom. The further south we went, the more obvious the difference was. When we got back, I drove into Lawrenceburg a couple of days later, and all the azaleas and dogwoods *there* were far advanced of ours, yet there can't be three hundred feet difference in our elevation. At the edge of spring, however, it makes that much difference. We're only seven hundred feet above Memphis, and at nearly the same latitude, but still we have far cooler weather, and summer nights that usually call for covers.

All that clover we've been planting for the past two years decided to come up all at once this spring. Y'all may remember that I am near-sighted and none too sharp of hearing, but I can smell a rose at six hundred yards, so spring constantly intoxicates me. First comes the clover, then the faint, faint piquant smell of blackberry blooms. After that there is the sharp-sweet smell of rambling roses, then *wham!* The honeysuckle hits. Underneath it all is—I promise I'm not making this up—the pale, sweet, green smell of new vegetation.

The cows meantime believe they have died and gone to heaven, knee deep in clover. People complain about how troublesome moving cows can be, but now they're so well trained to my call that I can get them from one paddock to another in four minutes or less. In fact, they got away from me the other day and Billy Gobble, the man who is building Liberty and Johnny's house, hopped the fence to help me. After trying to herd them for a minute or two, he looked over at me disgustedly and said, "Those cows are too *tame* to herd."

CHRISTIAN FUNERALS

On Friday, May 17, my sister, Sandra van Drimmelen passed away. Only eight days before, we had visited her. Except for the impairment to her speech, she had seemed well. That next Sunday evening she slipped into a coma. She had a type of brain tumor that is both very subtle and very sudden. After MRIs in July and August had failed to show anything, in March they removed a tumor nearly as big as a baseball. An acquaintance of mine knew that my sister had fought against cancer since 1991 and conquered it. He remarked that apparently Dr. Gonzalez' nutritional therapy didn't work. I told him that was the wrong inference. First, this cancer was unrelated to the first occurrence in her breast. Second, the other three women who were operated on the same day were all dead two years later. Sandra survived eleven years. That doesn't sound like failure to me. Orthodox medicine might envy such a record of "failure."

Sandra wanted to be buried at the Palestine Cemetery near Pearson, Arkansas. My father and my mother's family are all buried there. Monday after the funeral service in Memphis we—my elder brother, Stan, my younger sister Virginia, several of my children and theirs, and Sandra's family—caravanned through Arkansas past Heber Springs to Palestine.

I hate death, but I love Christian funerals. Before our eyes they play out what Paul writes in I Thessalonians 4:13, 14: "But I would not have you to be ignorant, brethren, concerning them which are asleep, that ye sorrow not, even as others which have no hope. For if we believe that Jesus died and rose again, even so them also which sleep in Jesus will God bring with him."

The hope of resurrection changes everything.

FREIGHT TRAIN

For quite some time we have been looking for a hay-loader. Hooked up to the back of a sixteen-foot wagon, it can vacuum up all the hay and load it up on the wagon. Well, it doesn't really *vacuum*. "Forks" would be a better word. Think of a big tray, twelve feet long and eight feet wide, canted up on wheels so that it empties out onto the wagon towing it. Mounted over the tray are nine sticks that slide back and forth, powered by a cam geared off the wheels. There are metal forks on the sticks, which the cam lifts, then pushes up. The forks catch the hay and keep pushing it up the trough until it pours out onto the wagon. This thing cuts haying time by a factor of *five*. That's why we were so eager to buy one.

We had advertised for a hay-loader and driven hours only to find disappointment. Hot on the trail of another prospect, Justin and Wright left here on May 22 to drive nearly to Sparta, three hours away. They didn't get back until nearly dark, but piled up behind them on the trailer was a hay-loader. It was made in 1947 and had been put up in a barn some forty-five years, but it still worked like a champ. Almost. The first time they put it to work some of the sticks broke—dry-rotted. They cobbled together a fix, and by Friday were building a huge haystack. The horses seemed fine with this new setup, pulling the wagon and hay-loader attached without batting an eyelid.

WHAT FREIGHT TRAIN?

The first week in June we had friends staying with us. They are building a house nearby. We had a great time (and twenty-five people at supper for a week!), but when they left, I think they took all the luck with them. Monday morning I threw my back out in the most humiliating way. Headed for the chiropractor, I drove over to the Top, where I have an office in the back of Justin's farmhouse. I was talking to a customer on the telephone when I heard what sounded like a freight train.

"That's odd," I thought, "we don't have any railroad tracks around here, much less freight trains." I looked out the window just in time to see the tops of the horses' ears fly by, followed closely by the hay-loader at a speed I estimated at forty-five miles per hour.

"Gotta go," I mumbled, dropping the phone. "Runaway."

By the time I ran outside, the horses had stopped, or, more precisely, the wooden fence across the road had stopped the horses. They had broken out the top slat, after driving the wagon tongue about two inches deep into an oak tree. The wagon tongue was broken in two, locking the wagon in place. The wagon and hay-loader had come to rest squarely across the road. Since it had been in gear when the horses ran away, every stick but one was broken. One wheel was off the loader, both hubs were missing, and parts were scattered around freely.

Job's words flashed across my mind: "The Lord gave, and the Lord hath taken away."

The origin of this catastrophe and names of the guilty are better left undiscovered. Suffice it to say that it arose from anger and fear, and the blessed aftermath was, I trust, the greater sanctification of the wrongdoers. Either that, or we'll have to shoot 'em.

Of course, that ate up my day because while the boys were straightening up that mess, I still had to go to town, but now I had to visit more than the chiropractor. After several other errands, I drove out of town six or seven miles to the Amish man from whom we bought the sixteen-foot

Hochstettler wagon. I knew I could get another tongue from him, and hoped I could get the hay-loader sticks as well. The Amish all use them.

Arriving at dinnertime, I could only wait for him to finish dinner. Amish don't get in a hurry. When he finally entered the shop, I held up the stick (1¾" x 1" x 10 feet) and said, "I need some of these. Can you help?"

The Amish man shook his head. "I don't have any wood." Since there seemed to be an abundance of the same stacked all around, I shook my head in wonder. "All I have is green. I didn't put up enough last year."

"What kind of wood do y'all use?"

"Poplar." I understood that. It's light, tough wood.

"What about oak?"

He shook his head. "It sags, just like green poplar. If it sags, the loader won't work because the forks drag on the tray."

I put that on hold just a minute and negotiated for a new wagon tongue. Then I went back to it. I didn't care how many roadblocks fell in my road; I was going to move them today. "Those original sticks were pine. Could we get any of that anywhere?"

"Lumber Company in town has some C grade pine that might work."

"Okay, what if I go and get the pine, and bring it back? Could you have the sticks done by Thursday?"

Long pause and reflection. "I guess I could."

I roared off in my 1984 F-150 pickup, headed for Lawrenceburg. When I got there the clerk assured me they had no C grade pine. *But* (this was the first break of the day) he would go with me out to the yard to see if we could find some knot-free 2 x 8s. We found four of them. I ran them back up to the Amish man, and got home a little before three. Okay, it didn't eat up the whole day, but what was left was only the rind.

Sanctification doesn't come cheap—or fast.

DON'T BE SURPRISED

The next day, Tuesday, the phone rang about 6:30 a.m. It was Ellen.

"Don't be too surprised when you come over here this morning. Somebody ran off the road last night and took out half the lattice fence and the barbed wire behind it."

That left me bewildered, since the fence stands on a perfect straightaway. The lattice fence is about nine feet tall. The boys spent nearly two weeks building it last year. The phone call didn't ease things much, once I saw the fence. Somebody had driven *down* the fence line, knocking out five or six uprights, several of them set in concrete, made kindling out of the lattice and cross-members, then drove through the barbed wire fence into the hayfield, necessitating stretching anew about two hundred feet of barbed wire fence. Car parts and fragments lay all around.

I thought my plate was about full when about ten o'clock the boys discovered the probable cause of the wreck: they found Sister's body out in the field. I guess she had been crawling toward the pond for water after she was hit. Sister was our Great Pyrenees out of Cleo's first litter. I hate to lose her. She was such a beautiful dog. Justin and Wright dug a grave back up on the hill, under the trees. We all went out there to bury her, and cover her grave with rocks. Later I wrote an e-mail to a friend:

> Today the need for peace has grown very great.
>
> Sister is buried, and with her all the joy and hope that she gave, the thrill to watch her stretch when she ran, the sweetness of her nodded greeting. Buried next to Kaiser and the others who have fallen victim to nature and the automobile.
>
> The malefactor disappeared, unpunished and unrepentant—further dissatisfaction.

JULY 2002

JACK GOES COURTING

Jack the Dalmador has disappeared now. Jack is not only a fighter; he is also a lover. Occasionally, Cupid beckons and Jack disappears. The last time, he returned looking like he had been stuffed through a sausage grinder. He had big plugs taken out of his hide everywhere, and couldn't walk on one of his legs for about four weeks. All he could do was lie up on the porch and groan, whacking the floor with his tail. I sprayed him with Mild Silver Protein, but that was it. Jack has already been hit twice and suffered two broken legs. Our thirty dollar puppy long ago became Thousand Dollar Dog. Jack's medical insurance has run out, according to the lady who insures our dogs (Susan).

Bear, our Australian Shepherd-Lab cross, is neither a lover nor a fighter. He is a strutter. Whenever anybody walks out the front door, he grabs something, anything, from a tin can to a log, in his mouth and struts with it. Bear used to accompanying Jack on his jaunts, but as a sensible dog, gave it up. Bull, our rat terrier, went off with Jack this last time. Why, I'm not sure, since anything big enough to whip Jack would consider Bull no more than an *hors d'oeuvre*. Bull has returned, but Jack remains missing. This worries me, because Jack, for all his follies, is still my dog, and he has taught me a lot.

He'll come back. He'll be skinny, and have plugs of skin and hair missing and new holes in his ears, but he'll come back. He always does.

BULLFIGHT

We have after much labor established strong stands of red clover in our pastures. Trouble is, without a lot of bees the clover doesn't yield much seed. There aren't many bees left, even out in the country where we live. Heavy agricultural pesticide use has killed lots of them, and about ten years ago the *varroa* mite, imported from Asia, invaded Tennessee. It killed about eighty per cent of the bees in two years. The mite can be controlled, but you have to keep after them.

Thus in need of bees, what to my wondering eyes should appear but an ad in the *Farmer's Exchange*. A fellow north of Chattanooga was trying to sell sixty or seventy hives of bees and all his equipment. My interest was piqued, but I had no idea what I would be buying.

Providentially, about that time I met Randall Staggs. Randall's son-in-law, Junior, was working framing up Liberty's house. He and Justin got to talking, and he mentioned that his father-in-law kept bees, and the long and short was that Justin bought some honey and made a new friend. And I met Randall.

Randall classifies himself as a "hobby beekeeper."

Personally, I class anybody who owns more than a couple of hives as "professional," let alone somebody who owns fifty, has been beekeeping since he was six, and is a third-generation beekeeper. Randall sandbags a lot. He energetically drove up to Altamont, about three hours away, where a Mennonite had the bees for sale. Randall and I worked out an arrangement where I would take a dozen hives and the equipment he didn't need. Randall negotiated a *very* favorable deal.

My mind began to work on *how* we would get sixty-two hives of bees from east Tennessee to us. No worry, Randall and his two boys know how to move bees. They drove two trucks with trailers (one a long cattle trailer). When we got there we loaded and loaded and loaded equipment. Then came time to load the bees. You have to wait until late in the day so that the bees all have a chance to return to the hive, else you leave them behind. Bees, as you might expect, do not move voluntarily. Randall and his sons suited up in bee suits while a friend and I watched from a safe distance. They just tacked a screen onto the front slot where the bees come out, lifted up the hives, and loaded them onto the trailer. We had to go to two different beeyards to get a dozen hives, but we did. This sounds easy, until you know that within minutes of donning it, a beesuit's internal temperature reaches three hundred degrees.

By the time we got back to the Top it was 10 p.m. and full dark. Justin, Zach, and Wright came out to help us unload. Randall's sons, Brad and Devin, hadn't arrived yet. We set up the stands and then were faced with the bees. Long acquaintance has left Randall somewhat *blasé* about dealing with bees. My sons, on the other hand, regard any flying stinging insect as a natural enemy meriting summary execution. They had to be *coaxed* into unloading the bees, even with the screens still on the ports. Every hive had a few stragglers clinging to the front. We had unloaded eight hives before Justin got stung. Zachariah quickly learned the principle of dealing with bees: do not mash the bee. Stand still. Actually, those were the only casualties. Randall's sons, Brad and Devin, showed up and suited up to take the screens off the hive entrances. Now Randall told me something interesting about bees. In transit, once they start moving they all hold on to each other. However, as soon as you stop, they begin to want out of the hive. We were soon to see what that meant.

Randall ordered all the lights out, because lights, even flashlights, attract the bees. At this point also they are *not* very rational or sweet tempered—"irritated" comes closer, or maybe "aggressive." No, downright *liverish*. By a flashlight I caught a glimpse. No sooner were those screens removed than a *carpet* of bees poured out of that hive and *covered* the front of it. I couldn't tell for sure, but it looked like they were bees with an attitude.

Randall told us it would take them a couple of days to settle down. First thing they do is look for water, and the nastier the better (nourishment for the brood). Their eating habits are pretty nasty, too. I saw them eating things I thought no self-respecting bee would eat. In fact, flies might think twice about it, but that's nature I guess. They calmed down pretty quickly. Now the air of our instant beeyard is filled with bees all day, but this story is not over by a long shot.

We still have to rob the bees.

RAINMAKER

I have figured out how to make it rain: cut hay. If that fails, just windrow the hay. We had a dry spell through most of June, and the clover I kept hoping that some rain would revive just got drier and drier. So we cut the hay, and it rained the next day. But not bad—not enough to ruin it. Next day Justin cut the rest of the hay, then windrowed it. That did it. In came a frog-strangling rain.

However, the hay did make great compost in the garden.

THE GREAT BULLFIGHT

We needed to move our cattle into Sunrise pasture, but couldn't leave them there without any shade. A small disagreement, let us say, divided us while we worked on a shade for the cattle. Unwilling to listen to reason or to me any longer, Susan and Wright got into the truck and drove down to the logging road to turn around. There they spied five heifers and a Black Angus bull running down the logging road that runs along the back of the big pasture we call Boaz. The Black Angus couldn't leave well enough alone. As he walked along the fence he taunted Pilgrim, our red Scotch Highland bull.

Susan and Wright tried to herd the strays west down the logging road, because they thought they belonged to our neighbor there. At length it dawned on them that they belonged to our eastern neighbor, so they began trying to turn them. Remember that Pilgrim weighs about eighteen hundred pounds, but like all Highland Cattle he is not very tall. He is also extraordinarily gentle—generally. At last, however, Pilgrim got fed up with that Angus bull's taunting. He walked through four strands of barbed wire fence like they were butter. You could almost hear him mumbling to himself, "I'm not taking any more lip from *this* sissy." If he had had sleeves, he would have been rolling them up.

About fifteen feet in front of Susan and Wright, Pilgrim lit into that Angus. It didn't last long. Pilgrim easily pushed him down into the ditch. The Angus came back, and Susan was afraid Pilgrim would just twist his head and his nearly four-foot hornspread would catch that Angus in the neck. But Pilgrim just pushed him back into the ditch. Then, with a look of disgust, he just turned around and strolled back through the fence.

Meanwhile, our young bull Flystrike had been watching, and thought it was now his turn. *Whoops*—he weighs about a thousand pounds *less* than Pilgrim. As is usual with cows, once things start going wrong, they go wrong fast. The five cows with the Angus bull disappeared into the woods beside the logging road, and our Highland cows started pouring out into the road behind Flystrike. One of our steers disappeared over the eastern ridge while Susan and Wright frantically herded cows back through the fence. Then Wright ran after the moving bull fight. Flystrike and Black Angus pushed back and forth, about evenly matched, headed east on the logging road toward Ella Gallaher Road.

There they met Justin, who started throwing rocks at the bulls to break it up. But his rocks kept bouncing over the Angus and hitting Flystrike in the head. The last rock was a little big, and smacked Flystrike right between the eyes. It nearly coldcocked him, and distracted him long enough to give the Angus time to turn and run. Fight broken up, Justin took the truck to go get the fencing equipment.

More than a quarter mile away, I couldn't see all this happening. I could only tell cows were out. We have trained our cows to come when we call. Somebody recently asked me how I did that, and I explained, "I call them in German. That intimidates them." Actually, I do call them in German, but nothing intimidates them. (Anyway the German and the Scots dialect words for cow sound the same.) You just have to call them and feed them right afterward, and after about a week of training, believe me, they come a-running. So from where I was I started calling, and the Highland steer that had disappeared over the hill came running out of the woods and went back into the pasture nice as you please. Susan and Wright then herded Flystrike back in, him shaking his head all the way.

The comedy of errors had not yet ended. Because it was blazing hot, Susan volunteered to trek the half mile to Liberty's to bring back water for Wright and her while they were waiting for Justin to come back. Upon her return she found no Wright. He had disappeared chasing after Justin, who had come back with the truck but instead of turning down the logging road had driven down Ella Gallaher a half mile and parked. Then he hiked through the woods to tell our neighbors that their cows were out. The vision of Susan still standing next to the break in the fence without any tools never danced in his head. By this time from afar I had seen Justin drive down the road. Assuming that he had gone chasing our cows, I went after him, stumbling across the cutover, following the cow tracks and feeling much like Davy Crockett—or Marlon Perkins at least.

While I'm still in the woods, here come our eastern neighbors, Doyle and Diane Lopp, roaring up the logging road on their four wheelers looking for their cattle. Justin *had* alerted them. Susan directed them into the woods and headed up the mean hill toward the road on foot for the fourth time. At the top of the hill she spies Justin and Maxie Lopp in Maxie's truck. But where is our truck with the fencing equipment? By now it is getting dark fast. I was still in the woods, so I didn't hear exactly what she said to them. Mostly, I'm glad I didn't. I'd bet she was a mite peevish by then.

Next thing we're buying is walkie-talkies.

AUGUST 2002

Now we had to put the hay-loader back together. We were ready to put the hubs back on the wheels, but when I looked at them they were just filthy. I took some kerosene and started to clean them off. That's when I discovered the difference between today's work and yesterday's. The entire *inside* face of the hub was painted. The paint was so perfect that I couldn't even scrape it off with my screwdriver. Think about painting that carefully a part that *nobody would ever see*. Nor was there a single burr on any edge of any part. Neither was any part worn. Apparently they fit together so perfectly that after fifty years they were still like new.

I'm here to tell you, they do *not* make them like that anymore. Those folks had never heard of "planned obsolescence."

THE NOBLE SWINE

We knew that all of our sows were expecting; we just weren't expecting them to all farrow at the same time. Late on Monday I was out mowing when Zachariah passed by and hollered, "We've got some new pigs!"

"Where?"

"In the pine thicket."

"How many?"

"I counted fifteen."

A couple of months ago we moved all thirteen pigs from Pig Holler, which they had pretty well demolished, over to Sunrise, which is separated from the rest of the farm by a road. Imagine a long rectangle, and you'll get close to the layout. It's about five acres divided into four paddocks. The southernmost paddock was a wreck. Not only was it overgrown with briars and blackberries and infested with fire ants, somebody had also tried to build a pond there. They had scraped off all the topsoil and left it in a pile, liberally sprinkled with car tires, tractor tires, pallets, and what not. That left a pasture growing rocks and gravel. Another pile of tires and wood was in the front corner. The pond hadn't ever sealed, so every time it rained, it only drained to a swampy mess of cattails. Sound hopeless?

Never say "hopeless" to the noble swine. Land clearing runs in their blood.

We moved the pigs to Sunrise, and two months later they have turned over every rock, cleared most every briar, and sealed the pond. Those pointy trotters, carrying two hundred to three hundred pounds of hog, can bring a *lot* of pressure on a piece of ground. Of course, the pigs were in—I have to say it—*hog heaven* as soon as they saw that pond. Wallowing in mud comes as naturally to a pig as lying to a politician.

Right after Zachariah had delivered the porcine birth announcement, Justin and Wright rode up on Beulah and Hep, our Percheron fillies. They wanted to walk them to cool them off, so we all five headed down the road to Sunrise to view the new pigs. There they were, in the dust under the pine boughs, *fifteen* of the scrawniest, cutest piglets you ever saw—black and white, red and white, and plain pink. We couldn't agree which two sows had delivered these two litters, or even if they were two litters or one. While we were arguing, one tiny pink pig emerged from the woods at the edge of the paddock and headed downhill toward the pond sixty yards away. I retrieved him and took him back to the others. When I walked down to the pond I saw something awful.

"Justin, look at that. We've got a dead pig." There on the dam, just along the water's edge, lay what appeared to be a dead sow. However, when I walked around to get a better view, I realized she wasn't dead at all, but had just given birth to a little piglet. When Justin and I got onto the dam above her, we could see that she had already delivered and lost one little piglet, floating face down. The other was in the mud and water, still attached by its umbilical cord. We poked at the sow to get her up, which she abruptly did, jerking free from the piglet. Justin picked him up and I followed the sow. She stopped. We stopped. It doesn't pay to push a sow in labor. Justin turned his head to holler at Wright and plop! Out drops another piglet.

"J.R.! Look at that! Another one!" I yelled.

"Where?" he said, "I turned my head and missed it!"

Now we had *two* piglets and a sow to herd. This was her first litter, and she hadn't done what sows usually do—spend a day chewing up straw and grass to make a nest. We tried to drive her into the pine thicket where the other two sows had delivered their pigs. We put the piglets up there, hoping to entice her.

That didn't work. She worked herself all the way across the paddock to the electric fence on the other side, and began scratching around in some tall grass, obviously nesting. She lay down and suddenly *another* piglet appeared. Justin retrieved the other two, sneaked up on her back side, and dropped them onto her. All three piglets began searching for a nipple to nurse. They are so hardy, so tough, it takes your breath away.

Susan pulled up with a camera, eager to take some pictures. About then it dawned on Justin that there were probably more piglets around. We went looking in the mound o' tires and behind the dam. Sure enough, I spotted two little ones behind the dam. We figured that the sow we had chased had started farrowing there, heard the call for evening chow, and tried to make it to the road when labor pains caught her crossing the dam. I took those two back up the hill to the sow where she was still producing more piglets, and Justin went to inspect the thicket on the mound o' tires . . .

where he found and quickly escaped a belligerent sow in person, guarding eight more piglets. At this point the full count was about twenty-eight piglets. I say "about" because it is nearly impossible to count piglets. Always shivering, they crowd together in a "pig pile" to stay warm, and they're always squirming, so a snout-count is tough.

In the morning we returned to do *something* about that sow. Pigs get sunburned. If we left her out in the open where she had delivered those piglets, the sun would kill them. Pigs, however, are *not* reasonable about their health, and recently postpartum sows are notoriously unreasonable about everything, especially about *your* moving their piglets. Morning found her with *eight* piglets. We drew off the sow when we fed the others, and quickly scooped her piglets into a bucket. These we tucked away in what seemed to us a very nice nest in the thicket. It seemed to *us* a very nice nest, but who knows how a sow thinks. Herd as we might, we couldn't get her near that thicket. We finally went back and got more corn and poured it out on the ground next to the mound o'tires. That got them all up, and we left, hoping the sow would find her piglets once we left. And by the way, before we left Justin found another sow giving birth behind the dam. He counted eight more, bringing the total up to thirty-nine.

Any of y'all looking to buy a feeder pig?

ROBBING HIVES WITH RANDALL

Friday two weeks ago I got up at 2:30 a.m., stumbled into my clothes, and drove over to Randall's house. I had promised Randall that I would drive up to Altamont to help him rob the fifty hives we had left up there— three hours away. "Robbing" is bee-speak for harvesting honey out of the hives. With Randall in one pick-up and his son Brad and son-in-law Junior in another, we set out. In preparation, I had bought my very own bee suit with veil and hive tool and smoker (to puff into the hive for calming the bees). The sun was still yawning and stretching when we arrived at the first bee yard. Once you get into your bee suit and it reaches its three hundred degree internal operating temperature, then you approach the hive. Randall puffed a smoker full of smoldering pine needles at the hive entrance. Then we pried off the top of the hive and the inner cover, and he puffed them again.

Picture how a beehive is built. There is a deep wooden cube on the bottom. Inside are hung nine frames, and onto the wax foundation sheet there the bees build brood comb. Above the hive body there are "supers" six or eight inches deep. These, too, are filled with frames, eight to ten. On these the bees build honeycomb. Contrary to expectation, the honey does *not* flow out of the comb when you move it, because the bees have capped every cell. Exactly according to expectation, the supers are *filled* with bees, and they weigh fifty pounds or more when full of honey. You have to set them on their side and blow out all the bees with a leaf blower before you pack them into the back of the truck.

Amazingly, the smoke *does* calm the bees. However, for the green-horn (me) to walk into the midst of a whirling cloud of bees, even with a bee suit and veil, creates a little uneasiness. Predictably, however, after we had driven from bee yard to bee yard without the bees piercing my defenses, I grew complacent. We tied into a gigantic hive with two hive bodies and five supers. Instead of those mild-mannered little yellow Italian bees, it was filled with irascible black Caucasian, a.k.a. Russian bees. They were imported after the *varroa* mite infestation began because they are resistant to the mite, but their temperament makes you suspect wasps lurk in their family tree. Through my heavy gloves I felt first one sharp sting, then another.

Now to sting you, a bee has to show *commitment*, the same way break-fast requires *cooperation* from the chicken and milch cow but *commitment* from the pig. When the honeybee stings you, he dies. Numerous bees commenced to die on my hands. They got after Junior and Brad, too, but Randall escaped—*laughing*. I have to admit, it was some funny.

By 10:00 a.m. we had sixty-eight full supers, two pick-up beds *full*. By the time we reached Lynchburg, I was hoping Randall wouldn't notice my head lolling on my chest as I drooled in my sleep, but hope was all I could manage. I'm just not used to waking up at 2:30 a.m. At Randall's we unloaded all the supers, and I promised to return with help. That next morning about 8:30 a.m. Susan, Justin, Mercy, Zachariah, and I showed up at Randall's garage. We brought our honey extractor (a centrifuge that slings the honey out of the frames) and a forty-gallon holding tank. Randall already had another extractor and an eighty-gallon holding tank. How does this operation proceed? Somebody pulls the honeycomb frame out of the supers, and hands it to the person at the capping tank. With a very hot electric knife he cuts the caps off the honeycomb, and hands the uncapped frame to somebody who places it into the extractor. Once the extractor fills with frames, you turn it on to sling out all the honey. While you're not doing any of these jobs, you drain out the extractor into a bucket and pour the honey through a strainer into a tank.

Imagine standing in front of all that honey. There's no resisting picking up a big piece of comb filled with honey—the sourwood honey is almost tart, and every frame tastes slightly different. The garage was *filled* with thousands of bees, and every time we took a frame out of a super, more bees were clinging to it. They really are gentle. Nobody got stung but Susan (twice) and Mercy (once). That hot knife is more dangerous than the bees. It will take the hide off your hand quicker than you can feel it. We worked until 6:00 p.m., and I mean *worked*, while those holding tanks kept getting fuller and fuller. By the time we finished we had one hundred and sixty-five gallons of the finest honey you ever saw. Randall claims his own honey tastes better, but can you trust a man who laughs at you when the bees sting you through your bee suit?

A SUCCESS STORY

Back when I was in the Yankee Army in 1971 and rolling in the dough making $185 a month, Susan and I bought an Osterizer blender in the

PX. At $29.95, it was fabulously expensive for people on my salary, but we could get it cheaper in the PX than anyplace else. Besides, we knew it would last forever. Well, *almost* forever. We have dragged that Osterizer blender all over the world and it still worked. Alas, recently the driveshaft of the motor wore down so slick that it wouldn't turn the blade any more. No help for it but to junk our thirty-one-year-old Osterizer and buy a new one for . . . $38.00! That's not much more than we paid for the original one, and still the same quality. I believe it's still made in the United States. If Oster can do it, why can't everybody else?

SEPTEMBER 2002

END OF AN EPOCH

Day before yesterday we pulled the last two rolls of Y2K toilet paper out of the barrel. I guess it's really over. We've used up the rice, the wheat, the cigarette rolling tobacco, and now the toilet paper.

An epoch has ended; a new age begun.

A LIFE FULL OF RICHES

The carpet o'pigs from the first litters is running all over the pig pasture, and spilling out into the road, raising the specter again of wandering hoards of piglets tearing up my neighbor's pastures. But we're not done yet. Dot, Louise, and Princess are still pregnant. Dot is almost too well-mannered to be a pig, and raises piglets just like her. In my mind there was a tug of war going on, trying to figure out whether Dot would: 1) have the piglets first or 2) explode. Last Saturday Dot resolved my inner conflict by farrowing—ten piglets, all fat and silky and not a runt among 'em. One is white all over with black polka dots. Dot is *some pig*. Louise wasn't far behind, farrowing the same day and delivering ten more piglets. You can really tell the difference in the piglets from these grown sows and those from first-timers. They had scrawny little piglets that shiver all the time and look like none of them will live more than ten minutes. Still, they have now begun to fill out and are bouncing around everywhere. Princess, our first and primary sow, has yet to farrow. So far, the piglets total about fifty (you'd have to chloroform them all to get a firm count), and Princess should boost that over sixty!

BODACIOUS HOEDOWN TIME

They came from New Hampshire, and Kansas, and Wisconsin, and Virginia, and Alabama, and Georgia, and Kentucky, and Indiana, and Ohio, and Tennessee, and Louisiana—some to eat, some to watch, but most to dance, at our annual Bodacious Hoedown. Everybody here has been getting up early and working late to bring everything to High Readiness. Wright, Justin, Zachariah, Mercy, and barefoot Tucker repaired the barb wire fence. That was the least part of all the work cutting and cleaning and mowing they did.

Then inside the ladies started ordering tents and chairs and portajohns—and cooking. Bushel baskets of peaches appeared, then disappeared into cobblers. Washtubs of squash appeared, then vanished into casseroles. Finally the pigs Big Red and Little Red disappeared, too, transported to A&D Processing at Chapel Hill for the penultimate step in their transmogrification from hogs into succulent barbecue.

By Friday everything was pretty well done, but last minute things always pop up. Friends came to help that day, and ended near sundown with the incredulous question, "Do y'all work like this all the time?" To tell the truth, I hadn't had time to notice. Okay, I'll admit I was somewhat disappointed in the turnout, which was only slightly larger than last year. All I can say is that those folks who passed up the Hoedown made the *biggest* mistake of their lives. Let me warn you to *attend* these functions, *not* to throw them, because throwing them will wear you down.

Tim Stulls brought two of his Border Collies over and herded our sheep with them. I cannot peel my eyes off his demonstrations. Watching Tim work those dogs mesmerizes me. They delight to do his will, and a simple word or whistle will send them hurtling over the hill after the fugitive sheep. Sure enough, in a little while that crouching little dog will hustle them back into sight. I really believe that in that blistering heat Tim's dogs would run themselves flat to death before they would fail him. How hard will they work? They live to work. One of Tim's best contenders was herding for him not long ago and fell dead of a heart attack. Only death can stop a Border Collie. Our friend Bill Willett came too. He logs with horses, and brought his Belgian stallion, Bud, and his mare, Dolly. Together with our two teams of Percherons—here is *not* the place to enter a discussion of the merits of Percherons relative to Belgians—we put on a show of mowing and gathering hay. Bill hooked up Bud and Dolly to our fancy wagon and drove people down the road to watch us loading hay.

All this may sound rather simple-minded to you, but as I tried to explain to the crowd what Justin or Wright or Bill was doing with the horses, I realized *how much* we had learned in the last three years. When we started, none of us knew a draft horse from Adam's off ox, but now we do. (The ox is the one with *horns*. The off ox stands on the *right* as you're looking at the team's rear.)

As the sun went down, the heat relented and we had a fine, cool evening for dancing. The 12th Louisiana String Band showed up right on time for a gigantic barbecue pork and chicken supper. I think either the band or some other folks had plastic-lined pockets. How else can you explain the disappearance of a hundred and fifty pounds of pork and sixty pounds of chicken, not to mention trenchers and trenchers of squash casserole, fresh coleslaw, potato salad, sliced tomatoes, and peach cobbler?

By the time the sun had almost set, everybody was itching to dance. Our friend James Bendowsky started things off playing his bagpipes (Great job, James!) just to get our blood up and running. It worked, and then the 12th Louisiana took over. Things get sort of hazy for me after that. That is, I can remember a *few* waltzes, but mostly I remember a blur of laughing faces whirling around and skipping up and down through Virginia Reels and patty-cake polkas and Gay Gordons. The Twelfth played and played, and when they finally quit, a lot of folks stayed and talked and talked. To top off the evening, the Twelfth's lead singer, Frank Walsh, brought out some huge bags of his own home-grown tobacco and showed us how to roll cigars. Believe it or not, they are as tasteful as, and much milder than, any cigar I have ever smoked.

THE EARTH IS FULL OF RICHES

There are some things you just can't tell, can hardly describe, because you have to witness them in person—like the summer Worth and I went to the League of the South Summer School near Charleston. We had Jim

Kibler as a guide when we toured Charleston. By the time we finished, it was already blue-skied evening, and we were near St. Michael's Church. I looked up into the deep navy sky, and there was a crescent moon shining behind a palmetto tree, just like the South Carolina flag. That picture is, as they say, indelibly etched in my mind.

Working on this newsletter last night I saw another of those inerasable sights. About 7:30 p.m. I stopped working and went outside. It was right warm, and although it was nearly dark, the boys were still gathering hay. We've had a terrible time getting in hay this year, and have very little to show for our efforts. I could hear, but not see, Justin raking the hay into windrows. I knew he would be driving the fillies, Hep and Beu, for that lighter work. From the haystack I could hear Zach and Wright talking as they unloaded a wagon full of hay. Silhouetted against the sky, I could see Zach twelve feet above the ground on the haystack. Now and then a great mound of hay would fly up from Wright's pitchfork. It was warm and dry as I stepped through Justin and Wright's new gate and into the field. Justin brought up the girls and I helped him unhitch them. "How are they driving?"

"Not well. When the rake dumps the hay, it gets lighter suddenly, and that makes them want to go too fast."

We finished and I strolled over to the haystack to help Zach and Wright. As I walked around in front of the horses, above the stack I could see what the Germans aptly call a *Sichelmond*—a sickle moon—just above the pole of the haystack, still orange from the strain of rising. Over the right shoulder of the haystack peeked red Mars, the only other point of light in the dusty sky. Silhouetted against them was haystack's ragged outline.

Sound crazy as it might, *that* is why I live out here, because just behind the edge of every minute lurks some glorious surprise—*Sichelmond*, sons, Mars, and haystack.

O LORD, how manifold are thy works! In wisdom hast thou made them all; the earth is full of thy riches.

— Psalm 104:24
(Reformed Episcopal Church, Book of Common Prayer)

WATCH FOR THESE ADDITIONAL VOLUMES
SCHEDULED FOR RELEASE IN 2013

———

VOLUME TWO:

BEST THING WE EVER DID

Breaking new farming barriers, Franklin and Susan go from making home-cured bacon, through Franklin successfully whispering bees into a hive, to Franklin finding himself in a chilling "discussion meeting" about the National Animal Identification System, where the government speaker confesses registering farm animals with the government is not about foot and mouth disease; it's about terrorists getting to our beef supply. Undeterred, Franklin keeps right on farming. The rewards are too great—a living legacy of farm know-how, land, and animals, right down to fruit trees for his great-great-great grandchildren to know him by.

VOLUME THREE:

THE SAGE OF DOGWOOD MUDHOLE

The Sage of Dogwood Mudhole begins with Franklin realizing he may have become a Jeff Foxworthy joke about how you know you're a redneck when there are two dead tractors, two junk trucks, and two grandchildren fighting in your yard, with an old man yelling at them from the doorway. Franklin seeks out, meets, and becomes fast friends with other likeminded sharers of an oral tradition of an older and happier—or sometimes newer and more satisfying—way of farming, reads old books about farming, restores his fields, sits vigil at his wife's bedside, and ponders love's perfection as she undergoes open heart surgery. When danger is over for now, Franklin ardently fells trees around his house, eyed warily by sons a little too willing to relieve an old guy of the work, all for the love of his wife and her desire for HDTV.

THE MONEYCHANGER™

The Moneychanger, Franklin Sanders' incomparable newsletter published each month except September, has served discerning readers for nearly 20 years. In addition to his *Dear Reader* column from which this series is drawn, each issue is filled with his gold and silver investing wisdom and projections, his deep knowledge of financial history, eye-opening interviews with alternative health pioneers, and of course, the latest news from the farm and family at Dogwood Mudhole—all written to help Christians prosper with their principles intact in an age of monetary and moral chaos.